CRIMINAL CAREER CONTINUITY

CRIMINAL CAREER CONTINUITY
Its Social Context

Lyle W. Shannon
Iowa Urban Community Research Center;
University of Iowa
Iowa City
with the assistance of:
Judith L. McKim
Iowa Urban Community Research Center
James P. Curry
Center for Health Services Research
Lawrence J. Haffner
Academic Computing, Harper College

HUMAN SCIENCES PRESS, INC.
72 FIFTH AVENUE
NEW YORK, N.Y. 10011-8004

Library of Congress Cataloging-in-Publication Data

Shannon, Lyle W.
  Criminal career continuity.

  Bibliography: p.
  Includes index.
  1. Juvenile delinquency—Wisconsin—Longitudinal
studies. 2. Crime and criminals—Wisconsin—Longi-
tudinal studies. 3. City and town life—Wisconsin—
Longitudinal studies. I. Title.
HV9105.W6S53 1988   364.3'6'09775   87-3214
ISBN 0-89885-387-7

CONTENTS

PREFACE

The question is often asked, "How did this research get started?" As with other events in life, it was partly by chance. Shortly after his term as chairman of the Department of Sociology and Anthropology at the University of Wisconsin, Professor Thomas C. McCormick asked Michael Hakeem and me (then Associate and Assistant Professors, respectively) if we would like to work with him on a study of changing trends in juvenile delinquency in Madison. As delinquency and crime were Hakeem's major interests, he readily agreed. I was a relatively new member of the faculty at Madison and in my first regular, full-time teaching position, and had on-going interests which included research in juvenile delinquency. Hakeem arranged a meeting with Chief Bruce Weatherly (who later became one of Madison's more controversial chiefs of police) and an agreement was reached to undertake a study of juvenile delinquency in Madison based on data from the police contact files of the juvenile bureau as they existed in 1955–56.

Several years later, before the findings from the Madison study had been published, I was in Racine as Co-principal Investigator of a project that later became "The Economic Absorption and Cultural Integration of Inmigrant Workers." I became acquainted with Chief Leroy C. Jenkins, who soon proposed that a companion study of delinquency be conducted in Racine. Such a study would be feasible because Racine and Madison had essentially the same system of police contact records.

The Madison study covered 1950 through 1955 and the Racine study 1950 through 1960. The findings, although based on samples of juveniles who had police contacts during the years included in the studies, generated numerous articles, research reports, M.A. theses, and Ph.D. dissertations.

Although I accepted a position at the University of Iowa in 1962, I continued my analyses of the Racine research data. It was decided that a follow-up study should be conducted in order to determine how many of the persons in each sample had continued their careers of police contacts beyond the age of 21. This was made possible with the cooperation of Dr. Paul H. Kusuda and Perry C. Baker of the Office of Systems and Evaluation of the Division of Corrections in the Department of Health and Social Services and Joseph S. Coughlin (then Chief of Administrative Services, Division of Corrections).

While those of us who worked together on this research had measured changing rates of police contact and referral (we knew how many persons between the ages of 6 and 18 resided in each school attendance center in both cities each year) and spatial variations in police contact and referral rates, we did not have complete data on the police contacts of everyone in the samples because data had been collected only on contacts during the 1950s. There was, of course, considerable variation in years of exposure as well because not everyone in the samples had resided in Madison and Racine during the entire period between the ages of 6 and 17. Our concern about years of risk led to some analyses with quasi-birth cohorts, for example, those from the sample who were born in 1938 in Madison and those from the sample who were born between 1943 and 1945 in Racine.

This research was supported by Small Research Grant ME 11367-01 and Grant MH 15627-02 of the Mental Health Small Grant Committee, National Institute of Mental Health, the Graduate College, the College of Liberal Arts, and the Division of Extension and University Services of the University of Iowa, the Research Committee of the Graduate School of the University of Wisconsin, and the Wisconsin Department of Health and Social Services.

As none of the scales measuring the seriousness of types of delinquent careers produced scores for the juvenile period that were highly correlated with adult criminal careers, we could only conclude that adult criminal careers were not extensions of any type, pattern, or degree of seriousness of juvenile careers. There was nothing in these juvenile careers that enabled us to predict adult criminal careers.

Earlier data had enabled us to describe the incidence of juvenile delinquency year by year in Madison and Racine, its changing nature, and its distribution in the city, the data were not adequate for a test of the hypothesis that careers commenced with minor misconduct at an early age, gradually developed into more serious types of misbehavior, and then continued into adult crime. Nor could we test the hypothesis that there were sociologically meaningful configurations or typologies of juvenile misbehaviors, of which some led to continuing careers and others did not. Having read Wolfgang, Figlio, and Sellin's *Delinquency in a Birth Cohort*, we concluded that *birth cohort* data alone would permit us to make adequate tests of these hypotheses.

The first grant for the longitudinal birth cohort research came from the Fleischman Foundation in 1974. This was followed by grants from the National Institute of Juvenile Justice and Delinquency Prevention, 1976–1979 (76–JN–990008, 76–JN–99-1005, 76–JN–00–0019, 79–JN–AX–0010).

During work on "The Relationship of Adult Criminal Careers to Juvenile Careers," interest in the hypothesized cyclical nature of change in crime and ecological structure was rekindled by the fact that the spatial distribution of juvenile delinquency and adult crime appeared to be following the changing ecological structure of the city. There was nothing new to this, of course, but it seemed that the importance of ecological research in developing a greater understanding of continuities in delinquency and crime had not received appropriate recognition in recent years. Since the ecological structure of Racine had been developed with block data for an earlier project on the economic absorption and cultural integration of inmigrant workers, it was possible to code police contacts by place of residence and place of contact and thus produce some intriguing tables on the changing spatial distribution of alleged offenses.

With some preliminary work completed and additional data sets available, we were set to do research that would have methodological as well as substantive value. The next step was to formulate our scientific concerns in a framework that could also produce answers that would be useful to persons on the firing line. To assume that positive prescriptions for action would be forthcoming might be to expect too much but, even if the results contributed only to a better understanding of the processes by which delinquency and crime continued in some areas but not in others or the processes by which new areas of delinquency and crime came into being, that would be an accomplishment.

Should the research strongly indicate that what the community was doing in the hope of dealing with a problem was only contributing to the continuation and extension of the problem, that would be a disappointing finding but one which responsible, concerned people must consider. We would conclude that more of the same, e.g., increasing the severity of sanctions and sanctioning even a greater proportion of the miscreants, would not be the solution to the problem.

Some of the numerous and complex findings of the ecologically-oriented research project, "The Relationship of Juvenile Delinquency and Adult Crime to the Changing Ecological Structure of the City," funded by a National Institute of Justice Grant, 79–NI–AX–0081, and the earlier longitudinal birth cohort prediction project are presented here, adding up to the conclusion that not only had the inner city hardened but that new areas were developing in which the residents had high offense rates and in which the rate of offenses committed had also increased.

Although the analyses described in this volume build on the earlier research and use these data sets as well as others, we cannot help but believe that we have only begun to unlock a vast store of information on the official careers of the three birth cohorts and the interviews conducted with persons from two of the three.

We hope that the reader will share our excitement about the findings described here and our continuing analyses of the data as we seek to determine the influence of the social milieu on the decision-making process of both youth and adults. Although we have completed five lengthy research reports for the National Institute of Justice and the National Institute of Juvenile Justice and Delinquency Prevention, have presented numerous papers at professional meetings, have conducted seminars, have published in professional journals, and had chapters in a number of books on delinquency and crime, this is the first book-length publication on the three birth cohort research. It is our first attempt to combine what we have learned about individual careers and the changing spatial distribution of delinquency and crime with the effects of the social environment on continuities in delinquency and crime.

January, 1988

ACKNOWLEDGMENTS

Several people have been associated with the Iowa Urban Community Research Center's Racine research for many years. Judith L. McKim (Senior Research Assistant, Social Science) and Emily J. Meeks (Programmer, deceased May 1980) were also involved in every phase of the earlier research on the economic absorption and cultural integration of inmigrants as well as the projects on juvenile delinquency and adult crime. Judith McKim planned the original records search from the cohort lists and the coding operation in the Racine Police Department. She supervised all stages of the research including data entry. Emily Meeks was responsible for programming, and for the accuracy of all data sets. She and Roger K. Sandness worked together on the original mapping programs. Judith McKim also assisted in the development of the interview schedule, the training and supervision of the interviewers, and supervised the final coding of interviews. She has participated in writing and rewriting numerous reports, articles, book chapters, and this volume.

Rachel E. Pezanoski (Field Director) commenced working with us as an interviewer and ended as Field Director. Most recently she supervised data collection in the Police Department and in other Racine offices. Among those who were also field supervisors at one period or another were: Michael R. Olson, Barney K. Pauze, Victoria F. Davison, Delores Luedtke, and Susan Shemanske. The following graduate and undergraduate research assistants were involved in various stages of the coding and analysis: Barbara A. Carson, Hugh S. Espey, Kathleen R. Anderson, Cheryl L. Garland, Sara Stolz, Eugene Kennedy, Vijayan K. Pillai, Tie-Hua Ng, Tina Yuk-Bing Abels, Shari Hessong Morgan, Shirley Nelson-Kilger, Allen Bluedorn, Michael

Altimore, Vernon P. Pitts, Joon-Ho Kim, Royal Caldwell, and Kathryn E. Smith.

Graduate students and others from the University of Iowa, the University of Wisconsin-Parkside, The Gateway Technical Institute in Racine, and other colleges and universities worked with diligence as interviewers and coders.

Of the many who were involved in secretarial, clerical, and tabular work are Mary Kathleen Stockman Zimmerman, Julie Burton, Debra J. Cobb, Debi S. Schreiner, Ruth Moderson, Margaret L. Bruns, Joanne Ament, Jane Perkins, Stephanie J. Yabsley, Deborra Cameron, and Regina Oni.

From 1980 through 1982 we were assisted in the analysis of data by James P. Curry (Assistant Research Scientist, Center for Health Services Research) and during the final phases of analysis by Lawrence J. Haffner (Director, Academic Computing, Harper College). James Curry completed the analysis for and wrote papers which constitute several major chapters in our reports to the National Institute of Justice. Portions of several of these are included in this volume.

Bonnie P. Lewin of LEAA (now with the Federal Bureau of Prisons) visited the Iowa Urban Community Research Center on several occasions. She and Pamela Swain have shown unusual comprehension of the problems involved in cohort research.

The Advisory Board for the projects described in this volume consisted of Karl Schuessler, Robert C. Hanson, Harwin L. Voss, Delbert S. Elliott, Robert M. Figlio, Roland Chilton, and Aubrey Wendling. All contributed valuable suggestions at one time or another. Robert Hanson, Harwin Voss, and William F. Skinner (Graduate Research Assistant) gave us detailed criticism of the preliminary version of the final report. Gwynne Nettler read an earlier version of this manuscript and has provided many suggestions for its improvement. We were very indebted to him. The defects which remain are those of the principal investigator, Lyle W. Shannon.

Chapter 1

THREE BIRTH COHORTS IN AN URBAN SETTING

Ecological and Sociological Perspectives

INTRODUCTION

Longitudinal birth cohort studies of the chains of experiences that people have as juveniles and adults enable us to better understand the process by which some persons come to engage in delinquent and then criminal behavior as a career, a way of life. The most important findings in this book are based on three birth cohorts totalling 6,127 persons born in 1942, 1949, and 1955 whose recorded police and court experiences were analyzed from early age into adulthood. The study covered a period of 28 years in Racine, Wisconsin.

These birth cohort and official time series data on delinquency and crime in Racine, coupled with an understanding of the city's growth and development, will make us less surprised that present efforts to deal with delinquency and crime are followed by continuing high offense rates in the inner city and interstitial areas. Likewise, knowledge of the ecology of the city will make the discovery of high delinquency rates more comprehensible in neighborhoods which have traditionally been expected to have little delinquency and crime.

UNDERSTANDING THE INDIVIDUAL IN A CHANGING URBAN SETTING

The importance of ecological research in accounting for juvenile delinquency and adult crime has not received appropriate recognition in recent years. In the course of this research it became all too apparent that, while only limited numbers of people had continuous careers in delinquency and crime, there were areas of the community in which law-breaking had become almost a way of life for a disproportionate number of the population and in which an even greater proportion of the population drifted in and out of delinquency more frequently than did the residents of most other areas of the community. Further, it was apparent that delinquency and crime occurred more often in these areas (a greater percent of the population had engaged in delinquent and criminal behavior more frequently), year in and year out, than in other parts of the community.

As the chapters unfold we shall 1) delineate and describe different types of urban areas and changes in their physical and demographic composition between 1950 and 1980 which were significant enough to alter the ecological structure or pattern of neighborhoods in the city, and 2) show how the changing ecological structure was related to the changing spatial distribution of juvenile delinquency and adult crime and the justice system's responses to them.

Our third concern, as we examined the problem in an ecological framework, was with the extent to which increasing rates of delinquency and adult crime were followed by population movement, institutional change, and changes in the physical condition of areas and then by further increases in delinquency and crime. In short, the relationship between delinquent and criminal careers, high delinquency and crime rates, and ecological structure was dynamic and self-perpetuating. Understanding this cyclical relationship required the analysis of change in ecological structure over time, the distribution of delinquency and crime in the city, and community reaction to changes in both.

It has long been recognized that areas in the community with the physical, institutional, and demographic characteristics (deteriorated and overcrowded housing, abandoned buildings, commercial-industrial establishments, numerous taverns, and a population that has neither been integrated into the economy nor into the broader social structure of the community) which have clearly marked them as areas productive of delinquency and crime continue to be productive of delinquency and crime as long as they and their residents are unchanged. These are areas whose residents are characterized by the lower-class value stretch, i.e., they are aware of the values of the larger society but compromise them from time to time to achieve their immediate wants.

As these areas expand or, as new areas develop with similar characteristics, the spatial distribution of delinquency and crime changes. At the same time, it may be that this combination of physical, institutional, and demographic characteristics and high rates of delinquency and crime generate population movement which further exacerbates the problems of these areas in terms of physical deterioration, institutional change, and the breakdown of social controls. Those adults who gave some stability to the area, whether White, Black, or Chicano, move to more desirable areas, taking with them their sometimes miscreant children whose behavior, rather than changing, merely results in enlarged or modified areas with high rates of delinquency and crime. There is an upper class value stretch, but its product does not show up as ordinary street crime.

In order to understand changing patterns of delinquency and crime in Racine we must understand how the social organization and ecological structure of the city changed and how areas that once had lower rates of delinquency and crime became populated by persons whose social circumstances and way of life created a setting in which delinquency and crime were generated and perpetuated. These areas may also have attracted commercial establishments which were targets for those who disvalued law-abiding behavior or may have developed attractions or facilities which transformed them into arenas for troublesome behavior by persons who had not been integrated into Racine's larger society.

The social organization of the community refers to the economic base of the community, the types of employment available, the race/ethnic composition of the population, and the distribution of each group within the various sectors of the economy. Changes in the social organization of the community are measured by changes in the proportion of the population employed, the proportion employed in the industrial sector of the economy, and the unemployment rate. Since delinquent and criminal areas persevere and expand (this has been demonstrated in a wide variety of cities and we have found it in Racine as well), the cycle of population movement, residential deterioration, and changing institutional land use continues to generate ever-expanding, new areas whose social and demographic characteristics are productive of high delinquency and crime rates.

Unless countermeasures to integrate youth and young adults into the world of work and responsibility are taken, unless steps to reduce population movement, property deterioration, and institutional change to break the cycle are taken, larger and increasing numbers of areas of the city will become multi-problem areas. Because measures of this nature are not taken or are not of such a magnitude as to be effective, the cycle continues.

Changes in the ecological structure of Racine for the years 1950, 1960, and 1970 are measured with block data aggregated into various statistical units or subareas: census tracts, police grids, natural areas, and neighborhoods. Patterns of delinquency and crime as measured by offenses committed and arrest data from the Racine Police Department for 1949 through 1979 for the entire city provide a temporal and spatial framework against which to view the three cohorts of persons on whom detailed data have been obtained.

These analyses concentrate on how change in the demographic, housing, and institutional characteristics of areas is related to change in indices of delinquency and crime. Rather than having only one set of units, we explore the relationship of change in a set of variables to change in another set of variables with each of the four sets of spatial units. In each case the cohort and official data for the entire city are transformed into comparable ecological and temporal analytic units. By this means it is determined if the same or similar results are obtained utilizing four systems of spatial units and various measures of delinquency and crime for: 1) the three cohorts and 2) annual statistics for the total population.

To understand the process by which some persons became legal delinquents and perhaps later criminals, we must utilize data which record the first step in the process as well as the steps which followed. Although behavior which may result in a recorded police contact is the first step in the behavior pattern, the police contact itself is the first step toward an official record. Thus, police contact data bring us closer to juvenile and adult misbehavior than do other levels of official data. The terms "juvenile delinquency" and "adult crime" or "delinquents" and "criminals" are used in a general sense and do not refer only to the behavior of those who have been adjudicated or convicted.[1]

One of the major goals of this research has been to provide more precise information about the nature of juvenile delinquency and its relationship to adult crime in an urban setting, i.e., juvenile and adult misbehavior. We were also interested in the extent to which decisions by authorities and juveniles have contributed to continuing or discontinuing patterns of delinquency and crime, the effectiveness of various forces (formal and informal) in deterring law-violating behavior, and in obtaining some indication of points in juvenile careers when intervention of one kind or another was most effective.

Although sociological explanations of delinquency have differed, all have perceived delinquency as learned by rational human beings in a social environment. Inner city life has been viewed as facilitating the acquisition of behavior which is socially unacceptable in the larger society through day-to-day observation of and contact with delinquent or criminal role models who appear to be more successful than their law-abiding counterparts. The finding that, in city after city, areas with high rates of delinquency had considerable crime overlap, whether the measure was police contacts, arrests, convictions, or institutional commitments, led to the inference that adult crime must certainly be an extension of juvenile delinquency.

If the empirical findings presented here are accepted, crime prevention and control programs must turn again toward consideration of how the organization of society may be used not only to prevent the perpetuation of delinquency and crime as a way of life in areas that have traditionally had high rates of police contact, referral, court dispositions, and sanctions but to deal with the development of delinquency in peripheral areas of the city as well.

THE STUDIES WHICH HAVE GUIDED US AND WHERE THEY HAVE LED US

Descriptions of the social ecology of the city by University of Chicago sociologists first emphasized affinity with delinquency and crime (growing up in an area where delinquency and crime were commonplace) as an explanation of delinquent behavior.[2] This was followed by attention to the consequences of affiliation with groups (gang membership) in which crime and delinquency were accepted patterns of behavior.[3] The numerous publications by Shaw, McKay, and others set the stage for a generation of research in which affinity and affiliation were in a sense the dominant explanatory themes. Sutherland went beyond this and specified four facets of association which, if operationalized, should enable us to predict which juveniles are most likely to acquire delinquent and/or criminal patterns of behavior.[4] The nature of one's associates is determined by the family into which one is born, by the neighborhood in which one grows up, by the proximity of one's schoolmates to one's neighborhood, by the nature of one's schoolmates even if they are not close by, and so on. Glaser added a social psychological component when he spoke of differential identification.[5] While related to Sutherland's intensity dimension, differential identification is really closer to that aspect of explanation referred to by Matza as signification.

Most delinquency is conceptualized in this study as a part of or product of the learning process.[6] Children grow up in a neighborhood or cluster of neighborhoods (if their parents move, they are likely to do so within similar areas) with more or less distinctive social characteristics, crime and delinquency levels, attitudes toward the police and the juvenile and adult justice systems, and patterns of interaction between juveniles, adults, and representatives of the larger society. If a juvenile is socialized in one type of ecological area, he/she is likely to acquire the attitudes and behaviors prevalent in that area. As time passes, juvenile misbehavior produces reactions by society, including society's label for the delinquent, as well as his/her self-definitions and consequent changes in behavior that are associated with a change from primary to secondary deviation.[7] This view of delinquency (as a chain of events in a hostile environment) has been supported by Ferracuti, Dinitz, and Acosta de Brenes in their Puerto Rican research on juvenile delinquency.[8] Wolfgang, Figlio, and Sellin's *Delinquency in a Birth Cohort* was, of course, our model for the design of this research.[9]

By the time that people are adults they no longer find themselves in situations which generate misbehavior or the behavior has been legalized, i.e., the behavior no longer constitutes a status offense. There is an element of "maturation" involved, not in a psychological sense but in terms of the availability of social opportunities and alternatives that were not present at an earlier age. It is not simply a matter of growing up or settling down and securing work that was previously unavailable, but of getting married, assuming various financial responsibilities, and acquiring statuses that obviate the likelihood of contact-generating behavior.

THE THREE RACINE COHORTS

The birth cohorts (males and females) consist of 1,352 persons born in 1942, 2,099 persons born in 1949, and 2,676 persons born in 1955. The data and official records collected on these cohorts encompass a period from 1948 through 1976, data on the 1942 Cohort commencing in 1948 and that for the 1955 Cohort ending in 1976. Data collection for each cohort began with the first contact with the police at or after the age of 6 and ended for the 1942 Cohort when they were 33, for the 1949 Cohort when they were 26, and for the 1955 Cohort when they were 22. In addition to checking the official police contact and court records for persons in each cohort, we conducted lengthy interviews with 889 persons from the 1942 and 1949 Cohorts during the summer of 1976.

Inasmuch as police records in Racine were well established by 1950 (when persons born in 1942 were eight years of age) and other records that could be utilized in selection of the cohorts existed for a 1942 birth year at the earliest, this group was selected as the first cohort.[10] The 1949 cohort was selected as insurance against the criticism that could be levied against a single cohort's representativeness; it would have at least seven years beyond the age of 18 in which to establish a young adult (age 18-20) and an adult record of police contacts, subsequent referrals, and court dispositions. While not a factor in the selection process, the 1949 Cohort, like the 1945 Cohort of the Philadelphia study, grew up entirely after the end of World War II and the early post-war period, the late 50s and 60s. This may help to explain differences between the cohorts.[11]

During the period in which we were making preparations for coding the police contact data, community leaders approached us regarding the possibility of selecting a still younger cohort, believing that it would differ from earlier generations. The birth year of 1955 was selected for a third cohort. At that time (1974) the 1955 Cohort had just passed the age of 18. Funds were not adequate for complete data collection on this group in 1974 but later funding allowed us to collect police contact data for the 1955 Cohort to September 1, 1977, three years beyond the age of 18.[12]

DATA COLLECTION

The cooperation of the police department exceeded what anyone might reasonably expect.[13] Information regarding juvenile and adult complaints was read and coded from the files of the Juvenile Bureau and the Records Division of the Racine Police Department under the supervision of the Iowa Urban Community Research Center's field directors.

Reasons for police contact were coded into 26 basic categories consistent with Part I and Part II offenses of the Uniform Crime Reports, but with added meaningful "conditions" for juveniles.[14] Many of these contacts were for very minor violations, or for Suspicion, Investigation, or Information or Traffic violations. It was necessary to code these as completely as we did the most heinous crimes on the assumption that becoming known to the police for any reason may have had some influence on the course of a person's career. No contact was coded if the record did not show personal contact between officer and cohort member, if the cohort member was merely mentioned in connection with an investigation, or if the incident was in the nature of an assistance call. Contacts as victims, as abandoned, neglected, dependent children, and many non-delinquent contacts considered safety measures, were recorded but are not included in these analyses.

Juvenile court and adult police contact records were read and coded for all persons with continuous residence whose police contact data indicated a referral.[15] In coding for juveniles, only those hearings relating to juvenile misconduct were included. For instance, changes in custody arising from problems within the family and not originating with the child's delinquent behavior were not considered part of the dispositions history. Once it had been determined that records of arrest dispositions in various courts were complete, these were coded as indicators of the severity of sanctions.

During the collection of data on police contacts the address at which the alleged offender lived at the time of each contact and the address at which the contact occurred were coded according to a block number system established by the U.S. Census in 1970. Cartesian coordinates were assigned to each Census block number so that home addresses of alleged offenders and places of contact could be computer-mapped or analyzed within any spatial framework by any other variable or set of variables.

The age of the individual at each contact and the date of each contact and police disposition are included in the data and permit determination of whether contacts and dispositions occurred in rapid succession with only a few days between them or whether they were spaced over a span of years.

The length of time each member of the cohort resided in the community was determined to permit differentiation between persons with partial careers and those with continuous residence. This has facilitated handling the problem of mortality in longitudinal studies. We were concerned with identifying those who entered the system later than their birth date (for all practical purposes later than age 6), those who left Racine before the age of 18, and those who left before the police contact cut-off date for their cohort. This painstaking location and verification process was continued

TABLE 1.   BASIC CHARACTERISTICS OF THE 1942, 1949, AND 1955 COHORTS AND PERSONS
           WITH CONTINUOUS RESIDENCE IN RACINE*
- -

	Males			Females			Total		
	1942	1949	1955	1942	1949	1955	1942	1949	1955
Cohort									
Number	679	1081	1369	673	1018	1307	1352	2099	2676
% by Sex	50.2	51.5	51.2	49.8	48.3	48.8			
% White	94.1	90.1	86.4	94.8	91.5	88.4	94.4	90.7	87.4
% Black	4.6	6.8	9.1	3.0	5.8	8.4	3.8	6.3	8.8
% Chicano	1.3	3.2	4.5	2.3	2.7	3.1	1.8	2.9	3.8
Total	100.0	100.1	100.0	100.1	100.0	99.9	100.0	99.9	100.0
Continuous Residence									
Number	356	740	1114	277	557	1035	633	1297	2149
% by Sex	56.2	57.1	51.8	43.8	42.9	48.2			
% White	94.9	91.5	86.3	96.4	91.2	88.6	95.6	91.4	87.4
% Black	4.2	5.9	9.5	1.8	7.0	8.3	3.2	6.4	8.9
% Chicano	.8	2.6	4.2	1.8	1.9	3.1	1.3	2.2	3.7
Total	99.9	100.0	100.0	100.0	100.0	100.0	100.1	100.0	100.0

* Absent from Racine no more than three years during the age period 6 through
the cut-off date for that cohort.

in Racine during the interviewing phase for anyone whose presence had
not been previously established by directory search.[16]

The married names of females in each cohort were obtained from the
records of the Racine County Health Department. The females were followed through the Records Division of the Racine County Police Department to ascertain the total number and nature of police contacts of each
in each cohort.

The residence duration coding from the age of 6 through 1976 identified
4,079 persons with continuous residence in Racine, those referred to, unless
indicated otherwise, in the analyses which follow. The race/ethnic and sex
composition of each cohort and the part of each cohort with continuous
residence in Racine (4,079) is shown in Table 1. Interviews with the 1942
and 1949 Cohorts confirmed that race/ethnic identification of cohort members was very accurate.[17]

AN INTRODUCTION TO THE COHORT RECORDS

Although the main thrust of this research had gone beyond race/ethnic
and sex differences which should already be known to persons familiar
with the literature, some consideration has been devoted to them in order

to obtain an understanding of their relevance in the Racine setting. Unfortunately, the number of Blacks and Chicanos in the 1942 and 1949 Cohorts made race/ethnic comparisons difficult across all cohorts. The data will still be able to show how recorded police contacts (juvenile delinquency and adult crime) involved Whites in most areas of the community, how the problem was shared in the inner city, and how there was more continuity for those who resided in the inner city whether they were White, Black, or Chicano.

During the period of their lives covered by our data collection, 68% of the continuous residents in the 1942 Cohort and 69% of the continuous residents in the 1949 Cohort had one or more police contacts. Although persons in the 1955 Cohort were only 22 years of age at the time of their cut-off date, September 1, 1976, 59% of the continuous residents had already had at least one police contact.

The proportion of contacts for each cohort in each of the 26 categories of police contacts is shown in Table 2, as are the proportions of contacts that were for Part I offenses and the mean number of police contacts for each person in the cohort.[18] Differences in reasons for police contact quite obviously varied from cohort to cohort. Because cohort changes will be explored more fully in later chapters, only brief mention is now made.

The proportion of contacts for Drug offenses increased markedly. There are also readily noticeable increases for Theft, Assault, Burglary, Robbery, and, during the juvenile period, for Incorrigible, Runaway and Truant. Even more apparent are the increases from cohort to cohort in the proportion of contacts for Part I offenses in each age period, particularly with ages 6 through 17 and 18 through 20. Reference to sex differences will be made whenever they are significant or useful in understanding overall changes in proportions or rates. Consistent with current concern about serious female delinquency is the increasing proportion of police contacts for Part I offenses by females from cohort to cohort. Although the female rate of increase exceeded that for males for the 6 through 17 and 18 through 20 groups, periods for which comparison was possible for the same number of years, the proportion of male contacts that were for Part I offenses remained about double that for females.

An Overview of the Chapters Which Follow

In the next chapter we shall look at the cohorts and cohort change against juvenile and adult trends for the entire city over a span of 30 years. The problem of measuring seriousness and a discussion of the nature of temporal change by race/ethnicity and sex will be presented in Chapter 3.

Chapter 4 describes the ecology of Racine and the characteristics of each of the units in the four spatial systems, culminating in the clustering

TABLE 2. DISTRIBUTION OF POLICE CONTACTS BY TYPE IN COHORTS AND AGE PERIODS

	Ages 6-17			Ages 18-20			Ages 21+			Total		
	1942	1949	1955	1942	1949	1955	1942	1949	1955	1942	1949	1955
Traffic	25.4	17.2	10.1	52.2	39.0	31.3	49.4	36.7	28.9	42.5	28.4	17.8
Disorderly Conduct	24.3	21.7	14.4	14.5	20.4	26.4	19.3	26.8	34.5	19.9	22.8	19.5
Suspicion, Investigation	16.6	19.9	15.1	16.9	25.1	12.2	21.0	22.4	15.1	18.9	21.9	14.2
Liquor	6.1	5.1	2.3	4.0	1.9	2.1	2.0	1.6	1.0	3.6	3.3	2.2
Theft	7.8	9.6	27.9	3.0	3.0	5.4	1.1	1.9	3.1	3.6	5.7	9.9
Incorrigible, runaway, Truant	9.6	14.0	26.5	1.0	.2	.3	.1	.2	---	3.2	6.5	16.9
Vagrancy	2.6	2.7	1.7	1.6	2.1	.7	.5	.7	1.3	1.4	2.0	1.4
Auto Theft	2.9	1.9	2.4	1.2	.7	1.5	.2	.1	.2	1.2	1.1	2.0
Sex Offenses	.6	1.2	.9	2.0	1.5	1.3	.9	1.2	1.0	1.0	1.3	1.0
Assault	.5	1.0	2.3	.2	1.0	2.4	1.2	1.8	2.1	.8	1.2	2.3
Burglary	1.6	2.8	6.2	.6	.6	3.8	.2	.4	.8	.7	1.6	5.1
Weapons	.5	.4	.7	.2	.4	1.4	.5	.4	1.2	.4	.4	.9
Violent Property Destruction	.6	.2	.7	1.0	.7	1.3	.1	.4	1.0	.4	.4	.9
Forgery, Fraud	---	1.0	.8	.2	1.2	1.9	.7	1.4	1.8	.4	1.1	1.2
Robbery	---	.4	.8	.2	.3	2.0	.5	.3	.3	.3	.4	1.1
Gambling	.1	.2	.1	---	.1	.2	.3	.1	---	.2	.1	.1
Narcotics, Drugs	---	---	1.5	---	.6	4.7	.3	2.2	5.9	.1	.8	2.8
Homicide	---	---	.1	---	.1	.1	---	---	.3	---	.1	.1
Other	1.0	.6	.6	1.2	1.3	1.0	1.6	1.3	1.0	1.3	1.0	.8
TOTAL	100.2	99.9	100.0	100.0	100.2	100.0	99.9	99.9	99.9	99.9	100.0	100.1
Percent Part I	12.7	15.9	24.6	5.2	5.6	15.3	3.2	4.5	7.2	6.5	10.0	20.5
Mean Contacts Per Person	1.3	1.9	2.1	.8	1.1	.9	2.2	1.2	.3	4.3	4.2	3.3
Number of Police Contacts	836	2511	4444	498	1383	2008	1370	1587	608	2704	5481	7060

of units within the different systems with emphasis on delineating areas in which rates of delinquency and crime should be relatively high and show continuity across cohorts over the years. The fifth chapter examines the spatial and temporal differences in delinquency and crime rates in Racine.

The relationship of the characteristics of areas within census tracts and police grids to offense and arrest rates within these spatial systems are described in the sixth chapter. How the inner city differs from other areas is clarified as a basis for emphasizing its effect on offense rates by place of residence of offender and place of occurrence.

Chapter 7 is important because we return to the cohort data to show how, cohort by cohort and decade by decade, Racine has developed the high inner city and interstitial area police contact, offense seriousness, referral, and severity of sanctions rates found in classical ecological research in the United States. Chapter 8 provides further ecological evidence for the "hardening" of the inner city.

The widespread prevalence of police contacts with juveniles will be contrasted with the concentration of delinquency and crime among multiple offenders in Chapter 9.

Chapters 10 and 11 are on continuity in careers and are followed by Chapter 12 on dispositions and the possibility of predicting future behavior from frequency of referrals. The relationship of severity of sanctions to future behavior, described in Chapter 13, indicates that the juvenile justice system has not operated as intended. Race/ethnic and sex differences in incarceration (institutionalization) and the consequences of incarceration are also examined in this chapter.

Chapter 14 provides a first look at the data obtained from interviews with persons from the 1942 and 1949 Cohorts, finding that some cherished explanations of delinquent behavior are not supported. Chapter 15 continues with the interview data to explain why most juveniles ceased to have trouble with the police before they were adults. Official and self-report measures of delinquency and crime are compared and combined in Chapter 16 to better predict official statuses.

The final chapter (Chapter 17) summarizes the research and sets forth some general recommendations for the police, the school, the courts, and the community.

NOTES

1. The terms *delinquent* or *criminal* behavior as used in this research may refer to officially recorded police contacts by juveniles or adults, referrals by the police, or court dispositions, and all interview data in which respondents describe their misbehavior.

2. A few of the earliest relevant studies are: Clifford Shaw, *Delinquency Areas* (Chicago: University of Chicago Press, 1929); Clifford Shaw and Henry D.

McKay, *Social Factors in Juvenile Delinquency* (Washington, DC: U.S. Government Printing Office, 1931); Clifford Shaw and Henry D. McKay, *Juvenile Delinquency and Urban Areas* (Chicago: University of Chicago Press, 1942); Walter B. Miller, "Lower Class Culture as a Generating Milieu of Gang Delinquency," *The Journal of Social Issues*, Vol. 14, 1958, pp. 5–19; John P. Clark and Eugene P. Wenninger, "Socio-economic Class and Area as Correlates of Illegal Behavior Among Juveniles," *American Sociological Review*, Vol. 27, December 1972, pp. 826–834; Roland J. Chilton, "Continuity in Delinquency Area Research: A Comparison of Studies for Baltimore, Detroit, and Indianapolis," *American Sociological Review*, Vol. 29, February 1964, pp. 71–83.

3. Matza's organization of theoretical explanations in terms of affinity, affiliation, and signification allows one to present sociological and social psychological models of the process of becoming delinquent in an historical perspective. David Matza, *Becoming Delinquent*, (Englewood Cliffs: Prentice-Hall, Inc., 1969).

4. Edwin H. Sutherland and Donald R. Cressey, *Principles of Criminology*, (9th edition) (Chicago: J. B. Lippincott Co., 1974); James F. Short, "Differential Association with Delinquent Friends and Delinquent Behavior," *Pacific Sociological Review* 1 (1958): 20–25; and James F. Short (ed.), *Gang Delinquency and Delinquent Subculture* (New York: Harper and Row, 1968).

5. Daniel Glaser, "Criminality Theories and Behavioral Images," *American Journal of Sociology* 61 (1956): 433–444.

6. Ronald L. Akers, *Deviant Behavior: A Social Learning Approach* (Belmont: Wadsworth Publishing, 1973).

7. We are concerned about the labeling process in terms of self-definition but we are even more interested in the process by which persons in the justice systems label those with whom they have contacts and apply "extra attention." See Charles Wellford, "Labelling Theory and Criminology," *Social Problems* 23 (1975): 332–345; Theodore Ferdinand and Elmer Luchterhand, "Inner City Youths, the Police, the Juvenile Court and Justice," *Social Problems* 18 (1962): 510–527; Edwin Schur, *Labeling Deviant Behavior* (Englewood Cliffs: Prentice-Hall, 1971); Richard Ward, "The Labeling Theory: A Critical Analysis," *Criminology* 9 (1971): 268–290; and Jay Williams and Martin Gold, "From Delinquent Behaviors to Official Delinquency," *Social Problems* 20 (1972): 209–227.

8. Frances Ferracuti, Simon Dinitz and Esperanza Acosta de Brenes, *Delinquents and Nondelinquents in the Puerto Rican Slum Culture* (Columbus: Ohio State University Press, 1975).

9. Marvin E. Wolfgang, Robert M. Figlio and Thorsten Sellin, *Delinquency in A Birth Cohort* (Chicago: The University of Chicago Press, 1972). In following almost 10,000 Philadelphia boys from age 8 to age 18, they focused attention on the need for longitudinal cohort studies.

10. Leland Johnson, former Director of Pupil Services in the Racine Unified School District, was supportive of our two longitudinal research projects in Racine commencing in the 1950s. Without his continued assistance and advice, none of the research conducted in Racine would have been possible.

11. Wolfgang, Figlio and Sellin, *op. cit.*, p. 29.

12. The term "cohort" will be used in the remainder of this presentation to signify those persons from each total cohort whose residence in Racine commenced at or before the age of 6 and continued without significant interruption until the cut-off date for data collection.

13. Chief Donald J. Dodge, Assistant Chief Milton Hagopian, Lieutenant George Kopecky (Superintendent of the Records Division), and Captain Kermit McDonald (Head of the Juvenile Bureau) were helpful in every possible way. Had Lieutenant Kopecky not developed such an excellent records division during the tenure of Chief Leroy C. Jenkins (1956–1972), the study would not have been feasible. Cooperation was continued after Chief Dodge retired under Acting Chief Hagopian and the next chief, Chief James J. Carvino. After Lieutenant Kopecky's retirement we were assisted by the new supervisor of records, Jeanine Botting.

14. The contact categories are similar to those in Delbert S. Elliott and Harwin L. Voss, *Delinquency and Dropout* (Lexington: D.C. Heath and Co., Lexington Books, 1974): 82. They were originally developed in 1956 for the Wisconsin research by Voss. The only significant difference is that Elliott and Voss did not code contacts for Suspicion, Investigation, or Information or for Traffic offenses in their California research. Categories used in the Racine research are also similar to those utilized by Wolfgang, Figlio, and Sellin, op. cit., pp. 68–69; they, however, coded contacts that were made in the course of police investigations but also omitted contacts for Traffic offenses and did not include Incorrigible, Runaway or Truancy nor did they code several low-incidence categories separately.

15. No one has been more interested in this research than then Juvenile Court Judge John C. Ahlgrimm (now Chief Judge of Racine and Kenosha Counties). His cooperation has been followed by that of other juvenile court judges.

16. We were fortunate in having a set of Racine City Directories for 1947 through 1975 present in our office and were able to borrow telephone directories from the Wisconsin Bell Telephone Company for the period covered by the study for Racine, Kenosha, and surrounding areas.

17. The 1960 U.S. Census reported that 4.3% of the persons enrolled in high school in Racine's urbanized area were non-Whites. We identified 3.6% of the 1942 Cohort as Black. This is about what one would expect because they were 18 years of age in 1960 and therefore did not have quite as large a proportion of Nonwhites as later cohorts still in high school. In the 1949 Cohort 6.3% was identified as Black. They were 11 years of age in 1960 and at that time 6.35% of the students enrolled in Racine's elementary schools were Nonwhite. The 1955 Cohort was 11 years of age at the time of selection from the 1966 records; 8.8% was Black and 3.8% was Chicano. This represents more than twice the percentage of Blacks as in the 1949 Cohort but less than the 12.6% Black and 4.7% Chicano composition of elementary school children according to the 1970 Census.

18. The distribution of contacts for those persons in each cohort with continuous residence was, with few exceptions, not significantly different from the distribution of those who did not have continuous residence. See Michael R. Olson, *A Longitudinal Analysis of Official Criminal Careers,* unpublished Ph.D. Dissertation, 1977, and *Predicting Adult Criminal Careers from Juvenile Careers,* multilithed Progress Report to LEAA, November 1976.

Chapter 2

CHANGING RATES OF DELINQUENCY AND CRIME IN RACINE

Police Contacts and Arrests as Measures of Crime

Before systematically presenting the analyses, including those which deal with the relationship of juvenile delinquency to adult crime, the data must be described more fully and examined in their historical context. We commence with the development of procedures for handling juvenile police contacts, changing emphases on law enforcement and police policies, and pertinent aspects of record-keeping that may, in one way or another, have influenced rates and trends in recorded delinquency and crime.

Because there has been considerable confusion about the operational definitions of police contacts, arrests, and referrals, even among persons familiar with the research literature on juvenile delinquency and adult crime, their specific referent for this study must be clarified. Police contacts may be initiated by citizen complainants, agency personnel, or by police officers who detect juveniles 1) in the act of committing what would be considered a crime had they been adult or 2) engaging in behavior which could be considered injurious to themselves or others and thus warranting intervention. An officer may also instigate a contact on his/her suspicion that something illegal is taking place, as part of an investigation, or in an attempt to seek information from a juvenile or juveniles about activity that has previously taken place.

It is seldom necessary to formally detain juveniles at the time of police contact; in most cases the juvenile is simply counseled and released. Juveniles are not usually told that they are under arrest and may not realize that being taken into custody for even a short time is the equivalent of being arrested. If an officer believed that more formal action was required he/she could call a juvenile officer to take the juvenile home (with the parents to be notified about the incident later if they were not at home when the juvenile was returned) or perhaps may even request parents to report to the Juvenile Bureau with their child. If the juvenile actually was brought to the Juvenile Bureau, the police disposition, rather than counseling and release at site of the contact, could be a decision to counsel and release at the station. During the first 15 years covered by this research the Juvenile Bureau was only in operation 5 days a week and then only part of the day. If the Juvenile Bureau was closed, the officer could contact a court worker from County Probation who would decide whether or not to place the juvenile in detention. Regardless of the handling of the contact, a report was made to the Juvenile Bureau about the incident. Since juvenile misbehavior often occurred when the Juvenile Bureau was closed, relatively few referrals were made directly to it during the earliest period of the study. Whichever way it worked out, a juvenile temporarily taken into custody did not share the same arrest experience as that of adults.

There were several alternatives available to juvenile officers when a juvenile was taken to the Juvenile Bureau. The first, as we have stated, was to counsel and release the juvenile. Another was to summon parents to the station and then, after counseling, to release the juvenile to their custody. If the juvenile's behavior at the time of contact was of a serious enough nature that officers of the Juvenile Bureau decided he or she should be placed in detention, this decision would be communicated to the parent and to a court worker or the judge. The Juvenile Bureau could also informally refer the juvenile to any other agency or person they thought might deal with the problem effectively.

In summary, police had contacts with juveniles and the juveniles were *counseled and released* or *referred* to County Probation or some other agency for assistance, as it is termed when dealing with juveniles.[1] As a result, the first level of cohort contact data consists of recorded police contacts and the second level consists of referral data. By contrast, official data published by law enforcement agencies (including the Racine Police Department) are usually based on offenses reported or known to the police and arrests. The juveniles included may or may not have been taken into custody as a consequence of contacts with the police, and they may or may not have been referred.

Offenses reported or known to the police occur at a far higher rate than arrests or referrals and only a proportion of the offenses reported or known to the police result in an arrest or referral. Crimes cleared by arrest are an entirely different matter because they constitute a proportion of the offenses which the police know have occurred and which have been solved by arrests. Numerous offenses may, of course, be cleared by a single arrest.

Whether cohort rates or rates developed from annual reports of the

Racine Police Department are used, an increase in police contacts may or may not have resulted in an increased rate of referral or an increase in the rate of arrests. At the same time, both referral and arrest rates may have increased without an increase in the rate of police contacts. The seriousness of the reason for a police contact, however, is the most crucial determinant of whether or not a juvenile was referred.

As most law enforcement officers and sociologists know, the arrest rate of juveniles (when we call taking them into custody an arrest) is much higher than that of adults. This is probably not because the offenses of juveniles are that much more serious than those of adults but because the nature of juveniles' offenses (high visibility) is such that they are more likely to be apprehended and taken into custody; thus they constitute a disproportionate share of those arrested. For example, between 1955 and 1977, 46% to 75% of the persons arrested in Racine for Robbery, Burglary, Larceny, and Auto Theft were under the age of 18. This figure has never been below 60% since 1965.

As juveniles go past the teens and even into early adulthood their pattern of misbehavior is such that the probability of being detected by the police is high. The offenses in which they are engaged in that period are the kinds which, to ordinary citizens, seem most threatening to life and property. This translates into the fact that teenage youth tend to be disruptive of the peace and quiet of the community. During this period the kinds of personal and property crimes which they commit, while not threatening to the whole fabric of the social order or to the economic organization of society, are disturbing to people at every socioeconomic level. Perhaps it is this traditional emphasis on crimes against property of a rather simple type, this traditional emphasis on dealing with thieves, burglars, and robbers, which has fostered the growth of the new criminology.

COHORT TRENDS VS. CITYWIDE TRENDS IN DELINQUENCY AND CRIME

A careful review of changing administrative policies between 1951 and 1977 revealed that some changes would tend to increase police contacts and referral rates and that other changes would decrease them. What may appear to be minor record-keeping changes might have had just as much impact on police contact, arrest, and referral rates as did policy changes.

Let us now turn to rates of police contact by cohort and age at contact as presented in Diagrams 1 and 2, where trends are plotted on a continuum of years from 1948 through 1976.

The shapes of each cohort's smoothed trends are very similar; the 1942 and 1949 Cohorts peaked at age 17 and the 1955 Cohort peaked at 16. Although the rate of contacts per person by year for the 1942 Cohort declined for a five-year period from a peak at age 17 in 1959, it rose again in 1965,

DIAGRAM 1

RATE OF POLICE CONTACTS PER PERSON
BY COHORT AND YEAR OF CONTACTS

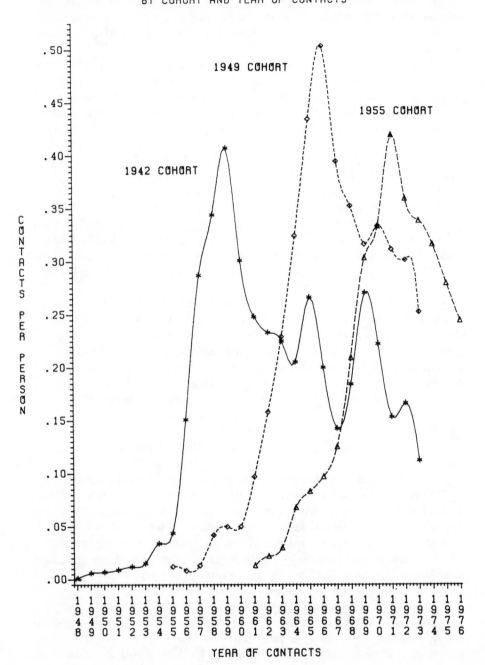

YEAR OF CONTACTS

DIAGRAM 2

RATE OF POLICE CONTACTS PER PERSON
BY COHORT, SEX AND YEAR OF CONTACTS

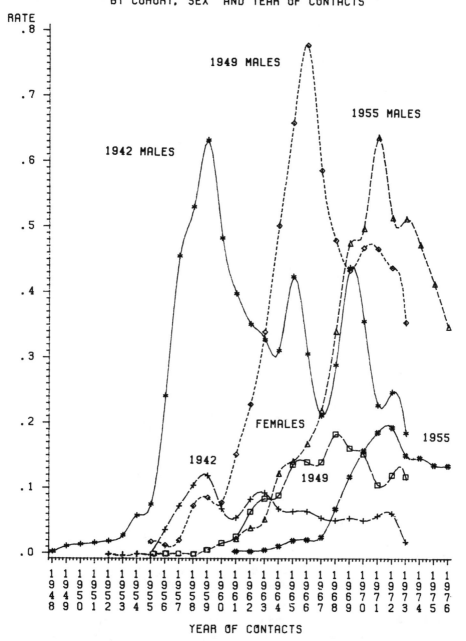

RATE

.8

.7

.6

.5

.4

.3

.2

.1

.0

1949 MALES

1955 MALES

1942 MALES

FEMALES

1942

1949

1955

YEAR OF CONTACTS

dropped to a low in 1967, and then was again at the same peak in 1969 that it had reached in 1965, thereafter declining to 1973. In 1966 the 1949 Cohort reached a higher peak than had the 1942 Cohort at its highest, again at age 17. Rates for persons in the 1955 Cohort rose in essentially the same way as did the other cohorts when they were at that age. The 1955 Cohort was too young to be directly affected by what was going on in the community, that is, the rise in arrest rates which took place in the city commencing in the 1960s.

Diagram 2 dramatizes these increases for the 1942 Cohort males and the rather higher peak for the 1949 Cohort males in 1966. It is also apparent that the females were relatively unaffected by events which produced rises in the 1942 Cohort rates in 1965 and 1969 and the 1949 Cohort's highest rates in 1966.

Table 1 of Chapter 1 showed that the percent of all police contacts that were for Part I offenses increased from cohort to cohort for persons from 6 through 17, 12.7%, in the 1942 Cohort, 15.9% in the 1949 Cohort, and 24.6% in the 1955 Cohort. The increase was from 6.5% to 10.0% to 20.5% for the entire period of years covered for each cohort. These changes suggested that serious juvenile misbehavior (the proportion of Part I offenses) increased from cohort to cohort.

Although it was not possible to produce police contact data for the entire city against which these cohort and cross-cohort changes could be viewed, other meaningful comparisons may be made. Diagrams covering a period of 25 to 30 years in Racine revealed that cohort increases in *police contact rates* for Part I offenses paralleled increases in *arrest rates* for all types of offenses.

In Diagram 3 we note that arrest rates in Racine for males from 6 through 17 went up sharply from 1963 to 1966, paused, then moved upward again, dipped in 1971 and 1972, and reached a peak in 1974. While female juveniles had been experiencing increasingly higher rates of arrest during these years, their rise was not nearly as sharp as that experienced by males.[2] Arrest rates for Part I offenses per 1000 juveniles are presented in Diagram 4. The scale for Part I offenses differs from that for all offenses since the latter had a much higher prevalence and incidence.[3] Here we find that the rise in arrests of juvenile males for Part I offenses was only slightly steeper from 1962 to 1974 than that for all arrests, and that the curve for females was somewhat flatter for Part I offenses. The net result was two quite similar curves.

The arrest data also revealed that persons aged 18 through 20 had experienced a sharper increase in arrests for all offenses than had those who were younger, commencing in 1963 and continuing through 1966, had reached a plateau, but rose again in 1973 to a peak year in 1975. This sharp increase was not found for Part I offense arrests for those 18 through 20 (Diagram 5). The diagram for all offenses also showed that persons 18

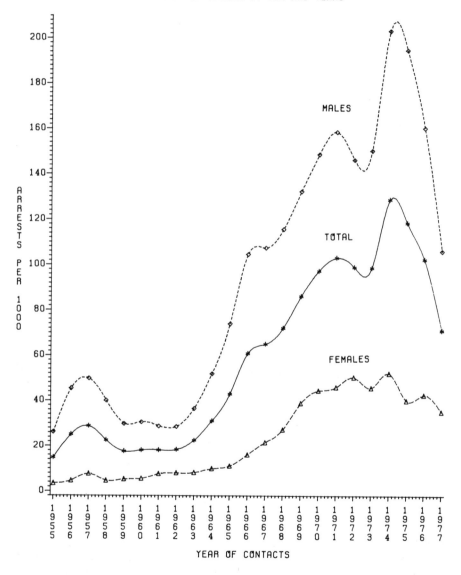

DIAGRAM 3

RATE OF ARRESTS PER 1000 JUVENILES
AGES 6-17 IN RACINE BY SEX AND YEARS

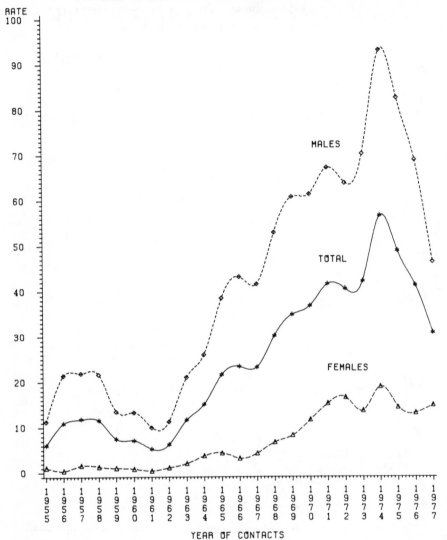

DIAGRAM 4

RATE OF ARRESTS FOR PART I OFFENSES
PER 1000 JUVENILES 6-17 IN RACINE BY SEX AND YEARS

through 20 had markedly higher arrest rates than those 6 through 17 and that the rise in rates was much higher by 1975 for those who were 18 through 20. The arrest rate for Part I offenses followed essentially the same pattern whether we were looking at persons 6 through 17 years of age or those 18 through 20 until 1974 where the downturn for the younger age group occurred a year sooner than that for the older age group. It is also clear that

DIAGRAM 5
RATE OF ARRESTS FOR PART I OFFENSES
PER 1000 PERSONS AGES 6-17 18-20 AND 21-44 IN RACINE BY YEARS

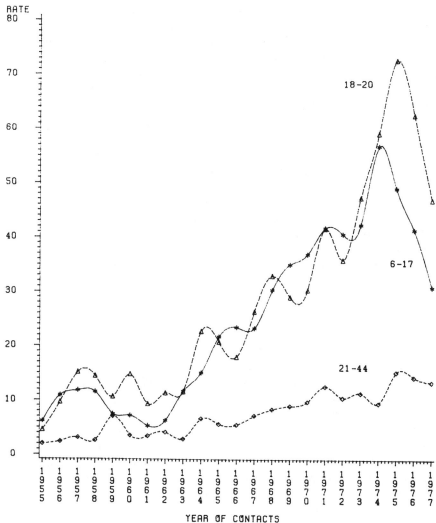

YEAR OF CONTACTS

the overall arrest rate reached a peak for persons in the 18 through 20 group in the middle 1960s and remained stable during a period in which Part I arrest rates were still increasing, but doing so more gradually.

Aside from the irregular differences but similar slopes of the curves upward for those 6 through 17 and 18 through 20, Diagram 5 makes it clear that the increase in arrest rates for Part I offenses was greatest for juvenile and youthful offenders when compared with the slope of those 21 and older. The five-fold increase in arrest rates for the ages 6 through 17 and 18 through 20 compared with a roughly two-fold increase for those 21 and older. *If* arrest data are an index of crime rates in Racine, then youthful crime has increased at a rate far beyond the increase for persons 21 years and older.

Diagram 6 has two curves, one for offenses and one for arrests. Each is on a different scale: 1) offenses reported per 1000 population and 2) arrests per 1000 population for Part I offenses. In 1963, for example, the arrest rate was approximately 4 per 1000 and the offenses reported per 1000 was slightly over 30. In other words, the rate for offenses reported was about seven times that of the arrest rate. In 1975 the arrest rate was 20 per 1000 and the offense rate was slightly over 100, or about five times as high as the arrest rate. This suggests that arrests for offenses reported were somewhat more likely in 1975 than they were in 1963 when placed on a per 1000 population basis. One interpretation that could be made is that the police had become more efficient. The public had been alerted to increasing rates of crime by front page treatment of serious and dramatic lawbreaking and increasing incidence rates produced by the FBI's Uniform Crime Reports during the 1960s and 1970s. Whether or not the latter were entirely accurate, there had been concern expressed. The increasing proportion of offenses resulting in arrest may also be interpreted as a hardening of police attitudes and fewer street-level settlements.

CHANGING COHORT RATES

Changing arrest rates in Racine should parallel cohort differences in the rates for police contact type within age periods for the rates presented in Table 1. The first set of rates was obtained by dividing the number of contacts of each type by the number of persons in the cohort. Similarly, the second set of rates was derived by dividing the number of contacts by the number of persons in the cohort who had contacts. This permitted an examination of changes in the cohort and changes in the reasons for contacts by people who had contacts. These are the bricks with which the structure is built.

From Table 1 we find that the rates for three categories of police contacts (Incorrigible, Runaway, and Truancy, Theft, and Burglary) increased from cohort to cohort during ages 6 through 17 more than did others whether the rate be for the cohorts or for those in the cohort with contacts. The rates for five other categories of contacts (Assault, Weapons, Violent Property Destruction, Robbery, and Drugs) also increased from cohort to cohort, although these are not high-rate categories. The rates for other offense categories, in some cases relatively high, either declined or revealed no steady increase across cohorts. In sum, however, Part I offense rates were higher

DIAGRAM 6

RATE OF REPORTS AND ARRESTS FOR PART I OFFENSES

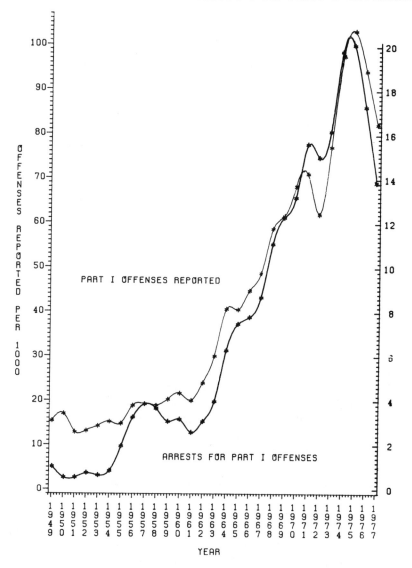

from cohort to cohort based on the number of persons in each cohort and for those persons in each cohort with contacts. Tables constructed for sex comparison revealed that contact rates for Part I offenses increased five-fold for females across cohorts but only three-fold for males from 6 through 17. Increases for specific offenses were even greater. There were no contacts for some offenses by female members of either the 1942 or 1949 Cohort,

TABLE 1. POLICE CONTACT TYPE: MEAN RATES BASED ON NUMBER OF CONTACTS DIVIDED BY NUMBER OF PERSONS IN COHORT

| | Ages 6-17 | | | | | | Ages 18-20 | | | | | |
| | COHORT | | | PERSONS WITH CONTACTS | | | COHORT | | | PERSONS WITH CONTACTS | | |
	1942	1949	1955	1942	1949	1955	1942	1848	1955	1942	1949	1955
Traffic	.335	.334	.209	.838	.694	.476	.411	.416	.292	1.300	1.041	.844
Disorderly Conduct	.321	.419	.297	.802	.872	.674	.114	.217	.247	.360	.544	.714
Suspicion, Investi-gation	.220	.386	.312	.549	.801	.708	.133	.268	.114	.420	.670	.328
Liquor	.081	.098	.048	.202	.204	.110	.032	.020	.020	.100	.050	.058
Theft	.103	.187	.267	.257	.388	.607	.024	.032	.050	.075	.081	.145
Incorrigible, Runa-way, Truant	.126	.271	.549	.316	.563	1.246	.008	.002	.002	.025	.006	.007
Vagrancy	.035	.053	.053	.087	.111	.080	.013	.022	.006	.040	.056	.018
Auto Theft	.038	.037	.050	.095	.077	.113	.010	.007	.014	.030	.017	.040
Sex Offenses	.008	.022	.018	.020	.047	.040	.016	.016	.013	.050	.041	.036
Assault	.006	.020	.047	.016	.042	.107	.002	.011	.023	.005	.027	.066
Burglary	.021	.055	.128	.051	.114	.292	.005	.006	.036	.015	.015	.104
Weapons	.006	.009	.014	.016	.018	.032	.002	.005	.014	.005	.012	.039
Violent Property Destruction	.008	.005	.015	.020	.010	.034	.008	.007	.012	.025	.017	.004
Forgery, Fraud	----	.019	.017	----	.040	.039	.002	.012	.012	.005	.031	.051
Robbery	----	.009	.017	----	.018	.038	.002	.003	.019	.005	.008	.055
Gambling	.002	.003	.001	.004	.006	.002	----	.001	.001	----	.002	.004
Narcotics, Drugs	----	----	.031	----	----	.070	----	.006	.044	----	.015	.128
Homicide	----	----	.001	----	----	.001	----	.001	.001	----	.002	.003
Other	.013	.011	.013	.032	.022	.029	.010	.014	.009	.030	.035	.027
TOTAL MEAN RATE	1.321	1.936	2.068	3.304	4.024	4.698	.787	1.066	.934	2.490	2.670	2.699
Part I Mean Rate	.168	.307	.510	.419	.638	1.158	.041	.060	.143	.130	.151	.413
Number of Contacts	836	2511	4444	836	2511	4444	498	1383	2008	498	1383	2008
Number of Persons in Cohort	633	1297	2149	253	624	946	633	1297	2149	200	518	744

but there were sufficient contacts throughout their careers for a rate for the 1955 Cohort's females who had even fewer years of exposure.

Police contact rates for Disorderly Conduct for those 18 through 20 not only had a high rate for the 1942 Cohort but increased to the second highest rate for the 1955 Cohort, whether it was the cohort rate or the rate for persons with contacts. Theft and Drug rates showed the next most notable increase across cohorts. Four other categories (Assault, Burglary, Weapons, and Robbery), although having relatively low rates of occurrence, also had higher rates across cohorts. Rates for Part I offense categories again increased across cohorts for both measures.

Numerically, there were no Drug contacts in the 1942 Cohort, eight in the 1949 Cohort, but 161 in the 1955 Cohort for those from 6 through 20. In sheer numbers, Burglary increased from 16 to 79 to 353, Assaults from five to 40 to 150, Armed Robbery from one to 15 to 77. Actually, it was numerical changes such as these which aroused the concern of persons in the juvenile and adult justice systems, as well as concerns of the public who learned about it in the media or experienced it as victims.

Despite seven years less exposure for the 1949 Cohort and 12 years less exposure for the 1955 Cohort, comparisons across cohorts for those 21 and older indicated that rates for Part I offense categories for persons with

AND NUMBER OF PERSONS IN COHORT WITH CONTACTS

	Ages 21+							Total				
	COHORT			PERSONS WITH CONTACTS				COHORT			PERSONS WITH CONTACTS	
1942	1949	1955	1942	1949	1955		1942	1949	1955	1942	1949	1955
1.070	.450	.082	2.027	1.152	.507		1.815	1.199	.584	2.630	1.734	.987
.417	.328	.098	.790	.840	.605		.852	.965	.642	1.233	1.395	1.086
.455	.275	.043	.862	.704	.265		.807	.928	.468	1.169	1.341	.792
.043	.020	.003	.081	.051	.017		.155	.138	.701	.224	.200	.121
.024	.023	.009	.045	.059	.055		.152	.242	.326	.220	.350	.552
.002	.002	----	.003	.006	----		.136	.275	.551	.197	.398	.932
.011	.009	.004	.021	.022	.023		.059	.084	.045	.085	.122	.076
.005	.001	.001	.009	.002	.003		.052	.045	.064	.076	.065	.109
.021	.015	.003	.039	.038	.017		.044	.053	.033	.064	.077	.056
.025	.022	.006	.048	.055	.038		.033	.052	.076	.048	.076	.128
.005	.005	.002	.009	.014	.014		.030	.066	.167	.044	.096	.282
.011	.005	.003	.021	.014	.020		.019	.019	.031	.028	.027	.052
.003	.005	.003	.006	.014	.017		.019	.017	.029	.028	.025	.050
.016	.017	.005	.030	.044	.032		.017	.049	.040	.025	.070	.068
.011	.004	.002	.021	.010	.012		.011	.015	.038	.016	.022	.064
.006	.001	----	.012	.002	----		.008	.005	.002	.011	.007	.004
.006	.027	.017	.012	.069	.014		.006	.033	.092	.009	.048	.155
----	----	.001	----	----	.006		----	.001	.002	----	.001	.004
.035	.016	.003	.066	.042	.017		.057	.041	.025	.082	.059	.042
2.164	1.224	.283	4.102	3.136	1.752		4.272	4.226	3.285	6.188	6.110	5.560
.070	.055	.021	.132	.140	.127		.278	.422	.673	.403	.610	1.139
1370	1587	608	1370	1587	608		2704	5481	7060	2704	5481	7060
633	1297	2149	334	506	347		633	1297	2149	434	897	1270

contacts remained almost the same; contacts for serious crimes were on the upswing from cohort to cohort. By the same token, it is revealing to note that the rates for Theft, Assault, Burglary, Narcotics, and the Part I offenses in general were higher from cohort to cohort for total years of exposure, while the total mean contact rate had declined. This, combined with the trend for other age periods, is evidence of consistent increase from cohort to cohort in the seriousness of recorded police contacts.

What we had were age, period, and cohort changes: 1) changes in individuals throughout the life cycle, 2) changes in the larger society associated with time periods, and 3) changes from cohort to cohort.[4]

In other words, there were problems of continuity and discontinuity among persons in a cohort, changes between cohorts, and changes generated by community-level changes in record keeping, police administration, staffing at various levels in the juvenile and adult justice systems, and changes in the orientation of the judges of various courts as they responded to community pressures. The interrelationship of these changes and the difficulty of identifying sources of change were problems of which we were constantly aware in the course of the analysis.

Although there were more or less linear changes in cohort offense rates and more or less linear changes in arrest rates for the entire community, there were also non-linear, rather abrupt changes in individual careers and in rates for the entire community. While we are concerned with linear changes that are related to the life cycle, there are also dramatic changes that must also be considered and explained. Some of the latter may be explained by changes in individuals that come about when they reached the age that new statuses were acquired, and consequently new roles, and others may be related to major changes in the focal concerns of subcultural groups or the larger community.

SUMMARY

The bricks upon which our findings are built consist of police contact records which may be influenced by administrative policy and changes in the eyes of the beholder, i.e., how police officers perceived and recorded the behavior of juveniles and adults. It is possible that behavior that was once handled informally and not recorded resulted in an official contact in later years. Nonetheless, these are the data that form the basis for daily reports that ultimately reach the crime-fearing public. These are the kinds of increases in delinquency and crime that generate public concern. And it is with these data that we must work in order to develop an understanding of the nature of delinquency and crime, their relationship to each other, and their relationship to the social organization of the community.

NOTES

1. It should be mentioned that a juvenile court intake section was established in 1974 and juveniles, instead of being referred to the Juvenile Bureau, are now usually referred to the juvenile court intake. Referral to Juvenile Probation now takes place only after there has been a referral to the Juvenile Court or juvenile intake. The District Attorney's Office now has a juvenile court prosecutor.
2. In order to compute the rates described in this chapter the 1950, 1960, and 1970 Census and projected population figures for Racine beyond 1970 were broken down into age groups and rates were based on estimates developed for each intercensal year and for years beyond 1970. We used ages 21 through 44 because the proportion of the population over 21 involved in crime is disproportionately composed of persons of this age group.
3. Incidence is defined as either the frequency of police contacts or an event such as arrest per person (rate) during a given age, year, or period of time. Prevalence refers to the proportion who had a police contact or experienced some other event during an age period such as 6 through 17, 18 through 20, or for a combination of age periods. The closer we get to the delinquent act in the process of recording careers, the more likely we are to understand and predict continuing

delinquent careers. This has been a concern of long standing: Fred J. Murphy, Mary M. Shirley and Helen Witmer, "The Incidence of Hidden Delinquency," *American Journal of Orthopsychiatry* 16 (1946): 686–695; Maynard L. Erickson and LaMar T. Empey, "Court Records, Undetected Delinquency and Decision-Making," *Journal of Criminal Law, Criminology and Police Science* 54 (1963): 456–469; John C. Ball, Alan Ross and Alice Simpson, "Incidence and Prevalence of Recorded Delinquency in a Metropolitan Area," *American Sociological Review* 29 (1964): 90–93; Stanton Wheeler, "Criminal Statistics: A Reformulation of the Problem," *Journal of Criminal Law, Criminology and Police Science* 58 (1967): 317–324; William Chambliss and R. H. Hagasawa, "On the Validity of Official Statistics," *Journal of Research on Crime and Delinquency* 6 (1967): 71–77.

4. For a discussion of age, period, and cohort changes in relationships to juvenile delinquency see Carl-Gunnar Janson, *The Longitudinal Approach, Research Report, No. 9,* Project Metropolitan, Stockholm University, Stockholm, Sweden, 1978; Thomas W. Pullum, "Parametrizing Age, Period, and Cohort Effects: An Application to U.S. Delinquency Rates, 1964–1973," in Karl F. Schuessler (ed.), *Sociological Methodology* (San Francisco: Jossey-Bass, 1978), pp. 116–140.

Chapter 3

THE PROBLEM OF MEASURING SERIOUSNESS
OF CAREERS

DEVELOPING ADDITIVE MEASURES OF SERIOUSNESS

Measuring the incidence and prevalence of delinquency and crime is a problem but the development of an index of seriousness of offenses and an index of the seriousness of careers are even greater problems. Whether we use officially recorded delinquency and crime or self-reported transgressions, an index of the seriousness of individual acts, as well as summary measures of careers, is essential.

The number of alleged offenses is not a completely satisfactory measure of the seriousness of a person's behavioral history or career. Some individuals commit one serious offense which suggests a high probability of continuing misbehavior or contacts with representatives of the juvenile and adult justice systems, while other one-time offenders have been involved in what is clearly a minor or even accidental offense.

Exactly how one should combine different types of offenses with different frequencies and degrees of seriousness has been a question of theoretical and practical concern for many years.[1] We have approached the problem of measuring seriousness in several ways in order to be sure that the findings are not artifacts of a single measure and to make sure that using one measure rather than another would not generate quite different findings.

42

Number of Contacts as a Measure of Seriousness

The simplest way to construct an index of seriousness for individuals is to add the number of police contacts that each has had during some appropriate age period (e.g., 6 through 17). The mean number of police contacts or the rate per 100 or per 1000 persons may be utilized as an index of the seriousness of delinquency or crime during an age period for any segment of a cohort.

Although the mean number of contacts or a rate for all persons in each cohort by age periods differs from the mean number of contacts or a rate by age periods for only those persons who had contacts during that period, both sets of means or rates are useful in describing group variation. The more restrictive procedure is selected when the objective is to determine if the members of one group who had police contacts had more frequent contacts with the police than another group of persons who also had police contacts.

Utilizing the proportion of police contacts that were for Part I offense categories or the number of Part I offenses per person or per 100 persons in the group are other simple approaches to indexing the relative seriousness of a cohort's police contacts during each age period or of those who had contacts in each cohort.

Type-Seriousness Scores as a Measure of Seriousness

As a first step in developing a measure of seriousness, the 26 categories of police contact were placed in six levels of seriousness in terms of whether or not the contact was a Felony Against Persons, a Felony Against Property, a Major Misdemeanor, a Minor Misdemeanor, a Juvenile Condition (status offense), or a contact for Suspicion, Investigation, or Information. This was a more or less arbitrary arrangement but is consistent with police reporting practices. The justification for using this scoring system rests on the legal distinction between felonies and misdemeanors. Criminal law specifies that illegal acts are treated as relatively serious (felonies) or as less serious (misdemeanors).

The scoring system used in developing this measure assigned Felonies Against Persons the highest (i.e., most serious) score of 6 and Felonies Against Property the second highest score of 5. Certain acts, although normally considered felonious, may be dealt with as misdemeanors under specific circumstances at the discretion of law enforcement officials. For example, Burglary is treated as a felony when a house is entered but as a misdemeanor when it involves a locked vehicle. In order to reflect this dual status, these offenses were designated as Major Misdemeanors and received a score of 4. Other acts are invariably regarded as misdemeanors by the law. For example, Vagrancy and Disorderly Conduct are never classified as felonies. These Minor Misdemeanors were given a score of 3.

With the advent of the juvenile justice system, age became a mitigating condition under the law. An offense committed by a juvenile is treated differently (usually in the direction of lenience) from one committed by an adult. Additionally, a new set of offenses evolved which could only be committed by the young, e.g., truancy, incorrigibility, runaway, ungovernability, the so-called status offenses. The catch-all vagrancy and disorderly conduct statuses are also frequently invoked to deal with youthful misbehavior. We have designated the juvenile status offenses and Vagrancy or Disorderly Conduct, when committed by those under age 18, as Juvenile Conditions and have given them a score of 2.

The final category of offenses consists of instances when individuals were stopped on the street for *Suspicion, Investigation, or Information* at the discretion of the police officer. No criminal allegations need necessarily have been involved. These relatively minor incidents received a score of 1. The content of each of these categories is shown in Table 1.

THE DISTRIBUTION OF SERIOUS CONTACTS

The distribution of contacts by the type-seriousness scoring system is shown in Table 2 by age period, sex, and cohort. Females in each cohort and in each age period had fewer police contacts than did males and male contacts more frequently fell in the three most serious categories in each age period for each cohort than did female contacts. It was apparent that the aggregated seriousness of male delinquency and crime exceeded that of the females. Furthermore, whether mean seriousness rates based on the number of serious contacts (Felonies Against Persons or Property and Major Misdemeanors) were computed for each age period for each race/ethnic|sex segment of each cohort for persons in that segment of the cohort or the number of persons with contacts, the mean seriousness of contacts was, with one exception, greater for males than for females. When persons in each cohort were classified according to their most serious reason for police contact (Table 3), a considerably higher proportion of the males than females from each cohort had Felonies Against Persons, Felonies Against Property, and Major Misdemeanors.

Comparison of seriousness based on frequency of contacts (incidence) and proportion of cohort with contacts (prevalence), mean frequency of serious contacts and proportion with serious contacts, and frequency of Part I contacts and proportion of cohort with Part I contacts (all by age period, cohort, race/ethnicity, and sex) revealed that in every comparison the means of males were higher than those of females. In fact, of 486 age,

TABLE 1.   SERIOUSNESS OF POLICE CONTACTS: ORDINAL RANKING OF SIX MAJOR
           CATEGORIES AND THE OFFENSES INCLUDED IN EACH

Score

6   Felony Against Persons: The following offenses were given a score
         of 6 when treated as felonies by the police.

                 Robbery   Homicide
                 Assault   Escapee
                 Sex Offenses   Suicide
                 Narcotics/Drugs

5   Felony Against Property: The following offenses were given a score
         of 5 when treated as felonies by the police.

                 Burglary   Forgery
                 Theft   Fraud
                 Auto Theft   Violent Property Destruction

4   Major Misdemeanor: The following offenses were given a score of 4
         when treated as misdemeanors by the police.

                 Forgery   Assault
                 Escapee   Fraud
                 Theft   Violent Property Destruction
                 Narcotics/Drugs   Burglary
                 Weapons

3   Minor Misdemeanor: The following offenses were given a score of 3
         when treated as misdemeanors by the police.

                 Obscene Behavior   Moving Traffic Violations
                 Disorderly Conduct   Other Traffic Offenses
                 Vagrancy   Gambling
                 Liquor Violations   Family Problems
                 Sex Offenses   Other

2   Juvenile Status: The following offenses were given a score of 2
         when the alleged offender was under 18 years of age.

                 Vagrancy   Incorrigible, Runaway
                 Disorderly Conduct   Truancy

1   Contact for Suspicion, Investigation, Information: The category
         was given a score of 1 when the complaint report indicated a contact
         for any of these reasons.

sex, and race comparisons for the three cohorts there were only two where
females had higher seriousness scores than their male counterparts.

Cross-cohort seriousness had not only increased, as indicated by the
percent who had ever had a Felony Against Property or Person (9.8% for
the 1942 Cohort, 12.1% for the 1949 Cohort, and 18.7% for the 1955 Cohort),
but seriousness scores had become higher across cohorts within age periods

TABLE 2. PERCENT OF CONTACTS IN SERIOUSNESS OF CONTACT CATEGORY BY COHORT, SEX, AND AGE PERIOD

Ages 6-17

	Males			Females		
	1942	1949	1955	1942	1949	1955
Felony Against Person	.5	.8	2.6	---	.9	2.5
Felony Against Property	5.3	6.2	11.5	1.0	.3	3.0
Major Misdemeanor	9.1	11.6	16.5	5.2	9.0	14.4
Minor Misdemeanor	47.6	41.1	25.0	33.3	28.8	23.8
Juvenile Condition	9.2	13.0	25.4	12.5	20.7	33.9
Suspicion, Investigation	28.4	27.4	19.1	47.9	40.2	22.4
TOTAL	100.0	100.1	100.1	99.9	100.0	100.0
Mean Seriousness	2.6	2.6	2.8	2.0	2.1	2.5
Number of Contacts	740	2188	3601	96	323	843

Ages 18-20

	Males			Females		
	1942	1949	1955	1942	1949	1955
Felony Against Person	.9	1.1	9.1	3.5	---	3.6
Felony Against Property	2.0	2.8	9.0	---	1.1	3.6
Major Misdemeanor	5.0	6.0	9.7	---	1.5	7.4
Minor Misdemeanor	46.0	40.3	44.4	35.1	42.6	47.3
Juvenile Condition	1.1	.3	.2	---	.4	.4
Suspicion, Investigation	44.9	49.5	27.6	61.4	54.4	37.7
TOTAL	99.9	100.0	100.0	100.0	100.0	100.0
Mean Seriousness	2.2	2.2	3.0	1.9	1.9	2.4
Number of Contacts	441	1113	1560	57	270	448

Ages 21+

	Males			Females		
	1942	1949	1955	1942	1949	1955
Felony Against Person	1.1	2.1	7.5	1.1	2.5	6.6
Felony Against Property	1.1	2.0	2.2	---	.7	2.6
Major Misdemeanor	3.3	5.5	8.3	1.7	3.9	5.3
Minor Misdemeanor	45.4	47.8	52.6	41.8	50.9	57.2
Juvenile Condition	---	.1	---	.6	.7	---
Suspicion, Investigation	49.1	42.5	29.4	54.8	41.4	28.3
TOTAL	100.0	100.0	100.0	100.0	100.1	100.0
Mean Seriousness	2.4	2.3	2.8	1.9	2.3	2.7
Number of Contacts	1193	1302	456	177	285	152

Total

	Males			Females		
	1942	1949	1955	1942	1949	1955
Felony Against Person	.9	1.2	4.8	1.2	1.1	3.3
Felony Against Property	2.6	4.2	10.0	.3	.7	3.1
Major Misdemeanor	5.4	8.5	14.0	2.4	5.0	11.2
Minor Misdemeanor	46.2	42.8	32.6	38.2	40.2	34.7
Juvenile Condition	3.1	6.3	16.3	3.9	8.0	20.0
Suspicion, Investigation	41.9	37.0	22.3	53.9	45.0	27.8
TOTAL	100.0	100.0	100.1	99.9	100.0	100.1
Mean Seriousness	2.3	2.4	2.9	1.9	2.1	2.5
Number of Contacts	2374	4603	5617	330	878	1443

TABLE 3. PERCENTAGE OF RACINE BIRTH COHORTS WHOSE MOST SERIOUS POLICE CONTACT WAS AT SPECIFIED LEVEL

Cause of Contact	1942 Cohort			1949 Cohort			1955 Cohort		
	Male	Female	Total	Male	Female	Total	Male	Female	Total
Felony Against Person	5.1	1.8	3.6	5.7	2.9	4.5	12.7	4.6	8.8
Felony Against Property	8.1	.4	4.7	9.5	.9	5.8	9.0	2.1	5.7
Major Misdemeanor	12.6	2.2	8.1	13.2	5.9	10.1	10.6	6.5	8.6
Minor Misdemeanor	40.4	19.1	31.1	37.0	19.6	29.5	24.8	16.0	20.6
Juvenile Condition	1.1	1.8	1.4	1.6	2.0	1.8	3.8	4.2	4.0
Suspicion, Investigation	16.9	22.7	19.4	14.6	21.0	17.3	10.9	12.0	11.4
Contacts of Any Type	84.2	48.0	68.3*	81.6	52.3	69.0	71.8	45.4	59.1
Number of Persons	356	277	633	740	557	1297	1114	1035	2149

* The percent who had ever had a contact was slightly smaller than in other tables because of loss in rounding.

TABLE 4. SUMMARY OF BASIC STATISTICS ON FREQUENCY AND SERIOUSNESS OF CONTACTS BY COHORT AND RACE/ETHNICITY

	Ages 6-17			Ages 18-20			Ages 21+			Total		
	1942	1949	1955	1942	1949	1955	1942	1949	1955	1942	1949	1955
Number in Cohort	633	1297	2149	633	1297	2149	633	1297	2149	633	1297	2149
Number of Contacts	836	2511	4444	498	1383	2008	1370	1587	608	2704	5481	7060
Number of Persons with Contacts	253	624	946	200	518	744	334	506	347	434	897	1270
% with Contacts	40.0	48.1	44.0	31.6	39.9	34.6	52.8	39.0	16.1	68.6	69.2	59.1
Mean Contacts per Person	1.3	1.9	2.1	.8	1.1	.9	2.2	1.2	.3	4.3	4.2	3.3
Mean Contacts per Person with Contacts	3.3	4.0	4.7	2.5	2.7	2.7	4.1	3.1	1.8	6.2	6.1	5.6
% Contacts Serious*	14.0	17.7	29.0	7.7	8.8	25.4	6.1	9.6	17.8	8.8	13.1	27.0
Mean Serious Contacts per Person	.2	.3	.6	.1	.1	.2	.1	.1	.1	.4	.6	.9
Mean Serious Contacts per Person with Contacts	.4	.7	1.4	.2	.2	.7	.2	.3	.3	.5	.8	1.5
% Contacts Part I	12.7	15.9	24.6	5.2	5.6	15.3	3.2	4.5	7.2	6.5	10.0	20.5
Mean Part I Contacts per Person	.2	.3	.5	-.1	.1	.1	.1	.1	-.1	.3	.4	.7
Mean Part I Contacts per Person with Contacts	.6	.6	1.2	.1	.2	.4	.1	.1	.1	.4	.6	1.1

* Serious Contacts = Felonies Against the Person or Property and Major Misdemeanors.

for males and females for almost every race/ethnic|sex group, no matter which measure was utilized.

The three additive approaches to seriousness that we have utilized are compared in simple form in Table 4. Seriousness became higher across cohorts in both earlier age periods and generally declined from age period to age period within each cohort, with cohort and age period differences maximized by use of the six-point seriousness scale.

GEOMETRIC SCALING WITH SERIOUSNESS CATEGORIES

The difficulty with additive measures is that, while the scores refer to number of offenses, they tell us nothing about how the score was generated. While the six type-seriousness categories did not generate a scale with the internal consistency of a Guttman scale (errors in reproducibility exceeded 20% for each cohort), most people had delinquent and/or criminal careers that fell into a relatively small number of types of careers, perfect or error types.

In order to describe careers parsimoniously we then constructed a Geometric scale, an extension of the Guttman scale technique which assigns every perfect Guttman type and every error type a distinctive score. To construct such a scale one simply assigns (in order of seriousness) 1 point to a contact for Suspicion, Investigation, or Information, 2 points to a contact for a Juvenile Condition, 4 points to a Minor Misdemeanor, 8 points to a Major Misdemeanor, 16 points to a Felony Against Property, and 32 points to a Felony Against Persons. Those who had a contact for each category received a score of 63, for example.

THE INTERRELATIONSHIP OF SCORES

Which measure is the best measure of seriousness of delinquent and criminal behavior? This depends on what is to be done with it.

If the simplest possible index of delinquency or crime is desired (how often someone has come to the attention of the police or been sought out by the police), then the number of police contacts is the best measure. The number of police contacts accumulated during any given period indicates how frequently a person's behavior had resulted in police attention. Computing this kind of "score" is not difficult for hard-pressed police department records divisions.

If the overall seriousness of a career as measured by frequency and reasons for contact is desired, then the six-point seriousness score has certain advantages over the number of contacts. The range of seriousness scores increased across cohorts following essentially the same pattern as did number of contacts except that when total careers were considered there was an even greater increase for the females than for the males. The mean seriousness scores of persons in each cohort increased from cohort to cohort more consistently for the younger ages (periods) than did the mean number of police contacts.

The range of Geometric scores (not computed for the 1955 Cohort because it was found that they did not permit greater efficiency in prediction beyond that possible with either number of contacts or seriousness of contacts) changed very little or did not change across cohorts, particularly for the males. The most noticeable change in Geometric scores was for juvenile females, whose change indicated that they had developed a greater range in patterns of juvenile misbehavior. The extent to which the females had changed in the direction of participation in more serious delinquency and crime, although apparent from observation of the entire range of Geometric scores, was better represented by the increased proportion of their contacts for Part I offenses or by the seriousness scale which we have already discussed.

When each measure was correlated with each other measure by age periods it was found that, while these measures were closely related (particularly for the males), number of contacts and seriousness of contacts had the highest correlations within each age period for both sexes; most were .96 or above. Furthermore, when scores for age periods for one measure were correlated with following age period scores for the same measure, the correlations were higher for number of contacts and for seriousness scores than for Geometric scores.[2] Since high correlations are a basic requisite (necessary but not sufficient) for predicting continuity in careers, we shall utilize the additive seriousness scale or number of offenses as measures of seriousness in the chapters which follow.

THE POSSIBILITY OF CONSTELLATIONS OF CONTACTS INDICATIVE OF SERIOUSNESS OF CAREERS

Before leaving the subject of measuring the seriousness of careers, further comment should be made in support of the decision to include Traffic offenses and contacts for Suspicion, Investigation, or Information in these measures.

Sociologists have been concerned about the possibility of developing a typology or scale which takes into consideration the interrelationship of various categories of offenses. Thus, each person's score would be based not on the number of contacts in each category and some simple weighting of categories as has just been done, but on weights related to the probability that a given category of contact-generating behavior would be part of a larger pattern of behavior typical of serious delinquency. These weights could be derived from regression analysis or some other multivariate technique. Factor analysis, for example, would not only provide a basis for assigning weights to different reasons for police contact, but should at the same time determine if there are groups of people who tend to share the same delinquent and/or criminal behaviors as represented by categories of police contacts.

The issue of offense clustering is related to that of offense specialization dealt with by Wolfgang, et al., through the use of stochastic modeling. They were concerned, however, with whether or not the probability of committing an offense was greatest when it was preceded by a similar offense. They utilized the categories of Non-index, Injury, Theft, Damage, and Combinations and concluded that there was some tendency to repeat the same type of offense but that the probability of repetition, except for Theft offenses, was low.[3] On the other hand, Bursik (using the same categories as Wolfgang) analyzed the careers of 750 Chicago youths who had been adjudicated delinquent by the age of 17 and found evidence of some specialization.[4] His sample differed from that of the Philadelphia and Racine cohorts, however, in that the adjudicated Chicago youth were more likely to have a greater proportion of serious contacts in their records than members of a birth cohort.

As Bursik indicates, even if transition probabilities to the same type of offense are not highly likely, transition to a different but related offense may be the pattern. It is for this reason that we were primarily interested in determining if the offenses of individuals were related, even though the analytic technique employed loses the sequential dimension.

Geometric scaling of 26 reasons for police contact (not the seriousness levels utilized in the Geometric scale presented here) revealed that the recorded contacts of most offenders were of an almost random nature and most combinations of contacts were not meaningful in that they did not involve related activities.[5] Since this issue is not central to our current research, we have not pursued it at this time.

As a result of our concern about the possibility of interrelatedness of types of contacts, contacts were arranged in 38 different categories based on type and seriousness then subjected to the SPSS factor analysis routine. This procedure failed to reveal any meaningful constellations of contacts for males or females in either the 1942 or the 1949 Cohort. There were no constellations of acts that could be considered indicative of a particular type of career. While some factors consisted of categories that would be expected to cluster together (and most of them were rather serious, i.e., felonies), these factors also contained reasons for police contacts that are not often considered serious. Moving vehicle violations were a part of Factor 1 (which also included Theft, Disorderly Conduct, Vagrancy, and Liquor offenses) for males in the 1949 Cohort, thus our decision to include police contacts for Traffic offenses in the career seriousness scale was supported.

Since the possibility of eliminating contacts for Suspicion, Investigation, or Information had also been raised (it, too, had been a part of either Factor 1 or 2 for the 1942 and 1949 Cohorts), even further attention was given to this problem. When all police contacts were divided into Traffic, Non-traffic, and Suspicion, Investigation, or Information categories, and the numbers of contacts in each category for each person were correlated, age period by age period and for total careers, we found relatively little linear correlation between any pair of these contact categories, although the highest correlations for either cohort were between Non-traffic contacts and contacts for Suspicion, Investigation, or Information.

Perusal of the tables from which these correlations were generated revealed that there were much stronger, non-linear relationships generating fairly high gammas for many groups. The highest relationships varied with age periods and with the particular variables being correlated. The most consistently high correlations were again for Non-traffic contacts and contacts for Suspicion, Investigation, or Information (ranging from .533 to .722), suggesting that persons who had Non-traffic police contacts were also likely to have been stopped for questioning during each period of their careers.

SUMMARY

Several measures of seriousness have been examined: number of police contacts, an additive score with weights based on the frequency of contacts at six levels of seriousness, the rates or proportions of Part I offenses, and a Geometric score derived from the six levels of seriousness but based on combinations of contact categories. Examination of the results led to the conclusion that a summary score based on the number of contacts in each seriousness category ranging from Felonies Against the Person to contacts for Suspicion, Investigation, or Information was a simple but useful measure of either seriousness during age periods or total career seriousness.

While number and seriousness of contacts as measures of seriousness of delinquency indicated an increase in seriousness across cohorts for the juvenile and young adult periods, the proportion or mean number of police contacts that may be classified as Part I offenses also highlighted across-cohort changes, particularly if those persons with contacts, rather than the number of persons in the cohort or of a race/ethnic|sex segment, were used as a basis for deriving a proportion or mean.

The extent to which Traffic contacts were intertwined with Non-traffic contacts indicated that, while separate analyses should be made of Non-traffic contacts where appropriate, Traffic contacts should be included in measures of seriousness. We shall, of course, conduct analyses in which only those police contacts for the most serious offense categories, such as felonies or Felonies Against Persons, Felonies Against Property, and Major Misdemeanors, are included. Thus, the concerns of those who wish to focus on only the most serious types of offenses and offenders will be considered.

NOTES

1. Sophia M. Robison, *Can Delinquency Be Measured?* (New York: Columbia University Press, 1936) made an early attack on the measurement problem. More recently, a variety of more or less sophisticated scaling techniques have been utilized: Thorsten Sellin and Marvin Wolfgang, *The Measurement of Delinquency* (New York: John Wiley and Sons, 1964); R. I. Martin and Malcolm W. Klein, *A Comparative Analysis of Four Measures of Delinquency Seriousness* (Los Angeles: University of Southern California, Youth Studies Center, 1965); Travis Hirschi and Hanan C. Selvin, *Delinquency Research: An Appraisal of Analytic Methods* (New York: The Free Press, 1967); Marvin E. Wolfgang, Robert M. Figlio and Thorsten Sellin, *Delinquency in a Birth Cohort* (Chicago: The University of Chicago Press, 1972); and Charles F. Wellford and Michael D. Wiatrowski, "On the Measurement of Delinquency," *Journal of Criminal Law and Criminology* 66 (1975): 175–188.
2. There is some question about the appropriateness of correlating Geometric scores with the other scores because the Geometric scores are not equal-interval scores and might more properly be considered rank-order or even nominal scores.
3. op. cit., Wolfgang, Figlio and Sellin, pp. 174–207.
4. Robert J. Bursik, Jr., "The Dynamics of Specialization in Juvenile Offenses," *Social Forces* 58 (1980): 851–864.
5. Lyle W. Shannon, "Scaling Juvenile Delinquency," *Journal of Research in Crime and Delinquency* 5 (1968): 52–65.

Chapter 4

THE ECOLOGY OF RACINE

Before any analyses could be conducted of the relationship of delinquency and crime to the changing ecological structure of the city, it was necessary to develop measures of ecological change.

Ecological areas of a city may be described and delineated in a variety of ways, using such spatial units as blocks, neighborhoods, natural areas, police grids, or census tracts, from the smallest to the largest. Block data from the U.S. Census were utilized in developing Geometric and factor analytic scores to represent the quality of housing in Racine, block by block, for 1950, 1960, and 1970. The variables included were: value of owner occupied housing, average contract rent, proportion of units renter occupied, proportion of overcrowding in block, and proportion of units lacking some or all plumbing. These block scale scores may also be considered a proxy for socioeconomic status and may be utilized with other variables to characterize each unit in each of the four spatial systems. Block census data for 1950, 1960, 1970, and 1980 enabled us to adjust the number of units in each spatial system for each 10-year period as the city expanded in area or population from 1950 to 1980.

The maps which follow show each of the four spatial systems. The first map shows the 1970 Racine Census Tracts superimposed on a computer-generated map of block Geometric scores in which commercial-industrial areas and parks and public use areas for 1970 are also delineated. The second map shows the Police Grids[1] for which we also aggregated census block data. The third map presents natural areas delineated to maximize the homogeneity of areas on a basis of housing quality scores for blocks.[2] This map also overlays the 26 natural areas on the housing and land use map.

Numerous efforts were made to generate small, homogeneous neighborhoods with sophisticated computer routines but the small homogeneous areas that we desired did not emerge.[3] The computer results and summary block scores (housing quality, vacancies, target density, and land use) did, however, enable us to delineate the 65 neighborhoods shown on Map 4, taking into consideration all natural and man-made boundaries that would discourage or even preclude social interaction. These neighborhoods average 20 blocks in size with each of the 55 predominantly residential neighborhoods (with only a few exceptions) containing from 1,000 to 2,000 persons in 1970. Areas which are predominantly commercial-industrial or parks and cemeteries (numbers from 60 to 70) are readily distinguishable from those which are primarily residential neighborhoods.

The interrelationship of the units in the four spatial schemes is shown on Table 1. Smaller units (neighborhoods) do not fit nicely within natural areas, natural areas within police grids, and grids within tracts. This table shows how complex the overlapping is between tracts and grids and also gives a glimmer of the difficulty encountered in developing a set of groups which may be described loosely as inner city, interstitial or transitional, stable residential middle and upper socioeconomic status (hereafter SES), and peripheral or outlying upper SES areas.

What becomes apparent is that the heterogeneity of the largest areas in one spatial system may generate scores or characteristics which markedly differentiate them from similar areas with which they overlap in another spatial system. While this is an old problem in ecological research, it is one which must be taken into consideration in assessing what may seem to be dissimilar scores for roughly similar areas.

The Social, Demographic, Land Use, and Housing Characteristics of Units in Each Spatial System

Data were obtained for the four spatial systems on 38 different land use, housing characteristics, and population characteristic variables, some for the units in each spatial system but others only for census tracts. Some of the data were available for 1950, 1960, 1970, and 1980 and some were unfortunately available for only 1970. These data were used to place individual spatial units in relatively homogeneous groups of units. Many of the variables were available only for census tracts. Because we wished to conduct parallel analyses based on four different spatial systems, we were limited to the use of block data for housing, land use, target density, racial

MAP 2

NATURAL AREAS OF RACINE
BASED ON 1970 CENSUS OF HOUSING DATA

GEOMETRIC SCALE SCORES

POLICE GRID AREAS

MAP 1

NATURAL AREAS OF RACINE
BASED ON 1970 CENSUS OF HOUSING DATA

GEOMETRIC SCALE SCORES

CENSUS TRACTS

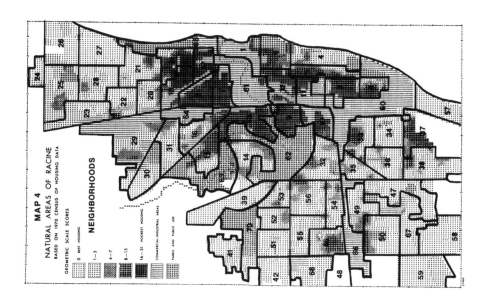

MAP 4
NATURAL AREAS OF RACINE
BASED ON 1970 CENSUS OF HOUSING DATA

NEIGHBORHOODS

GEOMETRIC SCALE SCORES

0 BEST HOUSING
1—3
4—7
8—15
16—31 POOREST HOUSING
COMMERCIAL-INDUSTRIAL AREAS
PARKS AND PUBLIC USE

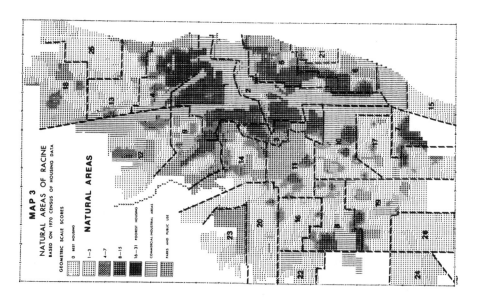

MAP 3
NATURAL AREAS OF RACINE
BASED ON 1970 CENSUS OF HOUSING DATA

NATURAL AREAS

GEOMETRIC SCALE SCORES

0 BEST HOUSING
1—3
4—7
8—15
16—31 POOREST HOUSING
COMMERCIAL-INDUSTRIAL AREAS
PARKS AND PUBLIC USE

TABLE 1.   RELATIONSHIP OF CENSUS TRACTS TO POLICE GRIDS, NATURAL AREAS, AND
           NEIGHBORHOODS

TRACTS	GRIDS	NATURAL AREAS	NEIGHBORHOODS
	Relationship of Tracts to Grids	Relationship of Natural Areas to Tracts	Relationship of Neighborhoods to Tracts and Natural Areas
Inner City			
1	12 (T2, 3, 4)[2]	--	1
3 (G12, 16)[1]	--	2	2, 3, 11, 12, 60
4 (G8, 9, 12, 13)	8 (T13)	1	7, 8, 13, 17, 61
5 (G9, 17)	13 (T4, 6, 12)	3	9, 10
Inner City and Interstitial to Middle SES			
2 (G12)	16 (T3)	5, 21, 6	4, 5, 6
13 (G5, 8, 9)	4 (T14)	13, 4	18, 19, 20, 21, 22, 65
6 (G13, 14)	17 (T3, 5, 7)	14, 11	32, 62
7 (G17)	21 (T8)	10, 17, 7	33, 34, 35, 36, 38
Middle to Upper SES and Outlying Areas			
12 (G2, 10, 13)	5 (T13, 14), 6	12, 9	15, 16, 29, 30, 31, 63,
	9 (T4, 5, 13)		64
10 (G14)	18 (T9), 19	22, 16, 8	46, 48, 54, 55, 46, 66
			68
9 (G18)	22, 23	19, 26, 24	47, 49, 50, 58, 59, 67
8 (G21)	20	15, 7	37, 57
Upper SES and Outlying Areas			
11	10 (T12)		
	14 (T6, 10, 13),	20, 23	39, 41, 42, 51, 52, 53,
	15		70
14 (G4, 5)	1 (T15), 2 (T12)	18, 25	14, 23, 25, 26, 27, 28
15			24

[1] Grid numbers in parentheses indicate that tract overlapped these grids or that tract overlapped additional grids besides the grid shown in the next column.

[2] Tract numbers in parentheses indicate that grid overlapped these tracts in addition to the tract in the first column.

composition, and some demographic characteristics in the grouping process for areas other than tracts.

Primary, secondary, and tertiary land uses for all blocks were coded according to eight categories: residential, business-commercial, schools, parks-playgrounds, cemeteries, institutions (hospitals, government offices, courthouses, etc.), manufacturing-industrial, and vacant. Targets (taverns, restaurants, grocery and liquor stores, and gas stations) were separately counted as they appeared in each block in 1950, 1960, and 1970. Target density is the average number of total targets per block for any of the four types of areas. Percent residential vacancy was developed from block census data. The housing exterior and interior scale and the housing picture match were taken from interviews conducted in 1971 as part of an earlier longitudinal study in Racine,[4] as were the attitudinal data.

ANOTHER LOOK AT THE MAPS

We had now arrived at the point where a basic decision was required. How did census tracts, police grids, natural areas, and neighborhoods interrelate or overlap to produce the final inner city?[5] Which areas made up the final set of transitional areas, those which were hypothesized to be changing physically and socially and, as a consequence, experiencing inordinate increases in delinquency and crime? And which areas, by their very nature, harbored relatively few criminals as criminals were perceived by the public? Depending on the spatial system utilized, four or five relatively homogeneous groups were produced.

The inner city could be delineated with each of the systems but a different size and shape was produced depending on the spatial system referred to, as shown on Map 5.[6] Interstitial areas in transition more or less clearly separated the inner city from older and newer stable residential areas which, in turn, were more or less surrounded by developing suburban fringe areas. Although life in the inner city and interstitial areas has a quality about it that differs from that in other areas, it must be remembered that if the beholder is from the middle or upper classes only the physical elements may be seen.

A THREE-DIMENSIONAL VIEW OF THE CITY

Now that the reader has some familiarity with the four spatial systems, we shall utilize several three-dimensional neighborhood maps to present a more dynamic picture of the ecology of Racine.

The land use score is a summary measure of the neighborhood's characteristics in terms of residential vs. manufacturing land use. The higher the peaks on a map, the lower the residential use of blocks in the neighborhood. The computer routine that produced these and other three-dimensional maps made the neighborhood with the highest score highest on the map without regard for the scores of other decades so that the rates shown must be taken into consideration in comparing decades. Since it is the three-dimensional shape of the city in which we are interested, this does not constitute a major problem. Maps 6, 7, and 8 revealed that as the city expanded and lost many of its inner city and interstitial dwelling units to non-residential use, the contrast between the inner city and outlying areas increased.[7] The contrast also became heightened as neighborhoods on the periphery of the city, some of which contained light industry and a few dwelling units in 1950, filled out as predominantly residential areas by 1970. The development of a commercial-industrial area on the southwestern periphery of the city suggested that rates of delinquency and crime would increase disproportionately in these peripheral neighborhoods to other peripheral neighborhoods.

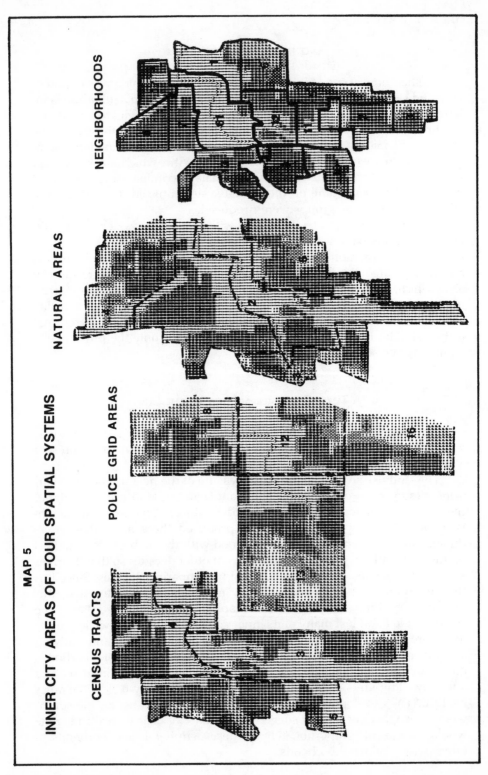

MAP 5
INNER CITY AREAS OF FOUR SPATIAL SYSTEMS

CENSUS TRACTS

POLICE GRID AREAS

NATURAL AREAS

NEIGHBORHOODS

MAP 6
MEAN LAND USE SCORE
BY NEIGHBORHOOD: 1950

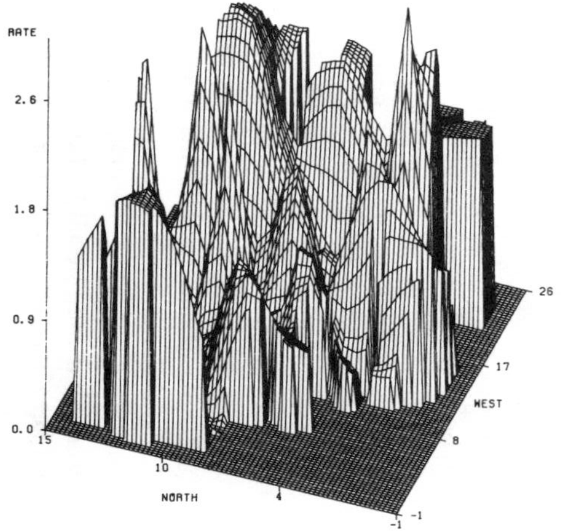

MAP 7
MEAN LAND USE SCORE
BY NEIGHBORHOOD: 1960

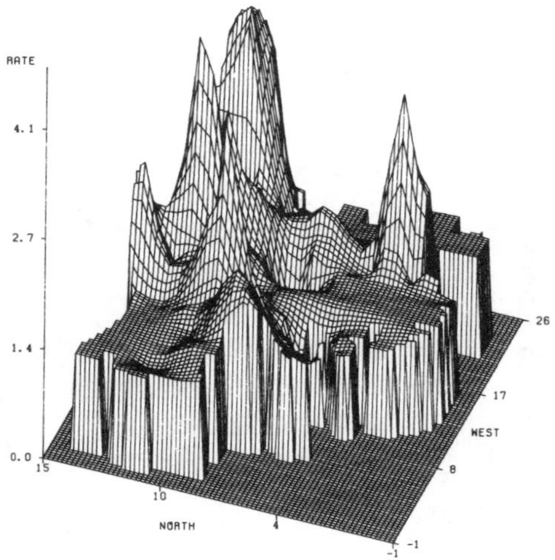

MAP 8
MEAN LAND USE SCORE
BY NEIGHBORHOOD: 1970

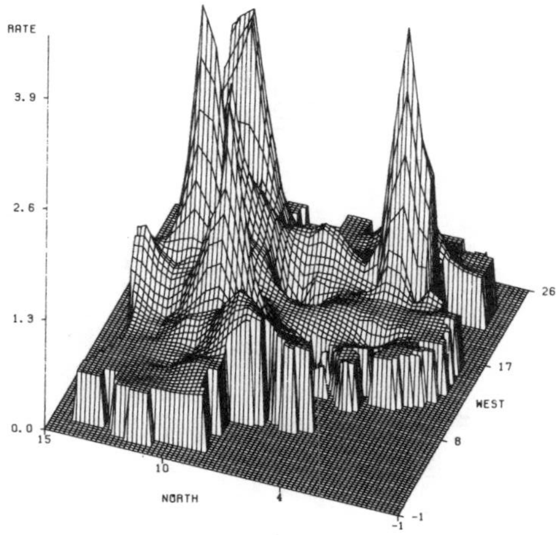

Other variables indicative of the changing ecology of the city were included as the analysis progressed. For example, residential vacancies in the inner city and interstitial areas represented a different phenomenon there than in other neighborhoods. By the 1970s it was apparent that outward movement made residential vacancies a more distinct characteristic of the inner city and interstitial areas than of other neighborhoods. Mean target scores were used to represent the number of taverns, grocery and liquor stores, restaurants, and gas stations per block. While targets had their highest concentration in the inner city and interstitial areas in 1950, their movement outward by the 1970s was dramatic.

A WORD OF CAUTION

We have been able to delineate spatial units whose characteristics were sufficiently different to permit them to be grouped in tables or dramatized in three-dimensional maps. The dynamic aspect of Racine's ecology has been demonstrated with three decades of data, best of all when the block data were aggregated into neighborhoods. Examination of delinquency and crime within the spatial framework that has been presented does not, however, imply that we have adopted a strictly ecological approach with the intent of explaining these phenomena entirely within this framework. The next several chapters do allow us to understand how the social organization of the city underlies its changing patterns of delinquency and crime.

NOTES

1. Police Grids were established by the Records Division of the Racine Police Department to facilitate the reporting of changing patterns of offenses known to the police in Racine.
2. School attendance centers were initially utilized in the 1950s because they were considered to be relatively homogeneous areas. From a race/ethnic standpoint most were. Block data were utilized as a basis for dividing and modifying these areas. To achieve greater homogeneity required even further modification of the manner in which areas were delineated and it was decided to call these areas Natural Areas because they were more or less bounded by natural or man-made barriers or by streets that had meaning to the residents of Racine.
3. Leo A. Schuerman of the Social Science Research Institute of the University of Southern California assisted us in this operation and provided a statistical package which enabled us to produce homogeneous areas from the block data. This technique is described in "Statistical Identification of Spatial Neighborhoods," presented at the Special National Workshop, Research Methodology and Criminal Justice Program Evaluation, Panel on Aggregation, Disaggregation, and Units of Analysis, March 17, 1980.

4. This study has been described in: Lyle W. Shannon and Judith L. McKim, "Mexican-American, Negro, and Anglo Improvement in Labor Force Status Between 1960 and 1970 in a Midwestern Community," *Social Science Quarterly*, July 1974, pp. 91–111; Lyle W. Shannon and Judith L. McKim, "Attitudes Toward Education and the Absorption of Inmigrant Mexican-Americans and Negroes in Racine," *Education and Urban Society*, June 1974, pp. 333–354; Lyle W. Shannon, "False Assumptions About the Determinants of Mexican-American and Negro Economic Absorption," *The Sociological Quarterly*, Vol. 16, Winter 1975, pp. 3–15; Lyle W. Shannon, "Some Problems in Measuring Changes in Occupation and Income (1960–1970) Among a Cohort of Mexican-Americans, Negroes and Anglos," *Pacific Sociological Review*, Vol. 19, January 1976, pp. 3–19; Victoria F. Davison and Lyle W. Shannon, "Changes in the Economic Absorption of Inmigrant Mexican-Americans and Negroes in Racine, Wisconsin Between 1960 and 1971," *International Migration Review*, Vol. 11, Summer 1977, pp. 190–214; Judith L. McKim, Victoria F. Davison, and Lyle W. Shannon, "Some Effects of the Community on Cultural Integration," *The Sociological Quarterly*, Vol. 18, Autumn 1977, pp. 518–535; Lyle W. Shannon, "The Changing World View of Minority Migrants in an Urban Setting," *Human Organization*, Vol. 30, Spring 1979, pp. 52–62; Judith L. McKim, Victoria F. Davison, and Lyle W. Shannon, "Becoming 'We' Instead of 'They': The Cultural Integration of Mexican-Americans and Negroes," *Urban Education*, Vol. XIII, Summer 1978, pp. 147–178; Lyle W. Shannon and Magdaline W. Shannon, *Minority Migrants in the Urban Community: Mexican-American and Negro Adjustment in Industrial Society*, Beverly Hills, California: Sage Publications, 1973, 352 pp.

5. There has been a lengthy literature on the consequences of using one spatial unit rather than another. See Calvin F. Schmid and Earle H. MacCannel, "Basic Problems, Techniques, and Theory of Isopleth Mapping," *Journal of the American Statistical Association*, Vol. 50, March 1955, pp. 220–239.

6. Delineating the inner city neighborhoods was in some respects a simpler operation than delineating other areas. The City of Racine had outlined what it considered to be the inner city for planning purposes and a smaller revitalization area which included part of this area but extended beyond it. Inner city neighborhoods within the city's designated inner city and revitalization area commenced at the top of the area with Neighborhood 17 and continued through 8, 7, 13, 61, 1, 6, 12, 9, 5, 10, 11, 2, and 3. The City of Racine had designated an area roughly similar to that encompassed by our inner city natural areas as an action area. The Southwest Revitalization area (approximately 25% of the larger action area) was composed of 104 city blocks, mostly within the city's action area.

7. Although the outline of the city remained the same from 1950 through 1970, some neighborhoods had not developed sufficiently for a score on the ecological variables (or were completely outside the area of urban development) in 1950. There were fewer neighborhoods for which scores were not possible in 1960. This in no way changes the images of the city that are here presented.

Chapter 5

MEASURING THE SPATIAL DISTRIBUTION OF DELINQUENCY AND CRIME IN RACINE

Which of the available measures of juvenile delinquency and of adult crime would best enable us to capture changes in offense rates and their relationship to the changing ecological structure of the city? Although several official data sets as well as the cohort data were available in the construction of measures of delinquency and crime for spatial systems based on census tracts and police grids, only the cohort data, official and self-report, could be used with the natural areas and neighborhoods which we had developed.

In this chapter we shall take a first look at changing offense and arrest rates within and across census tracts and police grids and across natural areas. While the interview and self-report data are briefly described, these data are not included in the analyses until later in the volume.

OFFENSES COMMITTED WITHIN CENSUS TRACTS

Property offenses had a rate of 5.8 per 100 persons in 1970 for Racine. They increased to a high of 8.6 in 1975 and declined to 7.0 in 1978. Offenses against persons had a rate of .9 per 100 persons in 1970, increased to 1.4 in 1974, and were 1.3 in 1978. This pattern of increase and slight decline was found for each of the crimes against property and persons with two exceptions: the rates for rape remained at the 1974 level with some fluctuation and the rate for homicide fluctuated because of the small numbers involved. When individual tracts were observed there was, of course, more variation and less stability in rates, particularly for crimes against the person. However, the high point for property offenses came in 1975 for nine of 14 tracts, with two reaching their peak in 1974 and three in 1976. Crimes against the person peaked in 1974 or 1975 for 10 of the 14 tracts, in 1976 for two others, but in 1978 for Tracts 11 and 14, the two tracts with the highest SES. Obviously there was a certain amount of idiosyncratic variation when less frequently occurring offenses were dealt with and there was a more patterned variation when Part I offenses were considered as a group.

In order to have a better idea of the consistency with which different offense rates varied over time, every offense rate for every year was correlated with every other offense rate for that year. Offenses against the person and against property had a Pearsonian correlation of .907. Within the offense against property category, burglary and theft were correlated .830, for example. Assault and rape correlated .942 but theft and homicide correlated only .306. Since frequently occurring offenses correlated quite well and there was considerable overall relationship between offenses against persons and property, we concluded that the analyses of variation in offenses committed within census tracts should be conducted with total Part I offense rates.

Very large and continuing differences in Part I offense rates were apparent from tract to tract. Inner city Tracts 1, 3, 4, and 5 had rates far above those for the city as a whole (marked with R on graphs), as shown in Graph 1. Note that Part I offenses had the highest rates in Tract 1, far higher than those for Tracts 3, 4, and 5. Tracts 3, 4, and 5 would have been overshadowed by Tract 1 had the scale in Graph 1 not been adjusted. Tracts 2 and 12 (Graph 2) had rates just above those for the city, while Tract 9 followed Racine trends very closely. Already we see that, aside from the inner city tracts, offense rates within tracts were not entirely consistent with expectations based on the categorization of tracts shown in Table 2 of the last chapter. This should be noted as a prelude to the analyses which we shall describe in chapters which follow. Tracts 6, 7, 8, 10, 11, 13, and 14 had rates slightly lower than those for the city, as may be seen in Graphs 3 and 4.

RESIDENCE OF PERSONS ARRESTED BY PART I AND II OFFENSES BY CENSUS TRACTS

Offenses were not broken down by type in these data but were available by sex and race/ethnicity. The 3.0 arrests per 100 population in Racine in 1966 rose to a peak of 6.1 in 1975 and declined to 3.9 in 1978. There was considerably more variation in year of peak arrest rates by tract of residence than there was for tract of offense. The arrest rate in Tract 1 peaked in 1970, in Tract 6 in 1972, in three tracts in 1974, in six tracts in 1975, and in three tracts in 1976.

While there was considerable variation in arrest rates by tract of residence, it was not as great as that by tract of offense, as shown in Graphs

GRAPH 1.

PART I OFFENSES PER 100 PERSONS
IN CENSUS TRACTS 3, 4, 5 AND RACINE

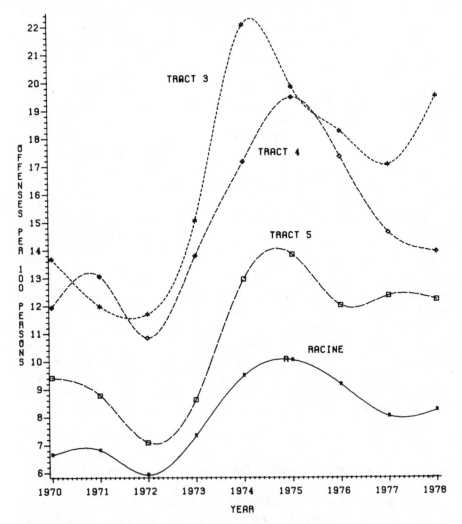

5 through 8. Inner city Tracts 1, 3, 4, and 5 (Graph 5) had rates which exceeded those for the city every year. Arrest rates for Tracts 2, 7, 8, and 9 (Graph 6) fluctuated just above or below rates for the entire city. Tracts 10, 12, and 13 had low rates (Graph 7) and Tracts 6, 11, and 14 had the lowest rates quite consistently (Graph 8).

It was also apparent that changes in the juvenile proportion of the

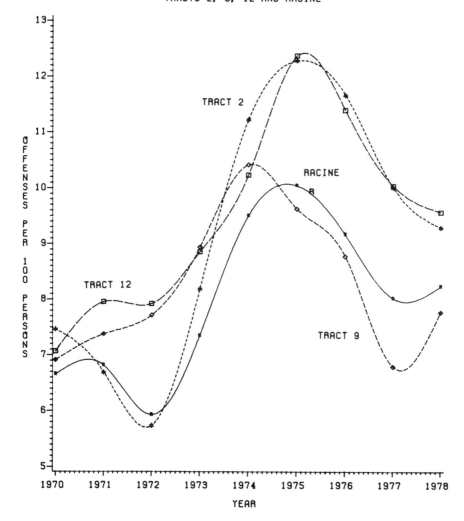

GRAPH 2.

PART I OFFENSES PER 100 PERSONS
TRACTS 2, 9, 12 AND RACINE

population from tract to tract over the years resulted in some interesting shifts in the proportion of all arrests that were juvenile arrests in some tracts. For example, Tracts 3 and 4 contained 15% and 26%, respectively, of the juvenile arrests in 1966 but this declined to 9% and 11% by 1978. Each of these tracts contained 19% of the adult arrests in 1966 but had shown less decline to 14% and 13% by 1978.

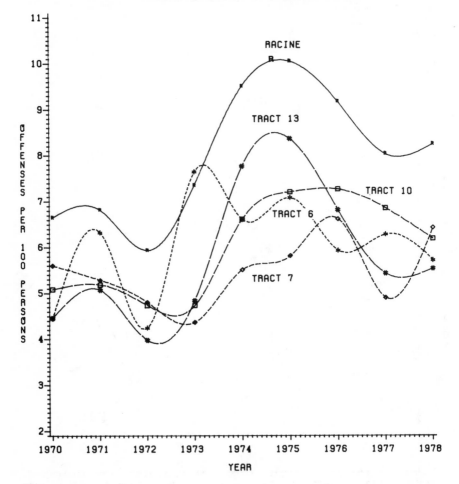

GRAPH 3.

PART I OFFENSES PER 100 PERSONS
TRACTS 6, 7, 10, 13 AND RACINE

Slightly over half of the adult male arrests in 1966 were from Tracts 3, 4, and 5 with a reduction to 40% by 1978. By contrast, well over half (56%) of the arrests of male juveniles were in these tracts in 1966 with a reduction to only 31% by 1978. Over half of the adult female arrests (61%) were of those residing in Tracts 3, 4, and 5 in 1966 with a reduction to 55% by 1978. Only 55% of the juvenile female arrests were from these tracts in 1966 but had been further reduced to 43% by 1978. In essence, male and female juvenile delinquency, as measured by arrests, moved outward more rapidly than adult crime.

GRAPH 4.

PART I OFFENSES PER 100 PERSONS
TRACTS 8, 11, 14 AND RACINE

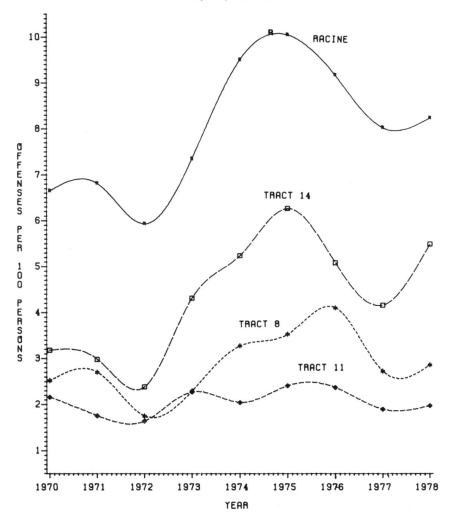

This may be seen another way by noting the percent of those arrested each year who were juvenile vs. adult. The percent of Racine males arrested who were juveniles commenced at 42.4% in 1966, rose to a high of 60.2%, remained at 55% or above until 1974, and then declined to 43.9%. However, there was immense variation from tract to tract in the proportion of juvenile vs. adult arrests and in the trend from 1966 to 1978. In only three years did juveniles constitute more than 10% of those arrested in Tract 1. In Tracts

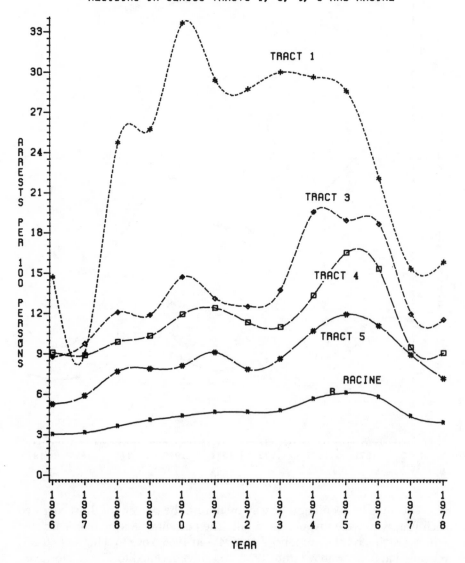

GRAPH 5.

PART I–II ARRESTS PER 100 PERSONS
RESIDING IN CENSUS TRACTS 1, 3, 4, 5 AND RACINE

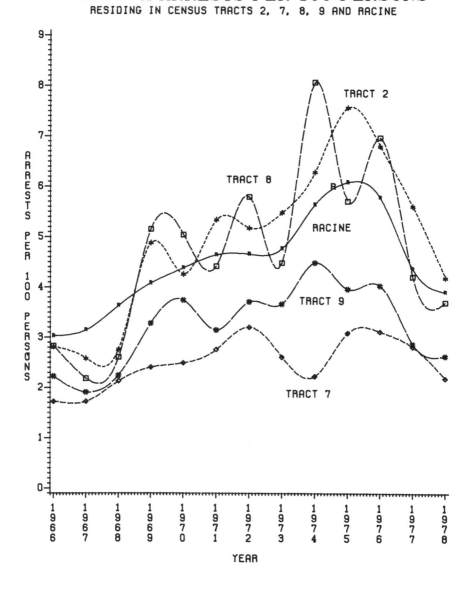

GRAPH 6.

PART I–II ARRESTS PER 100 PERSONS
RESIDING IN CENSUS TRACTS 2, 7, 8, 9 AND RACINE

GRAPH 7.

PART I–II ARRESTS PER 100 PERSONS
RESIDING IN CENSUS TRACTS 10, 12, 13 AND RACINE

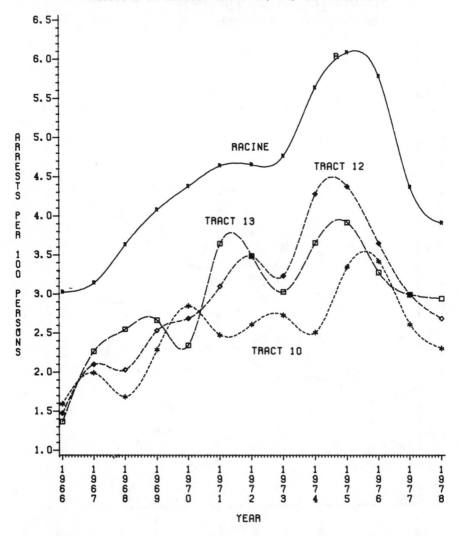

3, 4, and 5 the percent of the males arrested who were juveniles rose to its highest points in the early 1970s but declined to considerably lower proportions by 1978. By contrast, during the same period the proportion of juvenile arrests in Tracts 6, 7, and 8 showed significant increase. In Tract 8, the extreme case, the juveniles constituted 36.7% of the arrests in 1966 and reached 61.8% by 1978.

GRAPH 8.

PART I–II ARRESTS PER 100 PERSONS
RESIDING IN CENSUS TRACTS 6, 11, 14 AND RACINE

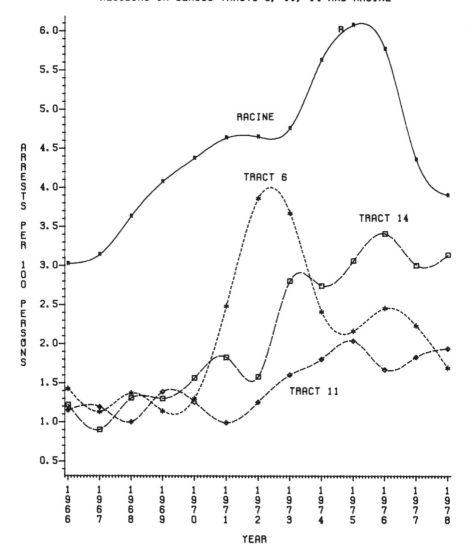

Similar changes took place among the females. Although they did not parallel the male changes in all tracts, in Tract 7 the juvenile proportion of female arrests increased from 33.3% to 61.9% over the 13-year period. There were also tracts in which the juvenile proportion of female arrests far exceeded the juvenile proportion of male arrests in a consistent pattern over a period of 13 years. In Tract 9, for example, there was not a single year when the juvenile proportion of the female arrests was below 50% and in most years it was above 60%; in Tract 10 it was 70.8% in 1966 and rose to 81.0% in 1978. In sum, the juvenile proportion of female arrests decreased in the inner city and interstitial areas but increased in all other areas.

Race/ethnic differences were also apparent. The percent of White juvenile arrests that were from Tracts 3, 4, and 5 declined from 35.8% to 14.8% between 1966 and 1978. The adult decline was from 34.6% to 26.8%. While most arrests of Blacks were of those residing in Tracts 3, 4, and 5 in 1966 (91.4% of adult arrests and 97.3% of juvenile arrests), the corresponding proportion of the arrests of Blacks had declined for both by 1978, more so for the juveniles than the adults (75.7% of the adult and 68.3% of the juvenile arrests were comprised of those who resided in these tracts). Decline in the proportion of arrests of Chicanos from these tracts followed a similar pattern, from 71.2% to 55.5% for adults and 82.0% to 56.7% for juveniles.

Although delinquency by residence of juveniles moved outward, the inner city tracts remained centers of delinquency and crime by place of offense and those who resided there continued to have high offense rates. It was concluded that variation in arrest rates by tract could be analyzed without controls for sex and juvenile/adult status because we were concerned with the basic overall change in arrest rates. Even though there were differences in rates by race/ethnicity and sex, the general pattern of change was there for all groups.

Place of Offense by Police Grids

With these data it was possible to look at Part I offenses by months and years from 1968 through 1979. One of the phenomena considered was the degree to which rates fluctuated seasonally and the fact that variation on a seasonal basis was as great as or greater than that found over longer periods of time. These fluctuations were plotted and it was found that January and July differences in number of offenses committed were, in many years, as great as or greater than the difference in number of offenses committed in January of 1969 and January of 1979. In Police Grid 12 (the extreme inner city area) seasonal fluctuation became greater and greater, particularly during peak years. In an area with a smaller number of offenses, Grid 4 for example, the fluctuation was even more apparent. The same pattern of seasonal fluctuation was found for theft for the city and for these grids. Since we wanted to know if trends in delinquency and crime were related to the changing social organization of the city as such change produced variation in the characteristics of areas within spatial systems, these seasonal fluctuations may be ignored for the purposes of this research.

When Part I in-area offense rates by police grids were considered, we again examined the problem of differences in rates by type of offense. Offenses against the person and property were correlated .905, assault and rape were correlated .921, and burglary and theft .880, the latter being the two offenses with the greatest frequency of occurrence, followed by assault. Although some of the less frequently occurring offenses had relatively low or inverse correlations with other offenses, the basic trend for crime within areas was well represented by Part I offenses regardless of type.

Keeping the analysis to a manageable form required that the rate for all Part I offenses be taken as an index for most of the analyses to be conducted. Several grids showed rates that were considerably above those for the city, Grids 6, 8, 12, and 22. Although graphs similar to these for census tracts were constructed, they are not included. The reader may wish to refer to Map 2 in Chapter 4 to keep the location of these grids in mind. Grids 8 and 12 were expected to have high rates but 6 and 22 were not. Rates for specific offenses showed that Grid 6, a low population, peripheral area that attracted large numbers of people for recreational purposes, had one of the highest robbery, burglary, and assault rates in the city in 1975 and the highest theft rate in 1975 and 1976. Grids 1, 2, 4, 14, 18, and 20 had relatively low rates and Grids 10, 21, and 23 had the lowest rates. All were middle and upper SES areas. We again concluded that a preliminary inspection of variation in offense rates found a considerably less than perfect relationship between rates and the ecology of the city.

A SPATIAL VIEW OF THE COHORT DATA

Maps 1, 2, and 3 are presented as preliminary examples of the spatial distribution of cohort police contact data. They were computed from data aggregated to the natural areas delineated on Map 3 in Chapter 4. Those who were socialized in the inner city or its interstitial subareas had the greatest mean number of police contacts throughout their lifetime, regardless of cohort.

Differences in the patterns of total contact rates between cohorts may be explained, aside from varying time at risk, by the changing nature of residential areas, by the expansion and changing locations of areas in which the least advantaged portion of the population was socialized, by the development of the areas containing the barrio, and by the development of a larger commercial-industrial area on the periphery of the city that had some elements of the way of life of inner city dwellers.[1] Each contact on this map was given equal weight, regardless of alleged offense seriousness.

Similar maps, based on the average seriousness scores of persons in each cohort (seriousness scores presented in Chapter 2) who grew up in each subarea regardless of the length of time that they lived in Racine, produced a pattern of even greater concentration in the inner city and its

AVERAGE NUMBER OF POLICE CONTACTS PER PERSON WITH CONTINUOUS RESIDENCE BY AREA OF JUVENILE RESIDENCE: NATURAL AREAS OF RACINE COMPUTER-CONTOURED

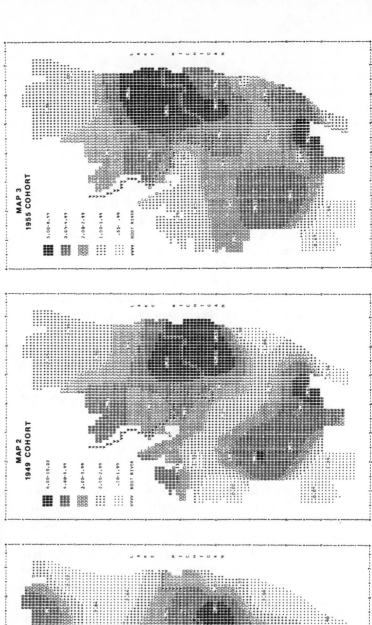

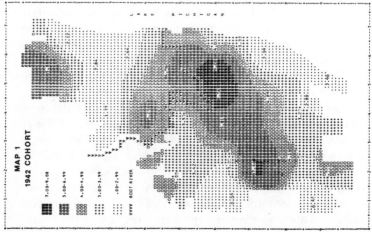

interstitial areas. Spatial patterns based on differences in grand seriousness scores (sum of career type seriousness scores) differed from the average number of contacts in that the sheer numbers of persons having repetitive contacts compounded by greater seriousness marked the inner city and its interstitial areas as the source of the disproportionate number of the felonies and major misdemeanors which are found in the city.

Although the spatial distribution of delinquency and crime in the cohorts has been described in other publications in which we were interested in change from cohort to cohort and were less concerned with spatial variation in time, more should be said about presentation of the cohorts in an ecological framework before concluding this chapter.[2] To facilitate some of the analyses presented in chapters which follow, it was necessary to code place of residence of all persons with continuous residence into a convenient set of time periods: 1950 through 1959; 1960 through 1969; and 1970 up to 1976. Thus, a usual place of residence for most people in the cohorts (even if they had no contacts) could be characterized with data from the U.S. Census.

This did not really solve all of the problems but it gave some idea of the extent to which members of the cohorts moved about the community and permitted determination if their distribution was roughly proportional to the distribution of Racine's population within each spatial system. The importance of the mobility problem is revealed by the fact that even after collapsing census tracts into six groups of similar tracts, 52.1% of the 1942 Cohort had moved to a different SES level tract between 1950 and 1960 and 38.5% of the 1949 Cohort had done so. When police grids were collapsed in six similar levels the figures were 53.5% for the 1942 Cohort and 35.8% for the 1949 Cohort. Slightly larger figures were obtained when the natural areas and neighborhoods were collapsed into seven levels.

When moves between 1960 and 1970 were dealt with in the same fashion we found that from 62.9% to 67.9% of the 1942 Cohort had moved to a different level, as had from 61.4% to 65.5% of the 1949 Cohort and even from 27.8% to 34.2% of the 1955 Cohort. In addition, as high as 9% of the 1942 Cohort and 14% of the 1949 Cohort had moved to tracts or other areas outside the city between 1950 and 1960, as had similar percentages of one or the other of the three cohorts between 1960 and 1970. All of this made it difficult to follow the delinquent and criminal careers of sizeable groups within each area of the various spatial systems over a period of time, a forewarning of the complexity of some of the analyses that will be presented with cohort data.

There is always a question as to whether a given cohort is representative of all cohorts that could have been selected. We dealt with that problem by selecting three cohorts. Thus, age, period, and cohort variation are captured by these data. The question remained, however, was there cohort spatial variability that generated problems when the analysis was directed toward changing patterns of spatial relations? We think not; rather, we see such variation in the spatial distribution of cohorts as indicative of population change in the city. A series of three cohorts facilitated a dynamic type of analysis, but, rather than attempt to settle the issue by argument, we examined the spatial distribution of the members of each cohort in relation to that of Racine's population at these same time periods.

Racine's population 1950 to 1980 by tract, grid, natural area, and neighborhood gave us an idea of what proportion of each cohort should have each area as their place of principal residence in each of the three periods. Although there were some discrepancies, the overall distribution of the three cohorts by census tracts was considered sufficiently close to that of the population to be representative by their places of residence. A similar approach was taken for police grids, natural areas, and neighborhoods, with the conclusion that the spatial representativeness of cohorts was not a problem that would distort findings.

THE INTERVIEW DATA IN AN ECOLOGICAL PERSPECTIVE

Interviews with 889 persons from the 1942 and 1949 Cohorts were utilized in showing the extent to which self-reports on delinquency and crime, self-concepts, explanations of delinquent behavior, reactions to detection and apprehension, and explanations of cessation of delinquent behavior were related to the social organization of the city.[3]

Self-report data (in addition to interview questions) were obtained from a separate check-off sheet. They are available for three age periods (6 through 17, 18 through 20, and 21 and older). Sixteen items were included ranging from running away from home to armed robbery. Scores on the scale were based on the frequency and seriousness of offenses reported.[4]

SUMMARY

Changing rates and patterns of Part I offenses were presented by place of offense for census tracts (1970–1978) and police grids (1968–1979) and changing rates and patterns of arrests for Part I and II offenses by place of residence of the persons arrested for census tracts (1966–1978). They indicated that further analyses would reveal a considerably less than perfect relationship between the changing ecology of the city and offense rate patterns. Although total police and court experience (official and self-report) of three cohorts may be described by census tracts, police grids, natural areas, and neighborhoods, we shall also expect considerable deviation in the distribution of rates from that which would be expected based on a concentric circle zonal hypothesis.

NOTES

1. There is an extensive and pertinent literature on delinquent and criminal subcultures which provides a background for our position. See: Walter B. Miller, "Lower Class Delinquency as a Generating Milieu of Gang Delinquency," *Journal of Social Issues* 14 (1958): 5–19; Richard A. Cloward and Lloyd E. Ohlin, *Delinquency and Opportunity: A Theory of Delinquent Gangs* (New York: Free Press, 1960); David J. Bordua, "Delinquent Subcultures: Sociological Interpretations of Gang Delinquency," *The Annals of the American Academy of Political and Social Science* 39 (1961): 120–136; LeRoy G. Schultz, "Why the Negro Carries Weapons," *Journal of Criminal Law, Criminology and Police Science* 53 (1962): 476–483; James F. Short and Fred L. Strodbeck, *Group Process and Gang Delinquency* (Chicago: University of Chicago Press, 1965); Solomon Kobrin, Joseph Puntil and Emil Peluso, "Criteria of Status Among Street Groups," *Journal of Research in Crime and Delinquency* 4 (1967): 98–118; Marvin E. Wolfgang and Frances Ferracuti, *The Subculture of Violence* (London: Tavistock, 1967); Paul Lerman, "Individual Values, Peer Values and Subcultural Delinquency," *American Sociological Review* 33 (1968): 219–235; Sandra J. Ball–Rokeach, "Values and Violence: A Test of the Subculture of Violence Thesis," *American Sociological Review* 38 (1973): 736–749; and Howard S. Erlanger, "Estrangement, Machismo and Gang Violence," *Social Science Quarterly* 60 (1979): 235–248. Erlanger's point that subcultural differences may readily and unintentionally generate police contacts in the larger society is well taken. This is particularly true if police and school personnel have little or no understanding of the minority subculture.

2. Lyle W. Shannon, "A Longitudinal Study of Delinquency and Crime," in Charles Welford (ed.), *Quantitative Studies in Criminology* (Beverly Hills: Sage, 1978): 121–146.

3. The 1960 and 1971 interview data were helpful in characterizing the areas in each spatial system, not only to reveal differences in people's attitudes from area to area but also to show that there was considerable heterogeneity within larger areas based on race/ethnic differences but also heterogeneity within race/ethnic groups within areas. This, if nothing else, demonstrated an awareness of the problem of aggregating people to spaces.

4. Respondents were given a check-off sheet on which they indicated the frequency in which they engaged in various behaviors for each age period, 6 through 13, 14 through 17, 18 through 20, and 21 and older. Scales were developed from the responses to these items based on frequency and seriousness of responses for each age period.

Chapter 6

THE RELATIONSHIP OF DELINQUENCY AND CRIME TO THE SOCIAL ORGANIZATION AND ECOLOGY OF RACINE

CRIME AND THE ECONOMY

Temporal changes in Racine's delinquency and crime as related to the city's changing social organization, particularly its economy, provided us with some perspective for further examination of spatial variation in juvenile delinquency and crime rates.

In 1949 there were 1.5 Part I offenses reported to the police per 100 population. This rate fluctuated but steadily rose to a peak of 10.4 Part I offenses per 100 population in 1975, declined for two years, then increased from the 1977 low to 8.5 Part I offenses per 100 population in 1979. These trends paralleled the Crime Index for the United States presented in the Department of Justice's Uniform Crime Reports, although Racine's rates were higher than those for the United States as a whole.[1]

In 1960, 5.0% of Racine's labor force was unemployed and in 1978 the unemployment figure was 5.2%. During this 19-year span Racine's unemployment rate fluctuated with low points of 3.6% in 1965 and 1974 and a high point of 7.0% in 1975.[2] While increases in the rate of unemployment sometimes seemed to be accompanied by increases in offense rates, the upward trend of offense rates was such that declines in unemployment were just as often as not followed by increases in the offense rate. Since unemployment did not show a long-term trend during the period under consideration and offense rates steadily rose, neither economic trends nor cyclical explanations of crime rate trends were supported for this span of years. Perhaps this is too superficial. More important, the number of 20-year-olds increased in Wisconsin from 1960 to 1980, thus the number of younger workers in need of jobs increased, the declining birth rate increased the proportion of women able to enter the job market, and fewer people were retiring from work than were entering work. The net result was probably more pressure for jobs than was reflected by unemployment rates.[3]

The ratio of manufacturing jobs to people fluctuated within a range from .29 to .36 during the 30-year period from 1950 to 1980.[4] It declined from 1950 through 1959, increased in 1960 but declined again during the 1960s to a point that was slightly lower than the 1959 low, increased again in 1970 but declined until 1974. Since then it steadily increased to its 1979 peak. It might be noted that we estimated that there were 31,628 manufacturing jobs in Racine in 1979 and that the Wisconsin Job Services estimated 31,600 for 1979. Although this ratio suggested decreasing competition in Racine for available jobs, the pressure probably remained about the same because the SMSA was the actual labor force area for Racine manufacturing jobs and its population slightly increased during the 1970s.[5] Again, we concluded that the increase in offenses reported to the police could not be explained by a simple index of jobs available or by unemployment rates.

The increase in offenses during this 30-year period was a complex phenomenon involving an increasing proportion of youthful members of the community who had neither been integrated into the world of work nor into other institutions in the larger and developing society. The extent to which the increasing heterogeneity of the population was related to the failure of youth to be fully integrated into the larger society will be considered in appropriate later chapters.

When the broader picture of offenses was considered the automobile played a role, not only in terms of traffic offenses but in terms of ancillary offenses which developed from its varied uses. Between 1941 and 1979 the number of vehicles registered increased threefold, from 20,100 to 59,938, compared to a population increase from 67,195 in 1940 to 85,541 in 1980.[6] The number of reportable accidents increased from 617 to 3,774, a sixfold increase. The number of persons injured increased from 377 to 1,509 during this period, a fourfold increase. When these were converted into rates per 100 vehicles registered, the reportable accident rate was 3.1 in 1941, increasing somewhat erratically to 5.6 by 1960 and 6.3 by 1979. This period was one in which youth obtained increasing access to the automobile, a phenomenon previously found related to higher rates of police contact, not only for moving vehicle violations but for other offenses as well.

Whether increased availability of the auto was the major factor in the increasing offense rate in Racine is problematical but offenders were no longer bound to their own neighborhoods and roamed more freely, finding themselves in a variety of difficulties far from home, just as the person who lived in a quiet neighborhood might find the miscreant at his or her doorstep. The auto was certainly one factor which modified earlier research findings on the ecology of delinquency and crime, i.e., rather than one pattern in which place of offense and place of residence were similar, we found two patterns, one based on place of offense and the other based on place of residence.

Another measure of the increasing involvement of automobiles in police contacts came from traffic flow data.[7] Weekday counts showed that the number of automobiles passing peripheral counting points more than doubled and even trebled on some major arterials between 1956 and 1978. On some extremely congested arterials the flow increased fivefold during that period. During a similar period mass transit passengers declined from 5,042,766 per year to a low of 525,681 in 1972 but rose to 1,541,007 by 1978, a figure still far below that of earlier years.[8] That some routes had twice the proportion of youthful riders as did others may explain differences in delinquency and crime patterns not otherwise accounted for.

Changes which may seem less prosaic were also bound to have their impact on patterns of delinquency and crime. New schools were built, others closed. Youth who resided in a given area no longer were sure that they would attend their neighborhood school, for better or worse. New parks, playgrounds, and Neighborhood Centers[9] were established, as were other recreational facilities which attracted youth, some of whom were perhaps well-mannered under most conditions and circumstances but less than docile under others.

The number of taverns and restaurants serving alcoholic beverages not only increased but areas previously without such establishments found them in their midst. Thus, we see that the community was growing in ways that were almost certain to generate increasing delinquency and crime quite apart from those patterns which were associated with deterioration and inner city decay.

CENSUS TRACT VARIATION IN OFFENSES AND ARRESTS

The problem of characterizing trends was mentioned as we noted that rates tended to rise from the late 1960s or early in the 1970s to 1975 at the latest in most cases. This turned us to the question of which year's rates should be used in describing trends (rates and changes in rates) within census tracts. Procedures for determining whether irregular data were best represented by a single slope or a two-segment slope were utilized in making this decision. Since 80% to 90% of the arrests were of males rather than females, tests were first conducted based on the number of adult males arrested by census tract of residence.[10] In only Tracts 1 and 6 was curvilinearity statistically significant. In all other tracts the best two-segment lines did not provide a closer fit to the number of male arrests than did a one-segment stable or upwardly-sloping line. The same procedures were next utilized in examining all arrests, juveniles and adults, males and females combined, still not taking differences in population trends within tracts into consideration, i.e., number of arrests were used rather than rates per 100 persons residing in an area. In all but three tracts the trend was best represented by a straight line.

Graphs were also constructed based on arrest rates for Racine and the individual tracts; rates for Racine were best represented by a straight line, with only Tract 1 better represented by a two-segment line. Rates for Tracts 2, 3, 4, and 5 rose from 1966 to 1974 or 1975 and then had a downward turn, in each case less sharp than that generated by number of arrests. Rates for other census tracts fitted a one-segment line even better than before. This suggested that even though we have mentioned tract rates as having increased during the late 1960s and early 1970s before declining, the downward trend in the last half of the 1970s may not be a significant feature in overall trends when considering arrest rates by place of residence of persons arrested.

Basic differences in arrest rates from one group of tracts to another were the most relevant feature of the tract data to be taken into consideration when describing the relationship of delinquency and crime to spatial differentiation within the city. The considerable annual variation in arrest rates for tracts was shown in Graphs 5 through 8 in Chapter 5. Similar trends were found for Part I offense rates within tracts as shown in Graphs 1 through 4 in the last chapter. Offense rates in most census tracts rose during the early 1970s to 1974 or 1975 and then declined to 1978, as highlighted by Graphs 1 through 4. For the purpose of the next set of analyses to be conducted it was decided that the periods 1966 through 1969, 1970 through 1974, and 1975 through 1978 should be separately characterized for arrest rates and that the periods 1970 through 1974 and 1975 through 1978 should be separately characterized for place of offense data.

POLICE GRID VARIATION IN PLACE OF OFFENSE

The police grid rates were divided into three time periods, 1968 through 1969, 1970 through 1974, and 1975 through 1979. In seven of the police grids, a two-segment line best fitted the temporal progression in rates, the downward trend coming in 1975 (two cases in 1974) and in 13 others a one-segment curve seemed most appropriate. Only one of the grids with a downward slope did not have a declining population and five of the seven were inner city or interstitial areas. Most importantly, every one of the seven had a high place of offense rate in 1975 even though there was a decrease after that. Also, considering the fact that the rate for the city declined after 1975, it was decided that, as with census tracts, concern should be with the basic differences in rates from one police grid to the other rather than with that segment in the temporal trend of some grids which was not characteristic of the area during the longer span of time for which data were available.

AN INITIAL PREDICTION OF OFFENSE AND ARREST RATES FROM THE CHARACTERISTICS OF CENSUS TRACTS AND GRIDS

One way to examine delinquency and crime and the ecology of the community was to make up a table in which an expectation of rates and trends was presented for each of the official sets of rates for census tracts and grids based on what we knew about each area. These data, when considered in reference to an ecological model of delinquency and crime, enabled us to specify areas in which offense rates would be highest (as was done in Chapter 5 when tracts and grids were considered) and in which residents would have the highest arrest rates.[11] This is consistent with traditional ecological theory with its emerging variants which suggests that delinquency and crime are more likely to be generated in one kind of milieu than in another and are the products of interaction among people in circumstances which make conventional behavior only one of the possible responses to life situations.

Table 1 presents an expected rate and trend and, opposite it, an observed rate and trend. In each column of observed rates and trends that rate or trend which differed from the expected has been underlined. In most cases what we expected was close to what we found. Nonetheless, it is apparent that this simplistic model of expected rates and trends did not take into consideration all of the variables crucial to explaining the rate of offenses in areas or the rates of arrests of persons who resided in them. While general relationships are represented by a table of this type, the relationship of specific variables to offense and arrest rates is still unknown, as is the relationship of the latter to the changing characteristics of areas within spatial systems. Whatever may be said about this initial look at relationships, it was apparent that offense rates and arrest rates for the period between the late 1960s and late 1970s were associated with certain static aspects of these spatial systems circa 1960 and 1970 and the dynamics of population growth, inner city expansion, and peripheral development.

A MORE DETAILED VIEW OF THE RELATIONSHIP OF THE CHARACTERISTICS OF CENSUS TRACTS AND GRIDS TO OFFENSE AND ARREST RATES

The next set of tables commences with an arrangement of areas by offense or arrest rates and determines if their milieu, as represented by selected variables, systematically differs.[12]

In Table 2, tracts have been arranged in four groups according to their

TABLE 1. DELINQUENCY AND CRIME RATES AND TRENDS: OBSERVED AND HYPOTHESIZED BY POLICE GRIDS AND CENSUS TRACTS

Police Arrest Rates for Part I and II Offenses by Census Tract of Residence

	Expected Rate and Trend Based on Population and Housing Characteristics in 1970	Observed Rate and Trend from Official Police Records 1966-1978*
Inner City		
1	High Stable	High Inc. to 1973
3	High Inc.	High Inc. to 1976
4	High Inc.	High Inc. to 1975
5	High Inc.	High Inc. to 1975
Heterogeneous Older Transitional		
2	Med. Inc.	Med. Inc. to 1975
15	Med. Inc.	Med. Inc., Fluct.
6	Med. Inc.	Low Inc., Fluct.
7	Med. Inc.	Low Inc., Fluct.
Middle to High SES		
10	Med. Inc.	Low Inc.
12	Med. Inc.	Low Inc. to 1975
8	Med. Inc.	Med. Inc. to 1974
9	Med. Inc.	Med. Inc. to 1974
Peripheral High SES		
11	Low Stable	Low Stable
14	Low Stable	Low Inc.
15	Low Stable	---

Part I Offenses Committed Within Census Tracts

Expected Rate and Trend Based on Population and Housing Characteristics in 1970	Observed Rate and Trend from Official Police Records 1970-1978
High Inc.	High Inc. to 1974
High Inc.	High Inc. to 1974
High Inc.	High Inc. to 1975
High Inc.	High Inc.
Transitional	
High Inc.	Med. Inc. to 1975
High Inc.	Med. Stable
Med. Inc.	Med. Stable
Med. Inc.	Med. Stable
Med. Inc.	Med. Stable
Med. Inc.	Med. Inc.
Low Inc.	Low Stable
Low Inc.	Med. Stable
Low Inc.	Low Stable
Low Inc.	Low Inc.-Med.
Low Inc.	---

Part I Offenses Known to Police in Police Grids

	Expected Rate and Trend Based on Population and Housing Characteristics and Change 1950-1980	Observed Rate and Trend: Official Police Records 1969-1979
Inner City		
8	High High	High Inc. to 1975
12	High High	High Inc
13	High High	Med. Inc.
16	High High	Med. Inc. to 1975
Transitional		
9	Med. Med.	Med. Inc. to 1975
17	Med. Med.	Med. Inc.
20	Med. Low	Low Fluct.
Stable Residential		
18	Med. Stable	Low Inc.
21	Med. Inc.	Low Stable
14	Low Low	Low Stable
4	Low Low	Low Stable
Peripheral High SES		
5	Med. Stable	Med. Inc.
6	Med. Inc.	High Inc. to 1975
22	Med. Inc.	High Inc. to 1974
19	Low Med.	Med. Inc., Fluct.
15	Low Low	Med. Inc., Fluct.
23	Low Low	Low Inc., Fluct.
Peripheral High SES		
1	Low Stable	Low Inc., Fluct.
2	Low Stable	Low Stable
10	Low Inc.	Low Stable

* Differences from expected are underlined

TABLE 2. RELATIONSHIP OF TARGET DENSITY, LAND USE, VACANCY RATES, HOUSING TYPE, AND CHANGE TO ARRESTS AND OFFENSES KNOWN TO POLICE BY TRACTS*

TYPES OF RESIDENTIAL AREAS	1950 TARGET DENSITY	1950 % COMM/IND	1950 % RES VACANT	1950 HOUSING SCORE	1960 TARGET DENSITY	1960 % COMM/IND	1960 % RES VACANT	1960 HOUSING SCORE	1950-60 CHANGE TARGET DENSITY	1950-60 CHANGE % COMM/IND	1950-60 CHANGE % RES VACANT	1950-60 CHANGE HOUSING	ARRESTS BY RESID 1966	ARRESTS BY RESID CHANGE 1966/69	1970 TARGET DENSITY	1970 % COMM/IND	1970 % RES VACANT	1970 HOUSING SCORE	1960-70 CHANGE TARGET DENSITY	1960-70 CHANGE % COMM/IND	1960-70 CHANGE % RES VACANT	1960-70 CHANGE HOUSING	ARRESTS BY RESID 1970	ARRESTS BY RESID CHANGE 1970/74	PLACE OF OFFENSES 1970	PLACE OF OFFENSES CHANGE 1970/74	ARRESTS BY RESID 1975	ARRESTS BY RESID CHANGE 1975/78	PLACE OF OFFENSES 1975	PLACE OF OFFENSES CHANGE 1975/78
Inner City																														
1	H	H	L	P	H	H	H	P	Inc	Dec	Inc	Det	H	H Inc	H	H	H	P	Dec	Dec	Dec	Det	H	H Dec	H	H Inc	H	H Dec	H	H Dec
3	H	H	L	P	H	H	H	P	Dec	St	Inc	St	H	M Inc	H	H	H	P	Dec	St	Inc	St	H	H Inc	H	H Inc	H	H Dec	H	L Dec
4	H	H	L	P	H	H	H	P	Dec	Inc	Inc	St	H	L Inc	H	H	H	P	Dec	Dec	Inc	St	H	L Inc	H	M Inc	H	H Dec	H	H Dec
5	H	H	L	P	H	H	M	P	Dec	Inc	Inc	Det	H	M Inc	H	H	H	P	St	Dec	Inc	St	H	M Inc	H	M Inc	H	H Dec	H	L Dec
Older or Transitional																														
2	H	M	M	G	H	M	M	M	St	Inc	St	Det	M	M Inc	M	M	H	P	Dec	Dec	St	Det	M	M Inc	M	M Inc	H	M Dec	H	M Dec
13	H	M	L	M	H	M	M	M	Dec	St	St	Imp	L	L Inc	M	M	M	M	St	Inc	St	Det	L	L Inc	M	M Inc	M	L Dec	M	M Dec
6	M	L	M	M	M	L	M	M	St	St	Dec	St	L	L Dec	L	L	M	M	Dec	St	St	St	L	L Inc	M	L Inc	L	L Dec	M	M Dec
7	M	L	M	G	M	M	L	M	St	St	Dec	St	L	L Inc	L	M	M	M	St	Inc	St	Det	M	L Dec	M	St	M	L Dec	M	L Inc
Growing Areas																														
10	M	M	M	G	M	L	M	M	Dec	Dec	St	Det	L	L Inc	M	L	M	M	St	St	St	St	M	L Inc	M	L Inc	M	L Dec	M	L Dec
9	L	M	M	M	M	M	M	M	Inc	Dec	St	St	M	L Inc	M	M	M	M	Inc	Dec	Dec	St	M	L Inc	M	M Inc	M	L Dec	H	M Dec
12	M	H	L	M	L	M	H	M	St	Dec	Inc	Imp	L	L Inc	L	M	M	M	St	Dec	Dec	St	M	L Inc	M	M Inc	M	M Dec	H	M Dec
Consistently Better																														
14	L	L	M	G	L	L	M	G	St	Inc	St	Imp	L	St	M	L	M	G	Inc	St	St	St	L	L Inc	L	L Inc	M	St	M	L Dec
11	L	L	L	G	L	L	H	G	St	St	Inc	St	L	St	L	L	M	G	St	Inc	Dec	St	L	L Inc	L	St	L	St	L	L Dec
8	L	L	H	G	L	L	L	G	Inc	Inc	Dec	St	M	M Inc	H	L	M	M	Inc	St	St	Det	H	M Inc	L	L Inc	H	M Dec	L	L Dec

* Ranked to achieve maximum homogeneity of groups on all characteristics.

residential and land use characteristics. Four different measures of the characteristics of census tracts and police grids were selected: target density, percent commercial-industrial, percent residential vacancy, and the factor analytic housing scores, each for 1950, 1960, and 1970 with changes between these periods for each measure. Arrest rate and offense rate changes were also included for selected years.

The inner city tracts (Tracts 1, 3, 4, and 5) had similar arrest and offense rates, physical characteristics, and population characteristics. Although there were some anomalies, it was evident that the cycle of deterioration and movement out of inner city areas was followed by increasing delinquency and crime rates, in turn followed by further deterioration and departure of people and targets from the area.[13]

Tracts 2, 13, 6, and 7 almost surrounded the inner city group and were characterized by lower target densities, lower commercial-industrial use, lower residential vacancy rates, and better housing scores than those for tracts in the inner city. Note that this group and the next one consisting of Tracts 10, 9, and 12 had many similarities. Yet, while their arrest rates were lower than those of the inner city tracts, most increased from 1966 to 1969 and some continued to increase from 1970 to 1974, although only one reached as high a level as the inner city rates before the decline which took place between 1975 and 1978.

The last group contained those very fine residential areas on the periphery of the city. They, as the inner city areas, were similar in many respects but did not have similar arrest or offense rates. Here, too, some of the similarities in characteristics within groups have been indicated on the table.

What was most apparent, however, was that even with tracts organized into somewhat similar groupings there were several patterns of arrest and offense rates and changes in rates within each group outside of the inner city. So, no matter which way the data were organized, a nice, orderly progression failed to materialize. But does it ever do so when the statistics are based on large, heterogeneous areas? Nevertheless, these tables do suggest that the analysis has moved along in such a manner as to capture the operation of the process of deterioration, decline, and increasing delinquency and crime, followed by further decline, the historic process which we have sought to document.

Unfortunately, the Southside Revitalization area in Racine, an area targeted for extensive community action (commencing in 1970 and involving local groups in the planning process) encompassed the lower half of Tracts 2 and 3 so that its impact on delinquency and crime could not be measured in terms of tract changes.[14] Table 3 presents the data as if characteristics of areas were the most powerful determinants of in-area offense rates, even though, as we have said, the automobile gave people a degree of mobility that they did not have in the olden times, when the hansom cab was the

TABLE 3. RELATIONSHIP OF TARGET DENSITY, LAND USE, VACANCY RATES, HOUSING TYPE, AND CHANGE TO COMMITTED PART I OFFENSES BY POLICE GRID AREAS*

TYPES OF RESIDENTIAL AREAS	1950	1950-60 CHANGE	PLACE OF OFFENSE	1960	1960-70 CHANGE	1970	PLACE OF OFFENSE
High Target Inner City							
8	H H M H	Dec St St	H H H St	H H M H	Dec Inc Inc St	H H H P	H H H H Dec
12	H H M M	Inc Inc Det	H M H Inc	H M H M	Dec St Inc Inc	H H M H	H M H L Dec
13	M H M M	St St Det	M L M Inc	M M H M	Dec Dec Inc Dec	H H M H	H M H L Dec
16	H H M M	Dec St Det	M M M Inc	H M H M	Dec Inc Inc St	H H M H	H M H M Dec
Transitional							
9	H H L M	Dec Inc St	H H M Inc	M H M M	St St St St	M H M P	M M H M Dec
17	H M L M	St Dec Det	M M L Inc	M H M H	Dec St Det Det	M M H P	M H M L Dec
Stable							
14	M L L G	St St St	L M L Inc	M L M L	Inc St St Det	M L L G	M M L L Dec
21	L L H G	St St Dec	L L L Inc	L L L M	St St Dec Dec	L L L M	L L M L Dec
4	L M M G	St Dec Dec	L L L St	L L L G	St Inc St St	L L M G	L L L M Dec
18	M L L M	Dec Dec Det	L L L Inc	M M L M	Inc St Inc Inc	M L L M	M L M M Dec
Peripheral Residential							
6	– – – –	– Inc Inc	H H L St	L L L G	– Dec Dec St	L H L G	H H H H Dec
19	– – – M	– Inc –	L H M Inc	L L M G	Inc St Inc Inc	M H L M	H H H L Dec
15	– – L M	Dec – Imp	M L M Inc	L L L M	Inc Dec Dec St	M H M M	H H St L Dec
5	M L – –	St Inc Imp	H M M St	M L M G	Inc Inc Dec Det	M M L M	M L M H M Dec
20	M M L M	Inc Inc –	H L L Dec	M L L M	Inc St St –	H H – M	H H M M Dec
22	M M L M	Inc Inc Imp	H H L St	M M L –	Dec – Dec Inc	H M – M	H M M M Dec
23	– – – –	– – –	L L L St	– – – M	– Inc Inc Imp	L – M G	L L L Inc
Highest SES							
10	L L L L	Inc Inc Imp	H L L Inc	L L H G	Dec St Dec St	L L L G	L St L St
2	H L – –	Dec Inc Inc	L L L Inc	L H L G	Inc St Inc Dec	L L L G	L L Inc M Dec
1	H M – M	Dec Dec Imp	L L L Dec	L L L M	Inc Inc Dec St	M L L G	M M Inc M Dec

* Ranked to achieve maximum homogeneity of groups on all characteristics.

mobile boudoir of the trysting genteel, but not as available to youth as the product of Ford's imagination has become to the young rascal of today.

When the data were organized by police grids, somewhat different results were obtained than for census tracts because several high rate areas, areas that were only part of much larger areas, were well separated from others by the grid lines, more precisely than they were by the boundaries of census tracts. Police Grid 6 is the best example. Its relatively small population and other characteristics which did not mark it as a high crime area had been overshadowed by the attraction of its recreational facilities which had generated a high rate of offenses.

As the years went by, every inner city and interstitial area plus those outlying areas which would draw people to them for reasons that might eventuate in delinquent or criminal behavior had high offense rates. Only one of the police grids that had a high offense rate by 1975 had a low target density (that was Grid 6 which we have just mentioned), only one had a low percent commercial-industrial, only two had low residential vacancy, and only three of the group were characterized as having good housing. While the total pattern suggested heterogeneity, a close look indicated that the evolving pattern of areal characteristics was related to high in-area offense rates.

Note that the characteristics of the inner city areas were quite similar but that, while these and the transitional areas eventually had high in-area offense rates, there were other areas with quite different characteristics which also had high offense rates.[15] Perusal of this table leads one to the conclusion that superficially similar areas did not have identical crime problems even though it appeared that combinations of variables may identify a milieu in which delinquency and crime were generated by either the residents or by those who were attracted to the area. It should be remembered that each month the *Racine Journal-Times* printed a map showing how many Part I offenses took place in each police grid with a lag of one month. Conversations with people over the years indicated that areas with frequent offenses such as larceny, burglary, robbery, and assault were perceived by many as dangerous shoals to be avoided while to others they carried all of the challenge of the thundering surf which must be passed through before reaching snug harbor.[16] Whether long time residents perused these maps avidly enough to identify patterns of change in the spatial distribution of delinquency and crime is another question.

ACCOUNTING FOR EXPECTED AND ANOMALOUS FINDINGS

While the process of decline and deterioration in the inner city was followed by delinquency and crime rates higher than those found for the city as a whole, evidence of disproportional increases in offenses and arrests was also found in census tracts and grids far removed from the inner city. These outlying areas differed from the inner city but they were similar in that they too functioned as arenas for trouble.

To be more specific, one may refer to taverns, parks and recreational areas, school yards, and beaches as arenas for delinquency and crime, yet each provided a somewhat different type of arena and there was variation in types of offenses and in the ages of offenders from one arena to the other. The reader may interject that tavern disturbances and stolen beach balls are not what we are concerned about and that the crimes about which we should be concerned are burglary, armed robbery, aggravated assault, and murder. Most of the offenses which took place in these arenas were not in the more serious categories, but these arenas did produce every type of offense from juvenile status offenses to the most gruesome murders. Thus, in order to conduct a statistical analysis, it was desirable to include all Part I offenses regardless of the level of seriousness and all arrests, whatever the reason for the arrest may be.

Target density, percent commercial-industrial, and housing quality scores consistently accounted for two-thirds to three-quarters or more of the variance in offense rates in census tracts. While change in tract characteristics accounted for a sizeable amount of the change in offense rates within tracts with offense rates held constant at the beginning of the change period, arrest rates did not follow the same pattern of change between 1970 and 1974 as did offense rates. Also, offense and arrest rates followed somewhat different patterns of change between 1975 and 1978. Tract 1, for example, had a decline in arrest rates between 1970 and 1974 and 1975 and 1978. While it had an increase in offense rates within the area between 1970 and 1974, it had the greatest decrease in offense rates between 1975 and 1978. It still, however, had the highest arrest and offense rates. Added to this is the fact that offense rate changes were larger than arrest rate changes in 1970 to 1974 but much smaller proportionately in the 1975 to 1978 period.

The crux of the findings was that there had been a developing relationship between the characteristics of census tracts and offense and arrest rates. Each year the characteristics of tracts accounted for much of the variation in tract offense and arrest rates. However, controlling for tract characteristics at the start of a period, and only considering that change which was disproportional to the position of a tract at the start of the period, added little to the proportion of the differences in arrest rates accounted for between two points in time.

Our next concern was with the extent to which findings utilizing police grids would duplicate place of offense relationships for census tracts. What we found were two almost completely different sets of correlations, the findings varying with the spatial system utilized. No wonder those who are engaged in research of this nature debate with fervor which unit of analysis should be used, particularly if there are relatively few units in each spatial system and considerable heterogeneity within the units of each system. Our position has been that a variety of spatial systems must be used with the same basic data in order to find out exactly how the findings differ.

Conflicting claims may be settled if it is demonstrated that the heterogeneity that seems to characterize larger units is behind the conflicting findings of research in the same and different communities. Conflicting findings are often artifacts of the data. No matter which periods were compared, the findings differed when tract and grid comparisons were made. Before turning to the cohort data we must again look at the impact of targets and, more specifically, taverns on offense and arrest rates.[17] In the course of this we shall obtain a better understanding of how such different results were obtained for tract and grid data.

The relationship of target density to vacant housing and trends for both and their relationship to Part I offense rates in police grids are shown in the first few columns of Table 4. Grids were placed in three groups according to target density and the trend for target density. Each of the high target density grids had originally or by 1970 acquired a relatively high percent of vacant housing and all had a high or medium and increasing in-area offense rate. The medium target density group included areas in which target density was increasing, decreasing, or stable, in which vacant housing trends were of all kinds, and in which there was also an assortment of offense levels and trends, although most of the latter were increasing. Note that the first six grids were inner city and interstitial and that all had high tavern densities.

Almost every tavern area included some which were considered by the police or by other persons in official positions as "trouble taverns." At the same time, these taverns were considered by persons who frequented them as places for rewarding interaction with their friends and associates.

Only one of the low target density areas shown in Table 4 had a high and increasing offense rate. This was not really an anomaly because, as we have mentioned before, it had formal and informal recreational attractions that drew the youthful population at all times except in the winter.

Residential arrest rates and in-tract offense rates in the second half of the table followed a pattern similar to that of police grids. These data also showed that the inner city tracts were characterized in the same way and had had the arrest and offense trends which were of concern. Here, again, the middle group was heterogeneous but in this group with characteristics much like the inner city were also the interstitial Tracts 2 and 13. What one must conclude was that combinations of factors distinguished these high offense and arrest rate areas far better than did single factors.

TABLE 4. RELATIONSHIP OF TARGET DENSITY AND CHANGE AND VACANT HOUSING AND CHANGE TO PART I OFFENSES COMMITTED IN POLICE GRIDS AND CENSUS TRACTS AND ARRESTS BY CENSUS TRACTS

TARGET DENSITY, HOUSING VACANCY, AND PART I OFFENSE RATES AND TRENDS BY POLICE GRIDS

	Target Density & Trend 1950-1970	% Vacant Housing & Trend 1950-1970	Offense Rate & Trend 1969-1970
High Target Density			
8	Dec. High	Inc. to 5.59%	High Inc.
12	Dec. High	Inc. to 8.30%	High Inc.
16	Dec. High	Inc. to 7.83%	Med. Inc.
17	Dec. Med.	Inc. to 4.09%	Med. Inc.
	(All had high tavern density.)		
Medium Target Density			
13	Dec. High	Inc. to 5.92%	High Inc.
9	Dec. Med.	Inc. to 3.89%	Med. Inc.
14	Stable Med.	Inc. to 2.10%	Low Stable
5	Inc. Med.	Dec. to 2.02%	Med. Inc.
22	Inc. Low	Dec. to -2.0%	Med. Inc.
2	Inc. Low	Dec. to -2.0%	Low Stable
15	Inc. Low	Dec. to -2.0%	Med. Fluct.
20	Inc. Too few blocks		Low Fluct.
	(13, 9, and 20 had high tavern density; 14, 15, and 2 had no taverns.)		
Low Target Density			
6	Stable Low	Dec. to -2.0%	High Inc.
10	Stable Low	Dec. to -2.0%	Low Stable
4	Stable Low	-2.0%	Low Stable
18	Stable Low	-2.0%	Low Inc.
21	Stable Med.	3.79%	Low Stable
23	Stable Low	Dec. to -2.0%	Low Inc.
1	Stable Low	-2.0%	Low Inc.
19	Inc. Low		Med. Inc.
	(4, 18, and 21 had low tavern density; 1 and 19 had no taverns.)		

ARREST RATES AND TRENDS FOR OFFENSES IN AND RESIDENTS OF CENSUS TRACTS

	Target Density & Trend 1950-1970	% Vacant Housing & Trend 1950-1970	Part I Offenses & Trend 1970-1978	Arrest Rate By Residents and Trend 1966-1978
High Target Density				
1	Dec. High	Inc. to 8.57%	High Inc.	High Inc.
3	Dec. High	Inc. to 11.47%	High Inc.	High Inc.
4	Dec. High	Inc. to 7.82%	High Inc.	High Inc.
5	Stable High	Inc. to 8.04%	High Inc.	High Inc.
	(All had high tavern density.)			
Medium Target Density				
2	Dec. Med.	Inc. to 4.25%	Med. Inc.	Med. Inc.
13	Dec. Med.	Inc. to 2.95%	Med. Stable	Med. Inc., Fluct.
10	Stable Med.	Inc. to 2.06%	Med. Stable	Low Inc.
14	Inc. Med.	Inc. to 2.95%	Low Inc.	Low Inc.
8	Inc. Low	-2.0%	Low Stable	Med. Inc.
9	Inc. Low	-2.0%	Med. Stable	Med. Inc.
	(13 had med. tavern density; 10 had no taverns.)			
Low Target Density				
6	Dec. Low	-2.0%	Med. Stable	Low Inc., Fluct.
7	Dec. Low	-2.0%	Med. Stable	Low Inc., Fluct.
11	Stable Low	-2.0%	Low Stable	Low Stable
12	Stable Low	-2.0%	Med. Inc.	Low Inc.
	(6 and 12 had low tavern density; 11 had no taverns.)			

NOTES

1. United States Department of Justice, F.B.I. Uniform Crime Reports. *Crime in the United States 1979*, Washington, D.C.: Government Printing Office, 1980. Other selected years were examined to establish trends.

2. Wisconsin Department of Industry, Labor and Human Relations, Bureau of Research and Statistics, Wisconsin Job Services.

3. Parker and Horwitz have recently reexamined the question of a linkage between unemployment and crime. Robert Nash Parker and Allan W. Horwitz, "Unemployment, Crime, and Imprisonment: A Panel Approach," *Criminology*, Vol. 24, November 1986, pp. 751–773.

4. *Racine Area Manufacturers Directory 1980*. Racine: Racine Area Chamber of Commerce, 1980. University of Wisconsin-Parkside Survey of Manufacturing Firms in Racine-Kenosha 1870–1972. The Racine Manufacturers Association and Wisconsin Job Services were very helpful in securing documents for us.

5. *U.S. Census of Population and Housing, 1970* and *Census of Population and Housing, 1980*. P.L. 94–171 Counts.

6. *City of Racine Vehicles Registered*.

7. *Traffic Maps—City of Racine*. State Highway Commission of Wisconsin in Co-operation with Bureau of Public Roads, U.S. Department of Commerce. 1956 and various years to 1979.

8. Southeastern Wisconsin Regional Planning Commission. *Racine Area Transit Development Program 1975–1979: Planning Report No. 3*.

9. Community Services Department and Department of Parks and Recreation, City of Racine, 1977.

10. Carolyn Rebecca Block, Senior Analyst, Statistical Analysis Center, Illinois Law Enforcement Commission, constructed numerous graphs which assisted us in determining whether data were best represented by a single or two-segment slope. Her extensive correspondence on this problem was invaluable.

11. The reader who wishes to investigate the very extensive literature on the ecology of urban areas would find Brian J. L. Berry and John D. Kasarda, *Contemporary Urban Ecology*, New York: Macmillan Publishing Co., 1977, the most comprehensive recent volume on this subject. Also see Vijayan Kumara Pillai, "Ecology of Intra-Urban Delinquency and Crime," *Journal of Environmental Systems*, Vol. 11, 1981–82, pp. 101–111.

12. Stanley Milgram, in "The Experience of Living in Cities," *Science*, Vol. 167, March 1970, pp. 1461–1468, argues that a cognitive map of the city could be constructed.

13. Data for the 32 largest U.S. cities for the period 1946–1970 suggests that White migration out of the central cities has led to social changes generative of high rates of delinquency and crime. See Wesley G. Skogan, "The Changing Distribution of Big-City Crime: Multi-City Time-Series Analysis," *Urban Affairs Quarterly* Vol. 13, September 1977, pp. 33–48.

14. The Southside Revitalization Plan for Racine has been described in detail in *Southside Revitalization Study: Development Plan for a Neighborhood of Racine, Wisconsin*, Citizens Advisory Committee and Llewellyn-Davies Associates, Racine, 1970.

15. The four variables selected for inclusion as representative of the characteristics of areas were available for blocks for all time periods. Other variables from the long list of characteristics of blocks or areas would have probably added little to the findings. With the exception of percent residential vacancy, each of the other variables was a composite score of several other measures.

16. Richard Block has pointed out that urban dwellers have known that some neighborhoods are more dangerous than others since at least the Renaissance. Although folk wisdom may reflect real crime counts, he goes on to show that the explanation of high rates of violent crime in some communities is not simple. See Richard Block, "Community, Environment, and Violent Crime," *Criminology*, Vol. 17, May 1979, pp. 46–57.

17. Lawrence E. Cohen and Marcus Felson explore our concern about targets in "Social Change and Crime Rate Trends: A Routine Activity Approach," *American Sociological Review*, Vol. 44, August 1979, pp. 588–608. In concluding, they state, "It is ironic that the very factors which increase the opportunity to enjoy the benefits of life also may increase the opportunity for predatory violations."

Chapter 7

COHORT DELINQUENCY AND CRIME RATES AND THE ECOLOGICAL STRUCTURE OF RACINE

THE PROBLEM OF AGE GROUP, TIME PERIOD, COHORT, AND SPATIAL VARIATION

Controlling for simultaneous variation in rates (age, period, and cohort) and describing the product of these variations as they generated changing spatial patterns of delinquency and crime according to four different systems was not a simple task. Each cohort had different police contact or seriousness rates holding age of cohort member and other variables constant. Rates varied over time periods. Police contact and other rates varied with the age of persons in the cohort. Rates varied according to the social characteristics of units within each spatial system.

There were four basic time periods for which we had the characteristics of each area for each spatial system, as shown in Diagram 1. The period before 1950 was probably, at least in the years close to 1950, what each area was like at that time; the cohort born in 1942 did not experience much of that period and the 1949 and 1955 Cohorts missed it. The 1950 through 1959 period became the first relevant period for the 1942 and 1949 Cohorts, and so on, with the 1960 through 1969 and 1970 and later periods relevant for all cohorts.

In order to examine the effect of place of residence on delinquent and criminal behavior and societal response to it with controls for age of cohort members, the age-by-age record of police contacts and cohort disposition were aggregated so that age groups did not overlap the 10-year time periods for which principal places of residence had been established. It was thus possible to measure cohort change within time periods for meaningful age categories as well as cohort change with age. This diagram facilitates com-

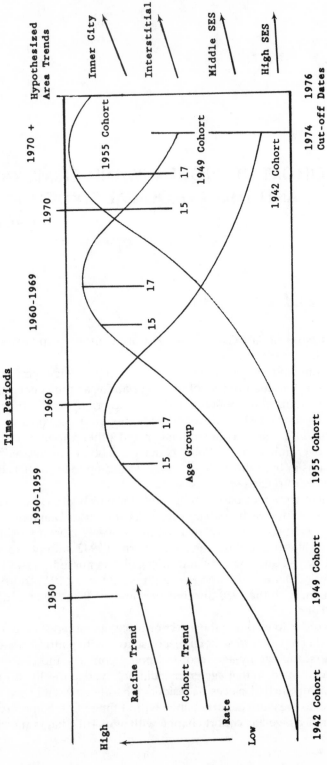

DIAGRAM 1. TYPES OF OFFENSE RATE VARIATION IN THREE RACINE COHORTS

prehension of the problems that were faced when selecting comparable age groups from each cohort as a basis for answering the questions addressed in this chapter.

Exactly which measure of any given phenomenon is the best is always a question for debate. If the problem is one of prediction, then that measure of the independent variable which results in the best prediction of the dependent variable is the best measure as long as everyone is satisfied that the dependent variable has been appropriately measured. Since we were involved in the description of relationships and changing relationships and were not oriented toward maximizing predictive efficiency at this point, several measures of each variable are presented in order to reveal how the findings varied with the measure of cohort delinquency and crime that was utilized.

TIME PERIOD VARIATION BY PLACE OF CONTACT

The simplest way to commence is to describe the location of police contacts by areas of each spatial system for the aggregated cohorts during the three major time periods commencing in 1950. There are a number of ways in which to compute time period rates, population as the base being the most usual. There are arguments for using the number of blocks in the area but this eliminates the population density factor and opportunities related to density. If the possibility of transition in household burglary rates had been our concern, justification might have been made for developing rates based on the number of residences in each area.[1]

It was decided that each area should be observed with two rate models in mind: 1) the census population in that area during each of the time periods and 2) the number of cohort members residing in the area during each of the time periods. Which of the two rates was used made some difference because the proportion of cohort members in each area in the inner city and interstitial areas would be less than the proportion of the total population in these areas and the opposite would be the case for peripheral areas. Rates for the aggregated cohorts by time periods are shown in Tables 1 and 2.

When considering the rates presented in these tables the 1950s rate includes persons from the 1942 Cohort ages 6 through 17 and the 1949 Cohort persons included are ages 6 through 10. The 1960s rate includes those who were 18 through 27 from the 1942 Cohort, 11 through 20 from the 1949 Cohort, and 6 through 14 from the 1955 Cohort. The 1970s rate includes only ages 28 and older (1942 Cohort), 21 through 27 (1949 Cohort), and 15 through 22 (1955 Cohort). Although rates cannot be compared across time periods without caution, the same general three-dimensional maps of the city were generated by the 1970s or for the 1949 and 1955 Cohorts, whichever measures were selected.[2]

TABLE 1. AGGREGATED IN-AREA COHORT POLICE CONTACT RATES BY TIME PERIODS FOR CENSUS TRACTS, POLICE GRIDS, AND NATURAL AREAS

CENSUS TRACTS

Area	1950s Per 100[1] Pop. 1955	1950s Per Cohort Resid.[2]	1960s Per 100 Pop. 1965	1960s Per Cohort Resid.	1970s Per 100 Pop. 1975	1970s Per Cohort Resid.
Inner City						
1	9.00	17.25	91.28	117.75	146.94	72.00
3	1.07	.59	11.12	2.97	16.12	6.03
4	1.04	.52	10.10	3.02	12.87	5.01
5	.98	.58	7.95	2.67	12.95	5.07
Transitional						
2	.75	.66	6.37	3.02	8.79	3.34
13	.14	.30	5.30	1.79	7.17	2.23
6	1.45	.84	5.67	1.59	6.98	1.67
7	.82	.39	4.36	1.30	3.87	1.04
Stable Residential						
10	.45	.23	4.51	1.19	5.58	1.61
9	.41	.27	7.32	2.04	7.55	1.97
12	1.22	.54	5.30	1.22	7.78	1.96
8	.76	.60	3.87	1.00	4.21	.66
Peripheral Middle to High SES						
14	.40	.22	3.28	.92	4.51	1.29
11	.49	.25	1.49	.37	2.71	.56
Mean	.91	.51	6.35	1.84	7.95	2.28

POLICE GRIDS

Area	1950s Per 100 Pop. 1955	1950s Per Cohort Resid.	1960s Per 100 Pop. 1965	1960s Per Cohort Resid.	1970s Per 100 Pop. 1975	1970s Per Cohort Resid.
Inner City						
8	.82	.40	8.56	2.47	10.88	3.56
12	1.77	1.71	16.17	8.33	23.24	9.18
13	1.05	.85	7.28	2.27	9.05	3.05
16	.75	.44	7.33	2.21	9.34	2.45
Transitional						
9	.95	.43	5.60	1.45	8.74	2.43
20	5.20	.23	10.47	.63	4.01	.54
17	1.45	.91	7.26	2.24	10.58	3.22
Stable Residential						
14	.68	.33	2.13	.52	3.10	.81
18	.52	.19	5.26	1.27	5.55	1.43
21	.58	.16	3.87	.70	3.34	.69
4	.36	.16	2.93	.87	2.40	.74
Peripheral Middle to High SES						
19	---	---	12.84	3.77	5.79	2.46
15	.00	.00	3.51	.54	5.18	1.16
23	---	---	1.41	.35	1.79	.58
5	.49	.25	5.50	1.51	9.26	3.02
22	1.45	.52	9.26	2.06	9.36	2.19
6	.00	.00	2.87	.45	15.59	2.52
10	4.76	2.00	3.95	.78	2.97	.70
2	.85	.80	1.91	.56	4.04	.98
1	1.00	.00	4.32	1.00	3.67	.89
Mean	.95	.47	6.55	1.74	7.90	2.26

NATURAL AREAS

Area	1959s Per 100 Pop. 1955	1959s Per Cohort Resid.	1960s Per 100 Pop. 1965	1960s Per Cohort Resid.	1970s Per 100 Pop. 1975	1970s Per Cohort Resid.
Inner City						
1	1.02	.59	7.54	3.05	13.48	5.61
2	1.83	1.00	17.41	4.67	29.98	10.44
3	1.20	.81	7.91	3.09	9.02	3.44
4	.57	.28	8.98		14.42	3.14
5	1.29	1.21	10.14	5.08	10.98	4.14
Transitional						
6	.35	.17	5.07	1.33	5.64	2.17
7	---	---	---	---	6.85	.92
8	.37	.20	5.85	1.47	6.11	1.78
Stable Residential						
21	.84	.73	4.27	1.48	3.75	1.34
13	.44	.22	4.35	1.33	5.22	1.63
12	.58	.28	5.37	1.27	7.79	2.06
9	1.45	.67	4.39	1.18	7.02	1.85
14	1.98	.95	5.79	1.48	4.23	.99
11	1.56	1.19	6.99	2.27	10.04	2.71
10	.78	.47	4.70	1.29	5.38	1.51
Peripheral Middle to High SES						
18	.50	.36	3.18	.88	4.03	1.11
19	.52	.33	9.00	2.02	8.93	2.08
16	.16	.08	4.35	1.01	4.67	1.15
20	.46	.14	1.68	.38	3.05	.75
22	---	---	---	---	5.69	2.81
25	.41	.21	2.88	.95	1.93	.78
17	.60	.25	3.80	.96	2.83	.71
23	---	---	---	---	1.85	.58
26	---	---	---	---	6.97	1.97
24	---	---	---	---	1.77	.63
Mean	.91	.49	6.26	1.83	7.76	2.26

[1] Police contacts in area by members of all cohorts residing there per 100 Racine population residing in area at mid-census year for during 10-year periods.

[2] Per aggregated cohort members residing in area during 10-year periods.

TABLE 2. AGGREGATED IN-AREA COHORT POLICE CONTACT RATES BY TIME PERIODS FOR NEIGHBORHOODS

INNER CITY

	1950s		1960s		1970s	
	Per 100 Pop. 1955[1]	Per Cohort Resid.[2]	Per 100 Pop. 1965	Per Cohort Resid.	Per 100 Pop. 1975	Per Cohort Resid.
17	.99	.40	12.52	3.05	14.15	4.55
8	.60	.25	7.71	2.41	10.35	3.80
7	1.00	.65	8.72	3.29	14.69	7.19
13	.35	.22	7.53	2.39	10.84	5.34
61	7.14	6.25	59.19	13.20	134.74	32.00
1	10.46	17.50	105.32	113.75	143.20	70.17
6	1.01	1.67	9.18	6.52	12.33	5.13
12	.77	.56	9.51	3.80	15.57	6.58
9	.95	.38	8.06	2.03	10.49	3.72
5	.52	.32	5.50	2.11	7.55	2.89
11	.62	.33	9.95	2.27	19.28	6.36
10	1.84	1.17	10.58	3.77	17.91	5.64
2	.93	.46	8.88	2.09	8.91	3.07
3	----	.06	11.00	.50	3.05	.33

TRANSITIONAL

	1950s		1960s		1970s	
	Per 100 Pop. 1955	Per Cohort Resid.	Per 100 Pop. 1965	Per Cohort Resid.	Per 100 Pop. 1975	Per Cohort Resid.
19	.52	.27	5.49	1.53	9.90	2.61
18	.72	.41	10.20	3.50	14.34	5.10
16	1.17	.67	4.78	1.52	10.53	3.08
4	.83	.77	4.72	2.04	6.53	2.29
65	4.81	5.00	32.23	17.00	29.52	24.50
64	5.48	2.67	19.49	7.67	44.44	10.00
46	1.25	.30	6.11	1.16	6.07	1.46
49	.79	.26	6.61	1.58	7.73	2.12
50	1.09	.33	5.58	1.26	7.37	1.80
54	.55	.18	4.28	1.08	4.38	1.54
66	----	.25	24.71	5.25	19.74	3.75
33	.94	.60	5.58	1.25	4.50	1.49
37	----	.00	----	.41	5.64	.96
60	2.63	1.80	22.03	12.71	46.23	23.00

STABLE RESIDENTIAL

	1950s		1960s		1970s	
	Per 100 Pop. 1955	Per Cohort Resid.	Per 100 Pop. 1965	Per Cohort Resid.	Per 100 Pop. 1975	Per Cohort Resid.
20	.74	.40	3.94	1.34	5.92	1.57
21	.29	.15	3.27	1.06	3.20	.90
22	.15	.08	2.19	.83	2.05	.72
23	.52	.32	5.15	1.40	11.10	2.67
29	.36	.13	6.04	1.64	9.47	2.59
30	1.94	3.00	8.70	2.71	9.84	3.03
31	.26	.12	2.88	.53	3.49	.81
32	.66	.39	3.25	.88	6.20	1.67
34	.51	.17	3.99	.83	3.91	1.00
35	.75	.44	3.22	1.05	4.19	1.17
36	.84	.31	3.92	.97	2.26	.51
15	.91	.32	2.65	.64	5.70	1.37
63	5.76	1.58	7.19	1.73	5.49	1.68
53	.57	.38	3.24	.79	4.74	1.10
62	4.80	6.00	15.77	12.46	21.85	7.50
56	.32	.21	3.70	1.12	4.30	.99
14	1.02	.47	4.35	1.08	3.07	.62

PERIPHERAL MIDDLE TO HIGH SES

	1950s		1960s		1970s	
	Per 100 Pop. 1955	Per Cohort Resid.	Per 100 Pop. 1965	Per Cohort Resid.	Per 100 Pop. 1975	Per Cohort Resid.
27	.21	.10	1.31	.40	1.29	.43
28	.53	.20	2.49	.61	2.62	.73
51	.43	.12	1.01	.26	1.74	.55
52	.39	.16	1.65	.40	2.92	.72
55	.26	.07	5.64	1.20	5.26	1.19
67	----	4.67	40.00	17.00	16.43	11.00
47	.38	.17	4.90	1.13	6.20	1.44
38	.25	.20	3.64	.90	2.93	.80
57	----	.00	----	.02	.95	.11
24	.00	.00	1.77	.68	2.95	.62
25	.42	.21	4.11	1.14	4.07	1.11
26	.00	.00	3.07	.72	2.53	.77
39	1.47	1.00	1.71	.40	1.81	.41
41	.00	.00	1.45	.26	1.32	.58
42	.00	.00	2.82	.57	5.62	1.51
68	----	----	----	24.67	49.33	24.67
48	----	.00	2.37	1.23	1.72	.87
58	----	.00	----	.21	2.07	.16
59	----	.00	.59	.44	1.55	.82
70	.00	.00	4.64	1.22	3.15	.59
MEAN	.95	.47	6.44	1.74	7.68	2.26

[1] Per 100 Racine population residing in area at mid-census year for police contacts in area but members of all cohorts residing there during 10-year period.
[2] Per aggregated cohort members residing in area during 10-year periods.

Census Tracts

All four of the inner city census tracts (1, 3, 4, and 5) had higher than average rates of police contact regardless of the rate model considered. At the same time that the population (and proportion of the city's population) and the number of cohort members (and proportion of the cohorts) residing in the inner city were declining, the proportion of Racine's police contacts generated in these areas remained the same or decreased only slightly.

These tracts, as in every other analysis, remained the core of the problem. They were, in cohort after cohort and time period after time period, the locale in which at least 40% of all police contacts took place. In the extreme case, while less than 6% of the 1942 Cohort still resided in these four inner city tracts in the 1970s, 48% of the police contacts took place in these tracts. For the 1949 Cohort 13.8% resided in the inner city in the 1970s but 45% of the police contacts by this cohort took place in the inner city in the 1970s. The 1955 Cohort had a larger proportion of its members residing in these inner city tracts in the 1970s (17.0%) and 36.5% of that cohort's contacts occurred in the inner city. Age differences from cohort to cohort played a part in the decline in the proportion of each cohort's contacts that took place in the inner city since younger persons (the 1955 Cohort) had a greater percent of their contacts closer to home, but still these rates remained higher than for other areas.

The census tracts that were considered transitional, with the exception of Tract 2, produced little systematic evidence that they differed from others. Tract 2 had more police contacts (higher than average rates during the 1960s and 1970s) than it should have had considering the number of cohort members residing there at different age periods, whichever model of expectancy was utilized. All other census tracts had lower than average rates in most time periods whichever model was employed.

Police Grids

Similar outcomes were found for the police grids, Grids 8, 12, 13, and 16 having higher cohort rates than the mean for most time periods, particularly Grid 12 (the most inner city area). Grids 9, 17, and 20, considered transitional, differed from other areas but were not perfect examples of police contact transition in that time period/cohort differences were irregular. Grid 17 had consistently higher mean rates than did Racine and Grid 9 had reached that point during the 1970s. Grid 20 had such a small proportion of either the city's or any cohort's population that its rates were based on numbers too small to accept as more than chance statistics. Aside from Grids 5, 6, and 22, all of which had higher than the mean rate of police contacts during the 1970s, the remainder had lower than average police contacts.

Natural Areas

As in other analyses which have been described, Natural Areas 1 and 2, the most distinctive inner city areas, had higher than average police contact rates. Not only that, but the proportion of each cohort's contacts which took place in these areas had increased while the proportion of each cohort who resided there decreased, time period by time period, i.e., there was a significant cohort by cohort impact on these inner city rates. Of the three other inner city natural areas (3, 4, and 5), all had high contact rates or, as in the case of Area 4, had made the transition in the 1960s. There was little evidence of transition to the status of being a trouble-producing area for areas which had been labeled transitional (Areas 6, 7, and 8), although there were time periods and cohorts for which a given area had more police contacts than would be expected considering its proportion of the city's or even a given cohort's population. Of the remaining areas, only Areas 11 and 19 had average police contact rates above the mean in both the 1960s and 1970s.

Neighborhoods

Maps 1–3 utilize the number of cohort members who resided in the neighborhood as the base. Whichever was considered, census population of the neighborhood or number of cohort residents, similar results were obtained except for the 1950s and both were most alike for the 1970s.

There were 14 neighborhoods which were considered part of the inner city. Almost all had high contact rates based on either the cohort's population who resided there each time period or the total population. If they did not have the inner city's disproportional number of police contacts in the early years or for the older cohorts, they had made the transition to disproportional police contacts by the 1960s and 1970s. Neighborhood 3 was the exception. While considered part of the inner city, it was the only area outside of the City of Racine's official inner city (it was part of the Southside Revitalization Area) that had been made part of our inner city configuration of neighborhoods. It had only six people in 1960, 194 in 1970, and 199 in 1980, very few people from any cohort, and very few of the police contacts were in this area.

The neighborhoods that were considered interstitial (14 of them) did not differ from other neighborhoods as clearly as did those in the inner city. While some fitted the transitional model with high contact rates in the 1970s, others had lower than average contact rates or were now experiencing a decline.

Six of the remaining 37 neighborhoods had a pattern of above average contact rates based on their cohort populations or their share of the community's population or were beginning the transition to becoming high delinquency neighborhoods. What this suggested (based on their location and institutional characteristics) was that neighborhoods may also have undergone change because they were located adjacent to parks and recreational areas.

TIME PERIOD VARIATION IN POLICE CONTACTS, SERIOUSNESS SCORES, REFERRALS, AND SEVERITY OF SANCTIONS BY PLACE OF RESIDENCE

We now turn to variation in contact rates, seriousness scores, referral rates, and severity of sanctions scores with aggregated cohort data for each of the spatial systems by place of residence of cohort members.[3]

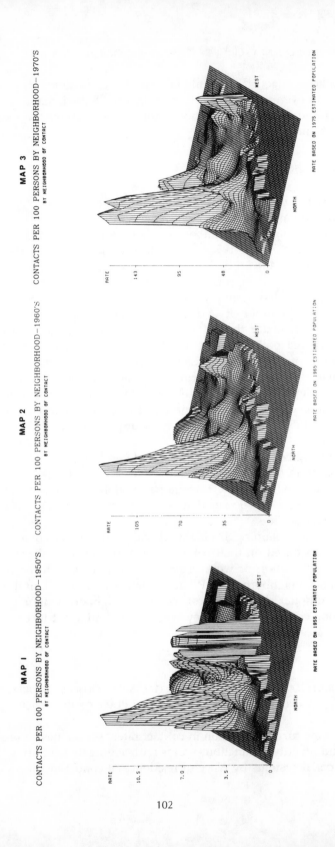

MAP 1

CONTACTS PER 100 PERSONS BY NEIGHBORHOOD—1950'S
BY NEIGHBORHOOD OF CONTACT

RATE BASED ON 1955 ESTIMATED POPULATION

MAP 2

CONTACTS PER 100 PERSONS BY NEIGHBORHOOD—1960'S
BY NEIGHBORHOOD OF CONTACT

RATE BASED ON 1965 ESTIMATED POPULATION

MAP 3

CONTACTS PER 100 PERSONS BY NEIGHBORHOOD—1970'S
BY NEIGHBORHOOD OF CONTACT

RATE BASED ON 1975 ESTIMATED POPULATION

Census Tracts

Table 3 shows the rate for each variable, computed with: 1) the number of cohort members residing in the area during each time period and 2) the number of persons with contacts, seriousness scores, referrals, or sanctions as denominators. Most of the anomalies in this table are a function of the fact that a given cohort may have had a few persons in an area with very lengthy records which markedly differentiated them from others in their area but having the effect of producing a higher than expected average in the 1950s.

What must be immediately noted is that the inner city became more sharply differentiated from other areas by average seriousness scores than by average number of police contacts. Regardless of the time period considered, inner city contact rates were generally higher than rates for other areas; this distinction was greater for the 1970s than for the 1960s, the time period with which comparison was most reasonable based on the average age of persons from the cohorts. While referral rates were generally higher in the inner city than in other areas, the difference was greatest when frequency of referral was considered for those who had been referred from each cohort. This is a factor which we believe has contributed to the "hardening" of the inner city, a process which was likewise noted when severity of sanctions scores were considered, particularly as seen in the rates for the 1970s.

Police Grids

While the inner city grids were sharply differentiated from most other areas on most measures, at least during the 1960s and 1970s, they did not differ from the interstitial areas to the extent that they did when census tracts were the spatial system. One need only remember that the inner city and interstitial areas as delineated by tracts were considerably different from those delineated by police grids to understand how this occurred. Rates for the inner city census tracts were higher in most instances than were the police grid inner city rates. The heterogeneity of police grids depressed the inner city rates, resulting in less difference between them and the transitional areas than in the case of census tracts. There was, of course, considerable in-group variation, particularly when rates were based on persons with contacts, seriousness, referrals, and sanctions, but this was not unexpected and appeared during the 1950s when fewer persons from the cohorts were in many of the police grids.

Even though there were more police grids than there were census tracts, it was again apparent that changing spatial differences in the distribution of delinquency and crime as measured by involvement with the police and courts were not captured as well by police grids as by census tracts.

TABLE 3. MEAN NUMBER OF POLICE CONTACTS SERIOUSNESS SCORES, REFERRALS, AND SEVERITY OF SANCTIONS BY TIME PERIODS FOR PERSONS WITH CONTACT HISTORIES BY CENSUS TRACTS*

	POLICE CONTACTS						SERIOUSNESS SCORES						REFERRALS						SEVERITY OF SANCTIONS					
	Cohorts			Persons w/PC			Cohorts			Persons w/SS			Cohorts			Persons w/R			Cohorts			Persons w/SOS		
	50s	60s	70s	50s	60s	70s	50s	60s	70s	50s	60s	70s	50s	60s	70s	50s	60s	70s	50s	60s	70s	50s	60s	70s
Inner City																								
1	---	---	5.33	---	---	6.40	---	---	17.00	---	---	20.40	---	---	2.50	---	---	7.50	---	---	13.83	---	---	41.50
3	.62	4.48	6.42	2.47	7.38	8.37	1.61	12.28	19.87	6.43	20.21	25.91	.14	1.37	2.79	1.70	3.76	5.68	.13	2.71	9.15	8.00	15.26	23.36
4	.76	3.55	5.10	2.93	6.47	7.04	1.90	9.71	19.57	7.33	17.70	27.03	.12	1.15	1.73	1.46	4.16	4.05	.21	2.42	8.16	16.00	18.40	20.75
5	.98	3.03	5.71	3.67	5.86	8.25	2.66	8.01	17.29	9.95	15.50	24.98	.28	.72	2.09	2.05	2.92	4.63	.55	2.10	7.38	26.67	17.55	20.06
Transitional																								
2	.55	2.18	2.22	3.47	4.57	3.86	1.47	5.64	5.96	9.33	11.80	10.66	.12	.75	.71	1.83	3.77	.54	.02	1.48	2.81	2.00	17.92	12.23
6	.70	1.68	1.07	3.39	3.75	2.60	1.84	3.98	2.71	8.96	8.89	6.58	.16	.36	.27	1.64	2.48	1.74	.17	1.24	1.27	9.50	15.72	9.94
7	.56	1.66	1.42	2.82	4.50	3.22	1.11	4.15	3.42	6.82	11.28	7.78	.13	.46	.40	6.33	2.85	1.88	.20	1.18	2.00	14.00	12.21	9.94
13	.53	2.19	2.08	2.13	4.75	4.83	.79	5.75	5.77	5.13	12.49	13.38	.06	.57	.71	1.57	2.98	3.63	.06	2.03	3.33	12.00	16.65	17.04
Stable Residential																								
8	1.20	1.76	1.79	3.00	4.42	3.56	2.40	4.24	5.07	6.00	10.67	10.08	.20	.48	.68	2.00	2.50	2.77	.00	1.58	3.31	.00	13.10	16.11
9	.91	2.38	2.29	5.00	5.20	4.32	2.27	5.91	6.32	12.50	12.94	11.90	.39	.70	.85	2.83	3.34	3.26	.09	1.76	3.61	4.00	13.70	15.39
10	.32	2.04	2.10	2.50	4.38	4.56	.78	4.91	5.90	6.06	10.55	12.74	.11	.43	.67	2.00	2.09	2.86	.11	1.08	3.16	14.00	10.31	14.45
12	.66	1.74	1.98	2.79	3.54	3.74	1.67	4.09	5.15	7.10	8.35	9.73	.20	.46	.56	2.08	2.28	2.40	.36	.81	2.81	22.00	8.16	13.30
Peripheral Middle to High SES																								
11	.75	1.05	1.08	4.20	3.31	3.04	2.01	2.36	2.68	11.27	7.42	7.55	.17	.21	.27	2.00	1.74	1.90	.10	.69	1.32	4.00	10.41	10.43
14	.60	.85	.48	3.50	2.74	1.14	1.35	1.93	4.12	7.79	6.23	9.86	.11	.21	.46	1.50	1.97	2.36	.00	.27	1.96	.00	7.00	12.31
15	---	1.82	1.16	---	8.00	2.47	---	4.41	2.76	---	6.47	5.88	---	.41	.32	---	1.50	1.22	---	.82	1.69	---	4.50	7.67

* Dashes (----) are used where there are fewer than 5 persons from the combined cohorts in the tract.

Natural Areas

Natural Areas 1 and 2, the most inner city areas of the inner city, also had rates which, for every variable, almost always exceeded those of the inner city areas as delineated by census tracts and police grids. This was the system that was developed from housing quality scores and if there was a shred of substance to the idea that delinquency and crime varied with changes in land use and the physical characteristics of areas as measured by housing quality, rates should have been noticeably higher for Areas 1 and 2 than for other natural areas. At the opposite extreme, the peripheral and high SES areas showed considerable in-group variation but were, with few exceptions, markedly different from the inner city and transitional areas, the anomalies occurring when rates were based on persons with seriousness scores, referrals, and sanctions scores. That the transitional areas were becoming similar to the inner city areas during the 1970s was apparent, but so were several peripheral areas, those which could be noted from inspection of the maps in Chapter 6 based on the distribution of contacts.

Neighborhoods

Neighborhood in-group variation characterized the cohort place of residence rates, albeit the inner city and transitional neighborhoods generally had the highest rates (table not shown). The average cohort and individual seriousness scores for the inner city neighborhoods were generally higher than those for the transitional areas and the transitional areas were, in most cases, higher than the stable residential areas, and so on. By the 1960s and even more so by the 1970s some of the inner city neighborhoods had mean sanctions scores which indicated that some of their residents had been more severely dealt with in the courts than had persons from stable and peripheral neighborhoods.[4] This was, of course, partly a function of the seriousness of the behavior and frequency of referrals for these people but suggested even more than did previous data that there was a "hardening" of areas within the inner city and interstitial areas at the same time that delinquency and crime had been increasing in some more stable and peripheral areas. While these rates were based on place of residence, it was not inappropriate to refer to "hardening" of inner city neighborhoods because most of the police contacts by persons who resided in these areas were committed in their area of residence.

Several series of maps, of which one is included for rates by neighborhood of residence, Maps 4–6, indicated how cohort residents of the inner city neighborhoods had become even more differentiated from other

MAP 4

MEAN NUMBER OF CONTACTS BY NEIGHBORHOOD—1950'S

BY NEIGHBORHOOD OF RESIDENCE

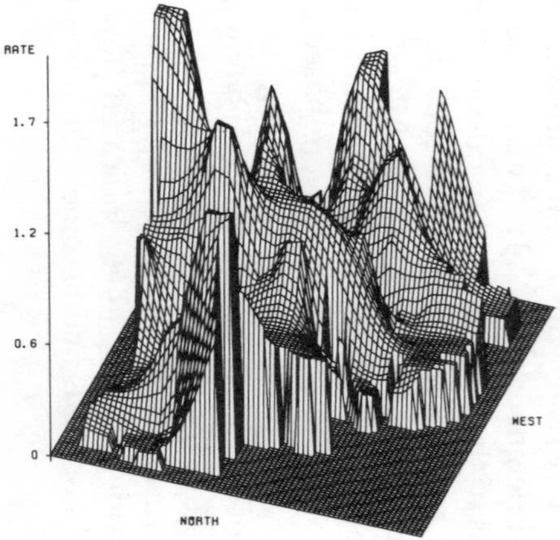

BASED ON COHORT MEMBERS IN NEIGHBORHOOD

MAP 5

MEAN NUMBER OF CONTACTS BY NEIGHBORHOOD—1960'S

BY NEIGHBORHOOD OF RESIDENCE

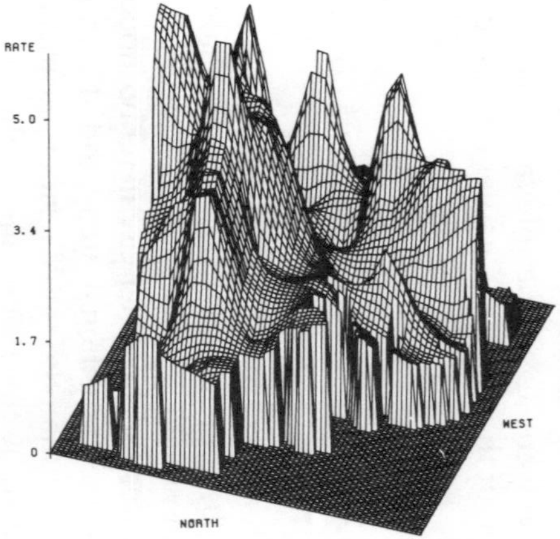

BASED ON COHORT MEMBERS IN NEIGHBORHOOD

MAP 6

MEAN NUMBER OF CONTACTS BY NEIGHBORHOOD—1970'S

BY NEIGHBORHOOD OF RESIDENCE

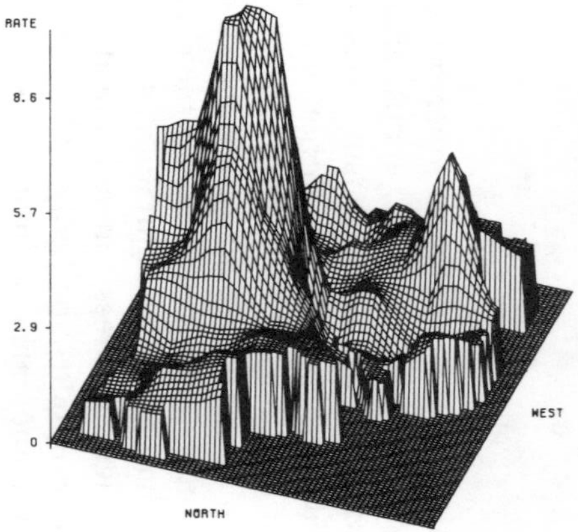

BASED ON COHORT MEMBERS IN NEIGHBORHOOD

neighborhoods by offense seriousness over the years. Inner city neighborhoods were also clearly differentiated by 1970 by another series which utilized only those cohort members with police contacts as a basis for determining the neighborhood's mean seriousness scores. Maps based on referral rates for neighborhoods were very similar to those based on mean seriousness rates.

It has been pointed out in earlier chapters that persons who resided in some areas outside the inner city and transitional areas were more likely to have had their police contacts in other areas, some far removed from their places of residence and in areas with targets or attractions not available close to home. Thus, as became apparent from examination of Table 4 in Chapter 6, there were neighborhoods throughout the city in addition to those in the inner city which constituted centers of trouble, some of which had previously been marked as having high rates of in-area offenses and others which have high rates of serious offenses by their residents. The location of these neighborhoods suggested that some not recognized as transitional areas by their land use and housing characteristics were in the process of transition to becoming delinquent neighborhoods.

SUMMARY

Police contact rates by place of contact for census tracts, police grids, natural areas, and neighborhoods, when examined in relation to time period and cohort models of change, revealed spatial variation that was fairly consistent with what would be expected, i.e., higher rates in the inner city, with lower rates in more peripheral, higher SES areas. The decline, however, from the inner city to the periphery was not marked by a high degree of regularity, although the pattern of inner city and interstitial high rates became more pronounced from decade to decade.

Departures from the model could be accounted for by the attractiveness of some areas as places of leisure time use or by the prevalence of targets for delinquent and criminal behavior. Similarly, tables and maps showing combined cohort, time period, and place of residence variation in police contact rates, seriousness scores, referral rates, and severity of sanctions scores revealed that none of these measures declined evenly with increasing distance from the city center during any of the periods observed. By the 1970s inner city and interstitial neighborhoods were more sharply delineated than they had been in the 1950s and 1960s. While in-area contact rates and place of residence rates were not congruent, it was also apparent that some inner city and interstitial neighborhoods had developed enduring patterns of delinquency and crime. A closer look at the dynamics of this process is taken in the chapter which follows.

Notes

1. The problem of meaningful rates has been discussed by Keith D. Harris in a paper presented to the Annual Meeting of the American Society of Criminology, Dallas, 1978, "Problems in the Development of Risk-Related Crime Rates," supported by Grant No. 78-NI-AX-0064 of the National Institute of Law Enforcement and Criminal Justice.
2. See Lyle W. Shannon, "Ecological Evidence of the Hardening of the Inner City," in Robert M. Figlio, Simon Hakim, and George F. Rengert (eds.), *Metropolitan Crime Patterns* (Monsey, New York: Criminal Justice Press, 1986): 27–53.
3. Stephen P. Lab, "Cohort Analysis and Changing Offense Rates: In Search of the Lost Method," unpublished paper based on the three Racine cohorts, has found that time period effects, especially for females, were greater than age group and cohort effects.
4. Some of the existing literature suggests that police, probation officers, and judges do not discriminate on a basis of race/ethnicity or socioeconomic status when controls for seriousness of offenses, previous record, etc., have been introduced. See Theodore G. Chiricos and Gordon P. Waldo, "Socioeconomic Status and Criminal Sentencing: An Empirical Assessment of a Conflict Proposition," *American Sociological Review*, Vol. 40, 1972, pp. 753–772 and Normal L. Weiner and Charles V. Willie, "Decisions by Juvenile Offenders," *American Journal of Sociology*, Vol. 77, 1971, pp. 199–210. Other studies suggest the opposite, for example, Theodore G. Chiricos, Phillip D. Jackson and Gordon P. Waldo, "Inequality in the Imposition of a Criminal Label," *Social Problems*, Vol. 19, 1972, pp. 553–572; Terence P. Thornberry, "Race, Socioeconomic Status and Sentencing in the Juvenile Justice System," *Journal of Criminal Law and Criminology*, Vol. 64, 1973, pp. 90–98; and Alan J. Lizotte, "Extra-legal Factors in Chicago's Criminal Courts: Testing the Conflict Model of Criminal Justice," *Social Problems*, Vol. 25, 1978, pp. 564–580.

Chapter 8

SPATIAL CONTINUITY IN DELINQUENCY AND CRIME

The Hardening of the Inner City

CHANGE IN PERCENT WITH POLICE CONTACTS BY AGE

Because professionals and laymen look at the prevalence, incidence, and seriousness of delinquency and crime by the age of offenders and by place of residence and, even more important, by areas and neighborhoods that are recognized as delinquent or criminogenic, the cohort data were analyzed on this basis for each of the spatial systems. The data for census tracts for each cohort and each age revealed a more or less gradual but steady chronological increase in the percent of persons who had a contact, more so in some tracts than in others. For example, the 1949 Cohort members in Tract 5 had a percent with contacts increase from the age of 6 (2.0%) to the age of 16 (30.7%) and from there on to the age of 24 at a level which moved up and down no more than 8%. Similar patterns of progression were found for *other* inner city tracts, grids, and natural areas.

While the highest proportion of persons from the 1955 Cohort with a police contact from any tract at age 19 was 38.2% (Tract 3), the highest proportion from a police grid was 40.7% (Grid 12), the highest proportion from a natural area was 37.8% (Natural Area 2), and the highest proportion from a neighborhood was 51.6% (Neighborhood 12), a neighborhood within Natural Area 2. The regularity of progression in percent of those who resided in any area was related, of course, to the number of persons residing in the area (progression percentages were smoother from year to year for areas with large populations) so that even though most neighborhoods had a peak proportion of their cohort members involved with the police in the

109

late teens, trends for neighborhoods within cohorts and cohort comparisons were more difficult to specify.

What one could note, although it only reinforced findings from the aggregated data previously presented, was that the inner city Tracts 3, 4, and 5 showed early involvement of persons in each cohort and reached the point that 30% or more of the cohort had police contacts each year by the age of 16 or 17. This level of involvement continued with some fluctuation so that by the ages of 30 or 31 for the 1942 Cohort, 24 for the 1949 Cohort, and 21 for the 1955 Cohort approximately 30% or more of each cohort residing in these areas was still having at least one police contact per year, a pattern found in no other census tract.

Those from the 1942 Cohort who resided in inner city Police Grids 8, 12, and 16 had a high and continuing level of involvement, although Grid 16 showed a decline in the proportion with annual police encounters by the age of 27. The 1949 Cohort presented essentially the same pattern of year by year progression for these grids but Grid 13 became one of those with continuity and high involvement with the police. The 1955 Cohort showed a similar pattern for all of these grids but Grid 9 was added. It was also apparent by this time that Grids 5, 6, 17, 18, and even peripheral Grid 22, were grids with continuity and relatively high police involvement on the part of cohort residents. The police grid tables for each cohort suggested that these changes were related to both cohort and time period progression.

Persons from the 1942 Cohort who resided in Natural Area 2 were involved early and their progression through the age of 31 was unmatched in any other area. From the age of 17 at least 40%, give or take 5% of the people who resided there, had at least one police contact every year until they reached the age of 28 and, of those who still resided in the area after that, involvement was as high as 70% at the age of 30. The 1949 Cohort residents of Natural Area 1 were similar to those in Natural Area 2. It was also apparent that early and widespread involvement and continuity had become the pattern for Natural Areas 4, 5, and 8.

While several other areas had relatively earlier and widespread involvement, continuity into adulthood for a large percent of the group had still not become the pattern. However, the 1955 Cohort showed that early involvement and continuity had become the pattern for a larger proportion of the young people in not only the areas that we have mentioned for the 1942 and 1949 Cohorts but for many areas bounding the inner city and interstitial areas as well.

The most extreme example in the 1942 Cohort was Neighborhood 9 where, at the ages of 18 and 19, over 70% of the youth had at least one police contact and had high involvement through the age of 26 for its young adults. While the involvement of persons who resided in Neighborhood 9 was one of the highest in the 1949 Cohort (although less than for the 1942

Cohort), there were other neighborhoods with comparably high involvement and for the 1955 Cohort there were even more neighborhoods with as high or higher involvement than that of Neighborhood 9. This does not mean that Neighborhood 9 was undergoing a decline in its youthful crime rate but that the 1955 Cohort was not contributing as large a proportion to the overall rate for the area as had some previous cohorts at their age of high involvement.

Neighborhood data made it possible to pinpoint areas which showed little involvement by cohort residents at early ages but which at a later period and for another cohort displayed high involvement. When these changes were congruent with changes in the distribution of targets and other changes in the neighborhood, as in the case of Neighborhood 46, we can see how increasing youthful involvement with the police was part of a larger transitional process that could be captured with units of observation smaller than census tracts and police grids, even though there were analytic problems involved when too few members of cohorts were found in some areas. It must be made clear that we are not, at the moment, talking about individual continuity, a different matter which has already been dealt with at considerable length and to which we shall again turn.[1] These data simply tell us that a larger proportion of the persons who resided in inner city areas were continuously generating police contacts than were those from other areas.

SPATIAL CONTINUITY IN SERIOUSNESS

Continuing our exploration of ecological correlations, the mean seriousness scores for cohort members residing in each area of each spatial system were correlated, age group by age group, in further assessment of the trend toward hardening of the inner city. Although prior analyses have shown that individuals had limited career continuity from age group to age group, such continuity that existed was greatest between adjacent age groups. We were here concerned about the extent to which seriousness had continuity in an area regardless of which members of the cohort resided there and would expect adjacent age groups to have had the greatest continuity. Four sets of correlations facilitated cohort comparisons within spatial systems and three sets facilitated spatial system comparison within cohorts.

Although relatively high correlations of seriousness scores, most in the .500s to .900s, were obtained for the earliest two age groups regardless of the spatial system for the 1949 and 1955 Cohorts, this was not always the case for the 1942 Cohort. This may have been because seriousness scores were lowest for the 1942 Cohort so that movement by some of its more troublesome members may have had considerable impact on the mean seriousness scores of smaller areas or simply have been because the inner city had not yet stabilized or hardened to such an extent that its average seriousness scores were always so high in contrast to other areas that the high correlations found at the earliest ages would continue. Inspection of the mean seriousness scores suggested that it was a combination of these factors.

Perhaps more important is the fact that age groups 11 through 14, 15 through 17, and 18 through 20 almost always had the highest correlations in the 1949 and 1955 Cohorts. If seriousness scores for earlier ages were regressed on seriousness scores for the 18 through 20 age group for the units of each spatial system, would we find a progressive impact suggestive of hardening through time?

Table 1 shows that for both the 1949 and 1955 Cohorts the 15 through 17 mean seriousness scores of areas had a significant impact on the 18 through 20 mean seriousness scores, regardless of the spatial system considered (but not for the 1942 Cohort). When the 11 through 14 age group was inserted during the second step, significant effects were still lacking for the 1942 Cohort with some changes for the 1949 and 1955 Cohorts. Still, the 15 through 17 age group accounted for the mean seriousness scores of areas during ages 18 through 20 in three of four spatial systems. Inserting the 6 through 10 age group in the next step resulted in very little change and we concluded that the mean seriousness of most recent prior age group for persons residing in an area accounted for more of the 18 through 20 seriousness of reasons for police contacts in areas than did seriousness of other age groups.

The Consequences of Movement

There has been considerable concern over the years about whether delinquent neighborhoods generate continuities in delinquency and crime or whether crime-oriented young adults gravitate to more crime-oriented neighborhoods as they leave their homes.[2] The cohort data enabled us to shed some light on this subject by looking at changes which occurred as people moved from one kind of neighborhood or spatial unit to another.

If the milieus to which members of a cohort moved were ones which had been assessed as more delinquency and crime producing (lower SES areas) than the ones which they had left, it would have been expected that those who changed milieu would have had increased involvement with the police and courts. Mean number of contacts for cohort members, persons with contacts, mean seriousness scores for cohort members, and so on, were calculated for those who stayed, those who moved up, and those who moved down. The mean score for those who moved down was usually higher during the following ages than for those who stayed or moved up but this did not mean that the move had had a proportionately greater

TABLE 1. REGRESSION OF SERIOUSNESS SCORES BY AGE GROUP AND PLACE OF RESIDENCE DURING JUVENILE YEARS ON SERIOUSNESS SCORES DURING YOUNG ADULT PERIOD

Dependent Variable: Seriousness 18-20	1942 COHORT				1949 COHORT				1955 COHORT			
	Tract	Grid	Nat. Area	Nghbd.	Tract	Grid	Nat. Area	Nghbd.	Tract	Grid	Nat. Area	Nghbd.
R	-.040	.144	.049	.266	.871	.922	.891	.810	.915	.691	.734	.813
Adjusted R²	.000	.000	.000	.046	.737	.838	.783	.648	.824	.448	.513	.655
Beta Age 15-17	-.040	.144	.049	.266	.871*	.922*	.891*	.810*	.915*	.691*	.734*	.814*
Multiple R	.563	.277	.335	.268	.905	.924	.892	.828	.917	.693	.766	.838
Adjusted R²	.165	.000	.001	.020	.783	.829	.772	.672	.812	.419	.538	.689
Beta Age 15-17	-.204	-.134	-.109	.285	.446	.789*	.817*	.483*	.825*	.744*	.419	.667*
Age 11-14	.585	.366	.367	-.037	.491	.148	.085	.370*	.109	-.075	.384	.248*
Multiple R	.716	.310	.546	.387	.913	.926	.896	.828	.945	.710	.797	.847
Adjusted R²	.330	.000	.158	.077	.779	.818	.766	.665	.862	.411	.567	.700
Beta Age 15-17	-.189	-.251	.027	.304	.413	.822*	.857*	.467*	.591*	.753*	.388	.603*
Age 11-14	.058	.605	-.118	-.346	.647	.029	.110	.361	.050	-.214	.205	.157
Age 6-10	.685	-.218	.619	.411	-.177	.109	-.106	.032	.366*	.205	.302	.177

* F-value indicates significance at .05 level or less.

113

impact on them than the effects of staying in the same type of area had had on others.

In order to determine whether or not a proportionately greater impact was there for those who moved down, an impact that would override whatever already acquired characteristics were present in the group who moved down, the after-move mean was divided by the before-move mean. If the hypothesis of changing milieu effects was correct, then the ratio should have been higher for those who moved to lower SES areas than for others.

Early and late moves down across natural areas were followed by disproportional increases in mean scores for the 1942 and 1949 Cohorts and higher means with some disproportional increases for those in the 1955 Cohort who moved down rather than staying or moving upward. And, of course, moves to higher SES natural areas produced proportionately greater decreases in most mean scores for those who made the move than for those who stayed or moved to lower SES areas for persons in the 1942 and 1949 Cohorts. Those in the 1955 Cohort who moved to higher SES areas had lower means on all measures during both time periods than did those who moved to lower SES areas but their increase in mean scores was not proportionately less on the cohort means for seriousness, referrals, and sanctions than were the increases for persons who moved to lower SES areas.

No matter which spatial system was utilized, census tracts or police grids, career changes for the 1949 Cohort were in the direction that one would expect based on milieu influences. The divergence from "expected" for the 1955 Cohort makes sense if we remember that some outlying areas had had increasing rates of delinquency and possible official over-reactions to them. Had we wished to stack the deck, rather than using lower or higher SES areas as a definition of moving down or up, we could have used moves to higher or lower delinquency areas.

THE IMPACT OF SERIOUSNESS OF CAREERS AND SEVERITY OF SANCTIONS ON LATER SERIOUSNESS

Multiple regression analysis was the next technique utilized to determine if severity of sanctions for the 15 through 17 age group had an effect on seriousness of reasons for police contact during the ages 18 through 20 beyond the effects of seriousness ages 15 through 17.

As a background to the multiple regression, the first-order correlations between seriousness during both age groups and severity of sanctions scores during both age groups, and several other sets of correlations, are presented in the lower section of Table 2. These correlations were based on the average seriousness of offenses and severity of sanctions scores for cohort residents of each area in the three larger spatial systems for these age groups, a shift from the individual level analyses.

TABLE 2. REGRESSION OF SANCTIONS AGE 15-17 AND SERIOUSNESS AGE 15-17 ON SERIOUSNESS 18-20 BY CENSUS TRACTS, POLICE GRIDS, AND NATURAL AREAS

Dependent Variable:	1942 COHORT			1949 COHORT			1955 COHORT		
	Tract	Grid	Nat. Area	Tract	Grid	Nat. Area	Tract	Grid	Nat. Area
Seriousness 18-20									
R	.046	.381	.187	.598	.834	.668	.903	.686	.648
Adjusted R	.000	.003	.000	.300	.679	.415	.799	.442	.396
Beta 15-17 Sanctions	-.046	.381	-.187	.598*	.834*	.668*	.903*	.686*	.648*
Multiple R	.046	.382	.230	.879	.922	.911	.931	.719	.735
Adjusted R	.000	.003	.000	.727	.832	.810	.839	.461	.501
Beta 15-17 Sanctions	-.042	.371	-.314	.129	-.040*	-.366	.246	.308	-.115
15-17 Seriousness	-.008	.019	.184	.797*	.958*	1.206*	.694	.435	.838*
Correlations									
Seriousness 15-17 X Seriousness 18-20	-.028	.225	-.032	.873	.922	.891	.927	.704	.734
Sanctions 15-17 X Sanctions 18-20	.367	.464	-.184	.610	.832	.785	.930	.665	.591
Seriousness 15-17 X Sanctions 15-17	.467	.555	.689	.589	.912	.858	.947	.869	.910
Serioiusness 18-20 X Sanctions 18-20	.244	.520	.737	.889	.954	.920	.951	.931	.896
Seriousness 15-17 X Sanctions 18-20	.263	.065	-.190	.871	.889	.939	.912	.757	.664

* F-value indicates significance at .05 level or less.

115

It should be noted that these age groups may not contain the same people for the 1949 Cohort since these ages straddled time periods. This has, of course, been a problem in several other analyses and has generated different results for the 1942 Cohort than for the 1949 and 1955 Cohorts, i.e., there has been less continuity in relationships from age group to age group. With this warning, what do these correlations suggest?

While there were some differences in the results depending on spatial system, trends were the same. None of the 1942 correlations were statistically significant but, since it could be argued that a cohort is not a sample, this may or may not be an important consideration. Whichever, all of the 1942 Cohort correlations were low, indicating that those members of the cohort who resided in a given area may have had a high average seriousness during the ages 15 through 17 but those who resided there did not have a high average seriousness for the ages 18 through 20 and the opposite. In other words, there was relatively little age group continuity in the seriousness of careers for the two age groups when frequency and seriousness of reasons for police contacts were at their peak. Police contact rates and seriousness were also lower for the 1942 Cohort and examination of the actual rates revealed that the inner city areas were not as highly differentiated from others as they were for those from the 1949 and 1955 Cohorts who lived there.

Similarly, severity of sanctions scores did not correlate significantly from age group to age group for the 1942 Cohort. In other words, there was not much relationship between the severity of sanctions scores for cohort members from age group to age group on a basis of where they resided and, although there seemed to be more relationship between age groups for sanctions utilizing police grids and census tracts, there was less for natural areas. But again, sanctions were not being administered very severely to juveniles at this time. The picture was very different for the 1949 Cohort during 1964 through 1969. All of the correlations were higher and statistically significant and the degree of change was considerable. Areas with high average seriousness scores and high average sanction scores were much more likely to have them for both age groups and the two larger inner city areas and some of the interstitial areas had become more highly differentiated from other areas in the city.

The 1955 correlations were somewhat lower for police grids and natural areas, not because the inner city had changed but because severity of sanctions had increased in some of the outlying areas for the ages 18 through 20, a consequence of increasing severity of sanctions throughout the community. The boundaries of census tracts were such that this was not captured and only the increased hardening of the inner city was shown.

The next set of correlations showed the relationship of seriousness of reasons for contact to severity of sanctions scores. We have dealt with these relationships in a more general way in earlier research but have not approached them in this ecological framework. The areas in which members of the cohort received more severe sanctions were those in which persons with high seriousness resided. In each case the 1942 Cohort correlations showed less relationship between seriousness of careers and severity of sanctions scores than did the 1949 and 1955 Cohorts. Our first concern was over what had happened in a given area and its relationship to the organization of society as it generated changes in areas and spatial patterns of phenomena. The emphasis focused on the cyclical nature of phenomena.

Our next concern was with correlations crossing variables by age groups, i.e., the correlation of seriousness of careers (15 through 17) with severity of sanctions scores (18 through 20). Since there was an element of lag involved, serious delinquency during earlier ages dealt with at a later age may have played a part in bolstering these correlations. The 1942 Cohort correlations suggested that seriousness in an area was not generally followed by severe sanctions in the next period or the reverse but the correlations for the 1949 Cohort were sufficiently high, as were most of those for the 1955 Cohort, to indicate that areas with high seriousness during one period had severe sanctions for their cohort members during the next period. Seriousness was followed by seriousness and seriousness resulted in sanctions.

Turning now to the first step of the regression analysis in the top half of Table 2, severity of sanctions during the ages 15 through 17 in police grids was followed by increasing seriousness ages 18 through 20 in the 1942 Cohort (but not in tracts and natural areas). The largest correlation produced was for police grids and in the opposite direction from what would be expected if severe sanctions were a deterrent to future seriousness in the area.

The 1949 and 1955 correlations are of greatest concern. Both tended to reaffirm what has been said about misconceptions of the effectiveness of severe sanctions. Severity of sanctions during the ages 15 through 17 and seriousness of careers at ages 18 through 20 were so highly correlated that one was inclined to conclude that severe sanctions contributed to the hardening of the inner city and interstitial areas as centers of delinquency and crime at the same time that diffusion to other areas was occurring. There was the problem of controlling for seriousness of careers 15 through 17 in further assessment of these findings but even then it appeared that severe sanctions no more led to less serious behavior than mild sanctions led to more serious misbehavior.

When seriousness of careers age 15 through 17 were entered in the multiple regression analysis the correlations were higher than before. The net effect of severity of sanctions on the relationship between seriousness of career 15 through 17 and 18 through 20 was positive in some cases and negative in others, varying with the spatial system utilized but in no case statistically significant. Again, the conclusion was that severity of sanctions was not having the effects desired, sanctions did not significantly reduce seriousness during the following ages. Severe sanctions were, in fact, followed by serious delinquency and youthful crime.

The more one analyzes the ecological data, the more sure one becomes that not only had the characteristics of the inner city and interstitial areas become more solidified but, to the extent that population movement outward had taken place, there had been some increases in delinquency rates in areas that had not previously had them and in areas which had not shown the elements of ecological transition.

Movement of families with children from the inner city to interstitial areas and to suburban areas was sure to have had an impact on patterns of crime. Rates in the inner city would be reduced (although they would still remain the highest) and rates in those more peripheral areas in which the housing supply fitted the purses of those not too affluent would increase. To the extent that Black youth make up a disproportionate number of the population (as well as a disproportionate number of the poor), Black offense rates for violent and property crimes will be higher than those for Whites and the continued concentration of Blacks in the inner city contributes to its hardening.[3]

COMPARISON OF POLICE CONTACT RATES FOR THE ENTIRE CITY AND THE THREE COHORTS

The reader may have wondered if the spatial distribution of delinquency and crime in Racine followed essentially the same pattern whether the various official series of rates or official contact data for the three cohorts were presented. Considerable congruence would be expected, of course, because the three cohorts are presumed to be as representative as any other three cohorts that might have been selected which included persons between the ages of 15 and 34 during the 1970s.

It has been mentioned earlier that whether in-area cohort rates were computed based on the Racine population or the in-area cohort population, the rates would be highly correlated and they were. However, and this is the important point, there was an almost perfect correlation between either set of cohort tract rates for the 1970s and the Racine Part I offense tract rates for 1970 through 1978 (.999 and .998). Both cohort police contact rates for police grids were highly correlated and both were highly correlated with Part I offenses in police grids (.998 and .875).

The Racine arrest rates series by census tract of residence (1970–1978) was also included in this analysis and was correlated with the cohort contact rates by place of residence (.815), mean seriousness scores (.883), and referral rates (.821). These three rates were highly correlated for cohort members by place of residence and each of these rates was in turn correlated with arrest rates by tract of residence. It was interesting that the correlations increased from .815 for contacts to .883 for seriousness, the measure which might be expected to correlate most highly with arrest rates because more serious reasons for police contact were more likely to culminate in arrests. Had we selected each year, commencing in 1970, for each official series and for each set of cohort rates, the year-by-year correlations would have ranged around those produced with aggregated data.

Traffic and Transportation and Changing Patterns of Delinquency and Crime

In Chapter 6 it was pointed out that automobile registrations and traffic had increased over the 30-year period at the same time that mass transit ridership decreased. While it is easy to draw parallels between measures of automobile usage and police contact rates, the volume of moving vehicles does not account directly for more than that part of the increase in contacts which derive from driving. On the other hand, many offenses were multiple and involved illegal or careless use of the automobile as well as liquor, sex, and other related violations.

As far as changes in offense rates in areas were concerned, perusal of a map with major arterials revealed that the "natural barriers" (large city parks and extensive industrial land use divided the city in half from north to south commencing on the west side of Census Tract 14 and extending down to Census Tract 8) were broached by half a dozen major thoroughfares, all of which led to the inner city and passed through interstitial areas on the way. Some of the differences in patterns of offenses by place of residence vs. place of contact were explained when maps were drawn showing where cohort members resided vs. where they had had police contacts. These have clearly shown that many police contacts took place along these major arterials as people drove from place of residence to areas of work and play and returned. Residents of more peripheral areas had contacts with the police which may have occurred during the trip and in the inner city or transitional area which was their goal. Those who resided in the inner city, transitional, or different peripheral areas had contacts with the police in transit and at their peripheral places of play. Comparison of traffic flow maps for 1956 and 1978, for example, revealed that between these years the number of vehicles arriving at several peripheral intersections had doubled and trebled.

Several bus routes (with high ridership of persons 16–24 years of age) facilitated the movement of those who did not have automobiles or access to them from the inner city and transitional areas to peripheral recreational attractions. More specifically, even without an automobile, peripheral areas to the northwest and southwest (with developing in-area offense rates) were readily reached by bus lines. Thus, the rhythmical, temporal movement of the population by auto or bus must be considered if one is to fully explain variance in delinquency and crime rates and their changing spatial patterns.

SUMMARY

Consistent increases with age through the late teens and into the early 20s in the percent of each cohort's members with police contacts was more characteristic of some inner city and interstitial areas than of others. Furthermore, it was also apparent that some inner city neighborhoods were delineated in such a fashion as to capture the extremes of the cohort, with as high as 70% of the youth having police contacts by the late teens and continuing involvement past the mid-20s.

A series of regression analyses provided confirmation for the concept of a hardening inner city. When the consequences of movement were examined, it became even more apparent that change in residence to crime-producing neighborhoods generated proportionately more increases in contacts, seriousness scores, referrals, and ensuing sanctions than were generated among those who moved to areas which were considered less likely to produce crime. While this was particularly true for persons from the 1949 Cohort, it appeared that discrepancies for the 1955 Cohort could be accounted for by the fact that some peripheral areas that had not been classified as crime-producing had, during the 1970s, experienced increases in indicators of involvement in the justice system and changes in land use which made them no longer milieus unlikely to increase the delinquent and criminal behavior of those who moved to the area.

Regression analyses of the seriousness of offenses and the severity of sanctions provided even further evidence that sanctions against members of a cohort who resided in an area were not followed by reductions in seriousness of offenses by cohort residents of the area during the following period. Moreover, it even appeared that severe sanctions were followed by increasing seriousness.

Other analyses described in this chapter revealed that the spatial distribution of offense rates for the entire population of Racine for the 1970s were highly correlated with cohort rates for the same period. It has also been shown that the expansion of the city and ensuing patterns of population movement played a part in the changing distribution of delinquency and crime.

NOTES

1. Robinson's article on the "ecological fallacy" (William S. Robinson, "Ecological Correlations and the Behavior of Individuals," *American Sociological Review*, Vol. 15, June 1950, pp. 351–357) raised doubts in the minds of many researchers

about the value of aggregate-level research but since that time, as pointed out by Scheuch (Erwin K. Scheuch, "Social Contact and Individual Behavior," pp. 133–155 in Mattei Dogan and Stein Rokkan (eds.), *Quantitative Ecological Analysis in the Social Sciences*, Cambridge, Mass.: M.I.T. Press, 1969), the ecological fallacy has been shown to be one instance of a family of cross-level observations including the "individualistic fallacy" (i.e., inferring the behavior of aggregates from observations on individuals).

2. For an even-handed treatment of both positions which leans toward the neighborhood as providing the milieu in which delinquency is a normal outgrowth of that way of life, see John Mack, "Full-Time Miscreants, Delinquent Neighborhoods and Criminal Networks," *British Journal of Sociology*, Vol. 15, 1963, pp. 38–53.

3. Skogan has dealt with the age and race composition of the population and their effects on crime rates in Wesley G. Skogan, Chapter 14, "Crime in Contemporary America," in Hugh Davis Graham and Ted Robert Gurr (eds.), *Violence in America: Historical and Comparative Perspectives*, Beverly Hills: Sage Publications, 1979. The impact of youthful offenders on offense rates has also been shown in Peter W. Greenwood, Joan Petersilia, and Franklin E. Zimring, *Age, Crime, and Sanctions: The Transition from Juvenile to Adult Court*, Santa Monica: Rand, 1980.

Chapter 9

THE CONCENTRATION OF DELINQUENCY
AND CRIME AMONG MULTIPLE OFFENDERS

CONCENTRATION OF CONTACTS

The developing concentration of police contacts within the inner city and interstitial areas in terms of contact location and place of residence of persons with contacts has been described in the past four chapters. At the same time, police contacts were widely *dispersed* spatially and more than one-half of the males, regardless of where they resided, had at least one Non-traffic contact sometime during their lives.

The concentration of contacts among a small proportion of the members of each cohort is described in this chapter. First of all, contacts for alleged delinquent and criminal behavior were highly *concentrated* among some individuals in each cohort in terms of the recurrence and the seriousness of behavior that generated them. Second, while a proportion of each group had *continuity* in their careers, most people had discontinuous careers or contacts during only one period in their lives.

The Proportion Responsible for Most Police Contacts

As indicated by the first line in Table 1, relatively few persons were responsible for a disproportionately large number of all police contacts in every cohort. In the 1942 Cohort 9.5% was responsible for 51.0% of the contacts. The concentration was somewhat greater in the 1949 Cohort, where 8.0% of the cohort was responsible for 50.8% of the contacts. Only 5.8% of the 1955 Cohort was responsible for 50.8% of that cohort's contacts.

Although cohort differences in the concentration of contacts appeared to be increasing, it must be remembered that the members of each cohort had fewer years at risk than the cohort before it and thus less likelihood that most of its members had engaged in behavior resulting in a police contact. Since the 1942 Cohort had the longest period of adult exposure, we would expect the least concentration of total contacts among a small portion of that cohort; they had more years of exposure to the possibility of contacts for Traffic offenses, offenses which showed less concentration than other types. All things considered, the concentration of contacts among

TABLE 1.   PERCENT OF COHORTS ACCOUNTING FOR PERCENT OF POLICE CONTACTS: TOTAL, BY SEX, AND BY RACE/ETHNICITY

	1942		1949		1955	
	% of Cohort	% of Contacts	% of Cohort	% of Contacts	% of Cohort	% of Contacts
All Contacts						
Cohort	9.5	51.0	8.0	50.8	5.8	50.8
Males	12.6	49.2	10.4	50.4	8.4	53.5
Females	8.7	51.5	7.7	51.1	6.7	53.8
White Males	12.7	49.1	10.9	51.0	8.0	52.2
Black Males	20.0	45.2	18.2	50.0	14.1	51.1
Chicano Males	----*	----	21.0	49.0	12.8	46.1
White Females	8.2	51.3	9.2	53.4	6.7	54.5
Black Females	----	----	12.8	50.0	9.3	49.8
Chicanas	----	----	----	----	12.5	54.3
Non-Traffic Contacts						
Cohort	7.4	52.5	6.0	52.6	5.0	53.6
Males	11.0	52.3	8.2	52.5	6.8	53.6
Females	4.7	55.4	5.4	55.4	4.2	51.8
White Males	10.6	52.5	7.8	52.4	5.9	52.8
Black Males	20.0	43.4	18.2	51.8	14.5	53.0
Chicano Males	----	----	21.0	53.0	19.1	61.8
White Females	4.5	57.0	6.1	58.6	4.0	53.5
Black Females	----	----	12.8	53.5	9.3	53.0
Chicanas	----	----	20.0	60.0	15.6	61.2
Traffic Contacts						
Cohort	11.1	50.5	15.5	60.1	13.0	61.5
Males	16.0	51.7	13.9	49.9	9.2	41.3
Females	13.7	63.6	8.8	48.0	4.6	39.7
White Males	15.1	49.0	12.5	46.2	7.9	37.0
Black Males	20.0	54.4	15.9	51.2	9.4	41.4
Chicano Males	----	----	21.0	45.4	21.3	59.4
White Females	13.8	63.1	8.3	46.8	4.2	36.7
Black Females	----	----	15.4	62.9	8.1	56.7
Chicanas	----	----	----	----	6.2	57.1

* Too few persons in cohort segment for this statistic (less than 15).

males probably differed less from cohort to cohort than indicated by the figures in Table 1.

Concentration of contacts was even greater among the females than among the males in each cohort. For example, 8.7% of the 1942 females accounted for 51.5% of the contacts by females in that cohort, while it took 12.6% of the males to account for 49.2% of their contacts. Similarly, 7.7% of the 1942 females accounted for 51.5% of their contacts but it took 10.4% of the males to account for 50.4% of their contacts. Among the 1955 females, 6.7% was responsible for 53.8% of their contacts, while 8.4% of the males was responsible for 53.5% of their contacts.

Police contacts were not nearly as concentrated among Blacks as among Whites in the 1942 Cohort; 20.0% of the Black males was responsible for 45.2% of their contacts in contrast to the 12.7% of the White males who accounted for 49.1% of their contacts. In the 1949 Cohort, 21.0% of the Chicano males accounted for 49.0% of their contacts and 18.2% of the Black males accounted for 50.0% of their contacts. Although concentration remained the highest among Whites, with 10.9% of the males accounting for 51.0% of their contacts and 9.2% of the females accounting for 53.4% of their contacts, only 12.8% of the Black females was responsible for 50.0% of their contacts. The concentration of police contacts among a small percent of the Blacks and Chicanos in the 1955 Cohort was higher than for the previous cohorts, only 12.8% of the Chicano males accumulating 46.1% of their contacts and 12.8% of the Chicanas accumulating 54.3% of their contacts. Likewise, only 9.3% of the Black females had 49.8% of their contacts and 14.1% of the Black males had 51.1% of their contacts. White male concentration had increased in the 1955 Cohort so that 8.0% accounted for 52.2% of their contacts while only 6.7% of the White females accounted for 54.4% of their contacts. Additional evidence of the concentration of contacts may be found by further perusal of Table 1, particularly as we turn to the percentages for Non-traffic offenses as compared with those for Traffic offenses.

Traffic vs. Non-Traffic Concentration

The data in Table 1 indicate that although Non-traffic contacts were generally more concentrated in a small proportion of the persons in each cohort than were Traffic contacts, there were some race/ethnic|sex segments of each cohort in which Traffic contacts were even more concentrated than Non-traffic contacts because a relatively small number of the group had access to an automobile. Suffice it to say that proportionately more males not only had access to automobiles but also spent more time driving around than did females, particularly Blacks and Chicanas. As a result, there was greater concentration of Traffic contacts among females than males. While Traffic contacts were less concentrated among White males who, of course, had greater access to automobiles than other race/ethnic|sex segments of each cohort, Non-traffic contacts were considerably more concentrated in the hands of a few persons.

The discontinuous nature of cumulative distributions for the proportion of people and proportion of contacts made it difficult to select precisely comparable cutting points for each race/ethnic | sex segment of each cohort but it was still possible to see that a relatively small proportion of most race/ethnic | sex categories accounted for a large proportion of each group's police contacts. The apparent decrease in the proportion of persons responsible for a cohort's contacts may, however, in part be attributed to the fact that later cohorts had fewer years in which to acquire contacts. The differential exposure factor would most strongly affect the number of persons who had acquired Traffic offenses, particularly the females.

Felony vs. Non-felony Concentration

When the concentration of contacts by whether they were Felonies or Non-felonies was examined, contacts for Felonies were even more highly concentrated among a small percent of the members of each cohort than were all Non-traffic offenses and Non-felonies. The concentration of Felonies was highest among the females and, within the female segments, among White females. Felonies were also highly concentrated among the White males, with 11.5% of the White males in the 1942 Cohort, 12.6% in the 1949 Cohort, and 16.4% in the 1955 Cohort accounting for all Felonies by White males in each cohort. Non-felony contacts showed less concentration among the males than the females, particularly the Blacks and Chicanas.

While there is an appearance of increasing concentration of contacts in Table 1, the opposite is found for Felonies. Some juveniles and young adults continued to steal automobiles or other property, to break into warehouses, or to engage in assaultive behavior of one sort or another. As the years went by (and this will be detailed in a later chapter), other persons in the cohort who had not had police contacts behaved in such a way as to have them for what were categorized as Felonies. Thus, the proportion of each cohort responsible for Felony contacts increased and produced a lower concentration of these contacts in a small proportion of the cohort.

MULTIPLE OFFENSES

The fact that a small percentage of each cohort produced most of the contacts for Felonies led us to wonder if these were the people who could be readily classified as chronic offenders. Further, were they the people who accumulated four or more or five or more contacts and among them the most serious offenses? In other words, were the frequent offenders (those whose offenses produced contacts) also the people who produced the bulk of the contacts for Felonies or Non-traffic offenses?

The answer to these questions may be found in Table 2. In addition to presenting the data for all contacts, the members of each cohort were categorized by the number of police contacts that they had had for Traffic vs. Non-traffic contacts and Felony vs. Non-felony contacts. We have utilized the same cutting points as Wolfgang, Figlio, and Sellin in order to facilitate comparison of our findings with theirs.[1]

TABLE 2.   CHRONIC OFFENDERS: PERCENT OF OFFENDERS WITH 4 OR MORE AND 5 OR MORE
           CONTACTS AND THEIR PERCENT OF THE CONTACTS

		1942		1949		1955	
		% of Cohort	% of Contacts	% of Cohort	% of Contacts	% of Cohort	% of Contacts
All Contacts							
4 or +:	Cohort	31.9	85.2	30.3	84.4	20.7	81.1
	Males	50.0	89.8	44.5	89.0	55.3	92.0
	Females	8.7	51.5	11.3	60.2	25.0	73.4
5 or +:	Cohort	26.2	79.8	23.5	78.0	17.1	76.7
	Males	42.4	85.3	35.4	83.1	26.7	90.1
	Females	5.4	40.6	7.7	51.1	6.8	64.9
Non-Traffic Contacts							
4 or +:	Cohort	18.6	79.8	20.9	83.0	16.4	82.5
	Males	29.5	82.7	30.4	86.1	24.4	86.6
	Females	4.7	55.4	8.3	65.9	7.8	65.8
5 or +:	Cohort	15.0	73.9	14.4	77.1	13.5	78.1
	Males	24.4	77.5	24.7	81.0	20.9	83.2
	Females	2.9	43.4	5.4	55.4	5.5	57.4
Traffic Contacts							
4 or +:	Cohort	16.0	61.3	8.6	42.7	2.3	19.8
	Males	27.0	68.5	13.9	49.9	3.9	22.4
	Females[1]	13.7	63.6	8.8	48.0	4.6	39.7
5 or +:	Cohort	11.1	50.5	5.3	31.6	1.3	12.4
	Males	18.5	56.3	9.1	37.6	2.1	14.0
	Females[2]	4.7	32.7	3.9	28.2	1.0	14.3
Felony Contacts							
4 or +:	Cohort	.6	27.1	1.7	44.1	3.5	63.8
	Males	1.1	29.2	3.0	48.6	6.4	69.8
	Females[1]	.4	28.6	.7	34.6	1.9	52.4
5 or +:	Cohort[3]	----	----	1.1	32.6	2.7	56.7
	Males	----	----	1.9	36.0	5.1	63.1
	Females[2]	----	----	.2	11.5	1.0	33.3
Non-Felony Contacts							
4 or +:	Cohort	31.6	84.4	29.8	83.6	19.5	78.4
	Males	49.7	89.3	43.8	88.2	30.2	84.0
	Females	8.3	50.2	11.1	59.9	8.0	57.2
5 or +:	Cohort	25.7	78.7	23.4	77.2	15.4	72.4
	Males	41.8	84.4	35.3	82.4	24.3	78.6
	Females	5.0	38.9	7.5	50.5	5.9	50.6

[1] Females with 2 or + contacts.
[2] Females with 3 or + contacts.
[3] Too few persons in cohort segment with 5 or more felonies for this statistic.

It should not be assumed that the designation of persons with two to four contacts as Recidivists and those with five or more contacts as Chronics has anything sacred about it. As a matter of fact, it was found that the characteristics of persons with no contacts, two to four contacts, and five or more contacts varied from cohort to cohort. Furthermore, the characteristics of persons who had police contacts for allegedly felonious vs. non-felonious behavior differed from cohort to cohort, as did those who had contacts for Part I vs. Part II offenses.[2]

Those males in all cohorts who had four or more contacts for Non-traffic offenses (30% or less) accounted for more than 80% of the Non-traffic contacts. Felonies were even more concentrated among males with four or five Felony contacts than were Non-traffic offenses, as shown in the lower section of Table 2. Similarly, females with four or more or five or more Non-traffic contacts accounted for a large proportion of the Non-traffic contacts among females but the concentration of Felonies was even greater than for Non-traffic offenses. While Table 2 does not show the concentration of contacts among multiple offenders by race/ethnicity, it was found that, although neither contacts in general nor those for Felonies were as concentrated among Black males as among White males, when those Black males with multiple Felonies were considered their proportion of contacts increased markedly, less than 25% being responsible for over 75% of the Felonies by Blacks.

CONCENTRATION OF SERIOUSNESS SCORES

The median seriousness scores of persons with five or more contacts were about four times as high as the median seriousness scores for persons with two to four contacts, 20.8 vs. 5.1 for 1942 White males, 20.4 vs. 5.3 for the 1949 White males, and 24.7 vs. 6.0 for the 1955 White males. Similar differences were found for Black males in the 1949 and 1955 Cohorts, 53.0 vs. 7.0 for the 1949 Cohort and 38.5 vs. 7.8 for the 1955 Cohort. The Chicano difference was 34.5 vs. 5.3 in the 1955 Cohort.

Although a number of contacts tended to produce high median seriousness scores for persons with five or more contacts, whether they were White, Black, or Chicano, male or female, it was clear that the median seriousness scores for persons with five or more contacts were not generated by contact categories at the lower end of the seriousness scale. This is particularly true for males; thus we have additional evidence to support the position that persons with five or more police contacts should be the subject of careful study.

Furthermore, it was found that Non-traffic contacts made up a larger proportion of the contacts among those with five or more contacts than of those with fewer contacts, regardless of cohort, race/ethnicity, or sex. Those with five or more contacts were responsible for a larger proportion of the

Felony contacts than were those with fewer contacts. We also found that the number of Felonies increased with seriousness scores for each race/ethnic group in each age period, i.e., increases in seriousness of careers were not based on number of contacts alone. Thus, the data told us again and again that persons with five or more contacts who had high seriousness scores, and who had probably committed a Felony, constituted a group upon which attention should be focused. We do not mean to imply that more severe intervention is called for at this point but that this is a group upon whom attention should be focused as a group more likely to exhibit career continuity.

Summary

While roughly 20% of each cohort's members was responsible for 80% of the Non-traffic police contacts generated by the cohort, an even smaller percent (8% to 14%) was responsible for all of the Felonies. Had the decision been made to identify those who were responsible for about 75% of the Felonies (and much of the other crime), the 5% of each cohort who had two or three Felony contacts would have been the target population.

Notes

1. Inclusion of the contacts for Suspicion, Investigation, or Information meant that 18.2% of the males with contacts who had 10 contacts or more accounted for 68.5% of the Racine contacts by the 1955 Cohort in comparison with 51.9% of the Philadelphia offenses accrued by 18% of their "delinquents" with five or more offenses. Since only 32.2% of the males in the 1955 Cohort who had Non-traffic police contacts had only one contact compared with 46.4% of the Philadelphia cohort, it was clear that regardless of the cutting points selected, multiple offenders would account for a greater proportion of the contacts in the Racine cohort.

2. Michael R. Olson ("An Examination of Criminal Typologies Based on Frequency and Seriousness of Contact with the Police." Unpublished manuscript, 1977). Analyses utilizing the three major age periods and combinations of them indicated that what was characteristic of individuals who had low or high frequency contacts with the law varied depending on 1) the way in which low and high were operationalized and 2) the period under consideration. Classification of individuals on the basis of frequency of contact with the police was essentially arbitrary. Furthermore, the results of discriminant analysis for various operationalizations of career seriousness indicated that the two cohorts differed more often than not within categories of seriousness, according to the definition of seriousness, and by age period.

Chapter 10

CONTINUITY IN CAREERS BY AGE PERIODS

THE DISTRIBUTION OF CONTINUITY BY AGE PERIODS

Continuity, in this chapter, refers to the relationship of the number and seriousness of police contacts of one age period to those of a following age period. Most pertinent to our concerns is the relationship of police contacts during the juvenile age period (6 through 17) to the young adult period (18 through 20), since the juvenile period was the one in which continuers would supposedly be singled out for special assistance because of their youth in contrast to the more stringent sanctions applied to adult offenders.

Just what proportion of each cohort had police contacts in each period, in none of the age periods, or in perhaps only one or two age periods? The frequency of contacts by years of age for each cohort (Diagrams 1 and 2) will enable the reader to see why these age-period cutting points were appropriate for the analysis presented in this chapter. The average number of contacts per person for each cohort was very low at the earliest ages and did not commence to rise until the age of 12 or 13, reached its peak at age 16 or 17 for males regardless of cohort, by 20 or 21 for the 1942 females, by 18 or 19 for the 1949 females, and by 17 or 18 for the 1955 females.

Other tables (not presented) revealed that, regardless of area of socialization, the age at which the largest number of persons had a police contact ranged from 16 through 18 with some race/ethnic exceptions. While more Blacks had contacts earlier than Whites, Whites socialized in the inner city had contacts earlier than those socialized in outlying areas. Females

DIAGRAM 1

RATE OF POLICE CONTACTS PER PERSON
BY COHORT AND AGE AT CONTACT

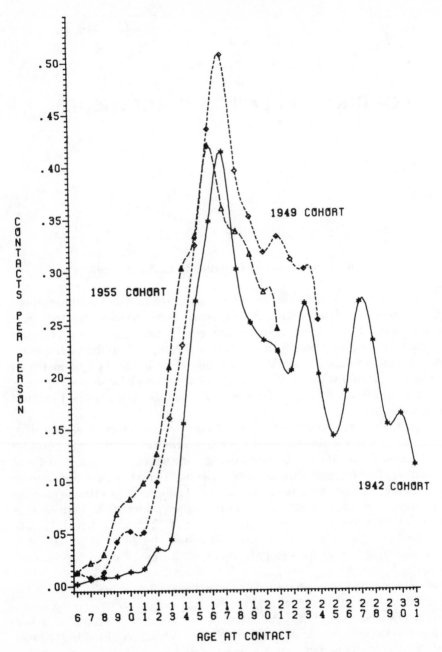

130

DIAGRAM 2

RATE OF POLICE CONTACTS PER PERSON
BY COHORT, SEX, AND AGE AT CONTACT

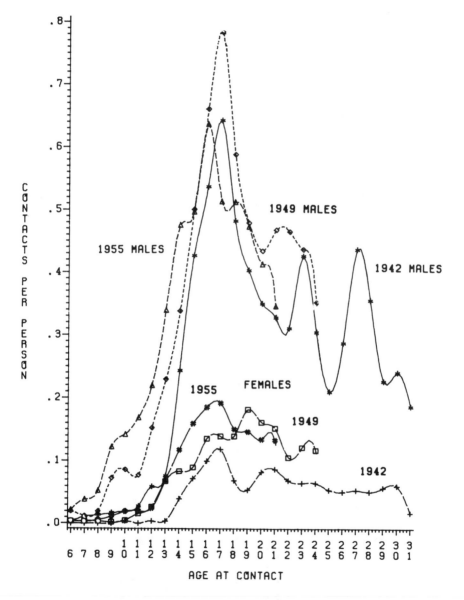

of all groups reached their peak proportion with contacts later than did males in their group, although this difference declined from cohort to cohort with the increase in police contacts by females. All of this suggested that, even though some variation existed between cohorts and within various segments of each cohort, the juvenile period was the one during which the number of persons with and the frequency of police contacts (prevalence and incidence) reached its peak. It was also apparent, particularly for males, that prevalence and incidence of contacts began to decline at the age of 18.[1]

Table 1 has been condensed from more detailed tables which controlled for race/ethnicity and area of socialization. Each cohort was distributed throughout eight continuity types descending from those with complete

TABLE 1. CONTINUITY OF CAREERS FOR TOTAL, NON-TRAFFIC, AND TRAFFIC CONTACTS BY COMBINATIONS OF AGE PERIODS AND SEX

Time Period/Continuity Contact Types			Total		Traffic Only		Non-Traffic	
Juv	18-20	21+	Male	Female	Male	Female	Male	Female
Yes	Yes	Yes	31.2	2.2	13.8	.4	14.0	1.4
Yes	Yes	No	3.7	2.2	2.5	.4	5.6	.7
Yes	No	Yes	14.9	5.4	9.8	2.5	9.8	2.5
Yes	No	No	6.7	9.1	8.4	4.0	14.0	7.9
No	Yes	Yes	7.6	3.6	14.0	3.2	5.1	1.8
No	Yes	No	3.4	5.4	5.1	5.8	4.5	2.2
No	No	Yes	16.6	19.2	20.8	18.8	16.9	6.9
No	No	No	_16.0_	_52.9_	_25.6_	_65.0_	_30.1_	_76.5_
			100.1	100.0	100.0	100.1	100.0	99.9
	1942 Cohort Ns		356	277	356	277	356	277
Yes	Yes	Yes	27.2	6.3	8.2	.5	15.3	3.8
Yes	Yes	No	12.2	3.9	6.4	.9	10.4	2.3
Yes	No	Yes	11.2	4.8	6.2	1.6	8.6	3.1
Yes	No	No	12.6	13.1	12.3	6.5	18.6	13.5
No	Yes	Yes	4.9	3.6	7.2	3.4	3.0	1.4
No	Yes	No	6.2	12.2	11.6	12.6	5.7	4.7
No	No	Yes	7.6	8.4	13.0	8.8	5.9	4.5
No	No	No	_18.2_	_47.6_	_35.1_	_65.7_	_32.4_	_66.8_
			100.1	99.9	100.0	100.0	99.9	100.1
	1949 Cohort Ns		740	557	740	557	740	557
Yes	Yes	Yes	12.3	3.2	10.6	1.4	12.1	3.2
Yes	Yes	No	20.5	8.3	16.0	5.1	19.6	7.8
Yes	No	Yes	3.5	2.1	2.7	1.4	3.3	1.9
Yes	No	No	19.9	17.3	7.9	4.7	15.5	13.7
No	Yes	Yes	3.3	1.4	2.5	.9	2.4	1.3
No	Yes	No	9.4	10.0	6.3	6.9	4.9	3.7
No	No	Yes	2.8	3.2	1.8	1.7	1.2	1.5
No	No	No	_28.3_	_54.5_	_52.2_	_77.9_	_40.9_	_66.9_
			100.0	100.0	100.0	100.0	99.9	100.0
	1955 Cohort Ns		1114	1035	1114	1035	1114	1035

continuity in each age period at the top to those who had never had a police contact.

Progressing from cohort to cohort we noted that 31.2% of the males from the 1942 Cohort, 27.2% from the 1949, but only 12.3% from the 1955 Cohort had a contact in each age period, the latter having barely gone beyond the age of 21. However, when the age periods 6 through 17 and 18 through 20 were considered, an additional 20.5% of the 1955 Cohort had contacts in both periods, compared with only 12.2% in the 1949 Cohort and 3.7% in the 1942 Cohort. Thus, at least one-third of each cohort had police contacts in both the juvenile and young adult periods. The pattern was, of course, quite different for the females. Perhaps the most interesting variation from cohort to cohort was the increasing proportion of males and females who had contacts during the juvenile and young adult periods.

There were fewer of either sex in continuity categories when only contacts for Traffic offenses were considered. The sizeable increases from cohort to cohort in males with no Traffic contacts at any period and the corresponding decrease in those with contacts only after becoming 21 was, of course, a function of the number of years of exposure to the possibility of Traffic offenses.

When police contacts for Non-traffic offenses were considered, the picture for both sexes was again different. There was more continuity than there was for Traffic contacts but, with the exception of the 1955 Cohort, about half the proportion of males with contacts in each period as there was when all contacts were considered. Most important is the fact that when the two categories indicating continuity for males between the juvenile and young adult periods were summed, 19.6% of the 1942 Cohort, 25.7% of the 1949 Cohort, and 31.7% of the 1955 Cohort had police contacts for Non-traffic offenses during both periods. Also of note was the larger proportion of males who had contacts as juveniles but none thereafter, 14.0% for the 1942 Cohort, 18.6% for the 1949 Cohort, and 15.5% for the 1955 Cohort. Still, and this highlighted the difficulty in prediction, 24.1% of the 1942 males and 34.7% of the 1949 males had contacts in either or both of the earlier periods but none as adults.

The higher proportion of females than males without contacts or without career continuity was further demonstrated by a comparison of the males and females for Non-traffic offenses. In the 1942 Cohort 34.5% and the 1949 Cohort 40.3% of the males fell in categories indicative of continuity in comparison to only 6.4% and 10.6% of the females.

The reasons for contact among those persons (varying from 7.6% of the males in the 1949 Cohort to 19.2% of the females in the 1942 Cohort) who had their initial police contacts at the age of 21 and older is worth noting. Of 528 such contacts, 321 were for Traffic, 95 for Suspicion, Investigation, or Information, 76 for Disorderly Conduct, eight for Liquor offenses, seven for Drug offenses, six for Theft, three for Fraud, three for Sex, and nine for Robbery, Forgery, Assault, Suicide, and so on.

Tables were also considered in which careers based on all contacts were utilized in determining a person's continuity type for the ages 6 through 17 which was then related to whether or not both contacts were acquired for Non-traffic reasons during either (or both) of the two following periods. This strategy resulted in considerably greater continuity in careers across all cohorts (for males more consistently than for females) than that obtained with Traffic or Non-traffic contacts alone, although not as much continuity as was found when total juvenile contacts were utilized in predicting total adult contacts. What it did suggest is that the best prediction of who would have Non-traffic contacts as adults should take both Traffic and Non-traffic contacts as juveniles into consideration. This seems reasonable because the data revealed that Traffic contacts were frequently tied in with other categories of offenses, particularly for juveniles.

CAREER PROGRESSION BY AGE PERIODS

Those persons from each cohort, male or female, White, Black, or Chicano, who had contacts during the juvenile and young adult periods had the greatest probability of having contacts as adults. In the 1942 Cohort, for example, 89.4% of the White males with contacts during the first two age periods had contacts after turning 21. While comparable percentages were lower for the 1949 and 1955 Cohorts, progression was still more likely for this group than any other. At the extreme opposite end of the scale in terms of continuity, was that 49% of those from the 1942 Cohort, 71.0% from the 1949 Cohort, and 91.8% from the 1955 Cohort, with no contacts by the age of 21 and no contacts afterward. Nevertheless, between these two extremes were over one-half of the males in each cohort and over 40% of the females in six different combinations of age period to age period continuity or lack thereof.

While the progression of females was far less than that of the males, the proportion (White females in particular) with contacts in the juvenile period who had contacts during the young adult period increased from cohort to cohort. But even though progression had increased for females, most had no contacts before the age of 21 and those who did were far less likely to have them after that age than their male counterparts.

FREQUENCY AND SERIOUSNESS OF CONTACTS AND CONTINUITY

We next examined the relationship between number and seriousness of contacts between age periods. In spite of the high percentage of persons with continuity as adults of those who had contacts during the preceding period, the number of contacts during any prior period had a relatively modest correlation with the number in the following period. For example, in Table 2 the correlation between the number of contacts during the juvenile (6 through 17) period and the 18 and older period was .503 for the entire city and .696 for inner city White males in the 1942 Cohort. The highest correlations in the entire table were .745 for Chicano males between the 6 through 17 period and 18 and older age periods and .714 for inner city White males between the 6 through 20 and 21 and older age periods. It is difficult to say that there was a trend from cohort to cohort in the relationship of early to later contact careers within the race/ethnic|sex subgroups because many of the differences were relatively small. It does appear that the sex differences among Whites were declining, particularly if one notes how the relationship between the number of juvenile and adult contacts for White males had declined from cohort to cohort but had increased for White females.

The relationship of seriousness scores in the early age periods to seriousness scores in the years following were more or less similar to those shown for contacts, varying by race/ethnic|sex groups and cutting points, again revealing a decline in sex differences among Whites.

CAREER TYPE BEFORE 18 AND SERIOUSNESS AFTER BECOMING 18

The association of number and seriousness found between age periods and differences based on area of socialization suggested that continuity types may provide a basis for determining which people in a cohort would have serious police records after the age of 18. Members of each cohort who were socialized in the inner city and interstitial areas vs. the rest of the city were selected for comparison. Everyone was placed in one of the career continuity types shown in Table 3. Tables were constructed for all cohorts but only that for the 1949 Cohort is shown.

These types consist of persons who (1) had No Contacts Ever, (2) had No Contacts Age 18 or After, (3) were Late Starters; No Contacts Before 18 or First Contacts 15 through 17, but Contacts at 18 or After, (4) had Intermittent Contacts Before 18 and Contacts at 18 or After, or (5) had Continuous Contacts Before 18 and Contacts at 18 or After. Although the distribution of persons by continuity type and place of socialization produced very little relationship for the 1942 Cohort (tau = .055) or the 1949 Cohort (tau = .088), it did produce a tau of .261 for the 1955 Cohort, significant at the .001 level. The latter was based on the highly disproportionate number of persons with continuous careers prior to the age of 18 among those socialized in the inner city and its interstitial areas in comparison with persons socialized in the remainder of the city.

Commencing with the 1942 Cohort, of those 11.7% who were socialized in the inner city and its interstitial areas and had what we termed a con-

TABLE 2. CORRELATION OF NUMBER OF POLICE CONTACTS BETWEEN AGE PERIODS BY RACE/ETHNICITY, SEX, AND NATURAL AREA OF JUVENILE RESIDENCE*

| | WHITE | | | | | | BLACK | | | | CHICANO | |
| | Males | | | Females | | | Males | | Females | | Males | Females |
	1942	1949	1955	1942	1949	1955	1949	1955	1949	1955	1955	1955
Entire City												
6-17 X 18+	.503	.559	.485	.274	.301	.467	.442	.548	.431	.447	.644	.478
6-20 X 21+	.526	.492	.364	.303	.403	.275	.479	.320	.504	.364	.379	.465
N	338	677	961	267	508	917	44	106	39	86	47	32
Inner City A-B												
6-17 X 18+	.696	.534	.465	.389	.530	.567	.406	.559	.434	.447	.745	.432
6-20 X 21+	.714	.489	.387	.444	.445	.222	.443	.318	.496	.369	.408	.484
N	126	213	178	94	132	182	42	103	38	86	37	26
Outer City C-D-E												
6-17 X 18+	.365	.569	.470	.144	.206	.418	---	---	---	---	---	---
6-20 X 21+	.394	.491	.334	.164	.386	.300	---	---	---	---	---	---
N	212	464	783	173	376	735	---	---	---	---	---	---

* Pearson's R computed with number of police contacts collapsed as 1, 2, 3, 4, and 5 or more.

TABLE 3. CAREER CONTINUITY TYPE BEFORE 18, CAREER SERIOUSNESS LEVELS, AND FELONY CONTACTS AT AND AFTER AGE 18 BY AREA OF SOCIALIZATION: 1949 COHORT

Continuity Type Before 18 and Seriousness Level 18+ Within Types	Inner City and Interstitial Areas					Middle and Outlying Areas					Total[1]				
	Continuity Type N	%	% In Level	% With Felonies In Level	% With Felonies In Type	Continuity Type N	%	% In Level	% With Felonies In Level	% With Felonies In Type	Continuity Type N	%	% In Level	% With Felonies In Level	% With Felonies In Type
No Contacts Ever	113	25.2				222	32.6				400	30.8			
No Contacts 18+[2]	35	7.8				101	14.8				153	11.8			
Late Starters	166	37.0			5.4	212	31.1			3.8	454	35.0			5.1
Low			63.3	.0				70.8	.7				66.1	.6	
Medium |18+ Seriousness			31.9	9.4				27.4	8.6				30.8	9.4	
High |			4.8	50.0				1.9	50.0				3.8	47.0	
Intermittent Career Before 18	48	10.7			8.3	65	9.5			9.2	118	9.1			8.5
Low			60.4	3.4				55.4	.0				56.7	1.5	
Medium |18+ Seriousness			29.2	.0				41.5	14.8				36.4	11.8	
High |			10.4	60.0				3.1	----				5.9	71.4	
Continuous Career Before 18	87	19.4			32.2	81	11.9			9.9	172	13.3			20.9
Low			23.0	.0				29.6	.0				26.7	.0	
Medium |18+ Seriousness			45.7	21.0				56.8	10.9				49.4	15.3	
High |			33.3	69.0				13.6	27.3				23.8	56.1	
Continuity Type Totals	449	100.1			9.1	681	99.9			3.2	1297	100.0			5.3

[1]Includes persons whose residence could not be categorized as primarily Inner City/Interstitial or Middle/Outlying (considerable movement from one type to the other).
[2]No contact before 18 or first contact 15 through 17.

tinuous career before 18, over half (53.5%) had a high seriousness score after reaching 18. No other area and no other continuity type had even close to 50% with this characteristic. Furthermore, 23.3% of the 11.7% socialized in this area had a Felony after turning 18 and 43.8% of this group who were serious offenders had at least one Felony after becoming 18. Here is a small number of persons with continuity prior to 18 and serious careers afterward; they are the persons whose total careers displayed continuity of the type that has been described in the early literature on the relationship of juvenile delinquency and adult crime. These are the atypical youth whose behavior resulted in the perception of delinquency as an ever-expanding, continuous type of phenomenon leading to a career in adult crime. While it is true that this type of delinquent exists, this type constituted such a small proportion of the total of each cohort that perpetuation of this model has resulted in considerable mischief if taken as representative of juvenile delinquency.

There was again a higher proportion of persons with continuous careers from the inner city and interstitial areas from the 1949 Cohort (Table 3), a greater proportion of them with high seriousness scores than in other areas, and the greatest proportion with Felonies after becoming 18 for those with high seriousness scores.

Almost half of those 1955 Cohort members who were socialized in the inner city and interstitial areas had a Felony after reaching 18, but the proportion of those with Felonies at 18 and older from all continuity types with a high seriousness score was greater than in the other cohorts. Since we have previously remarked about the increase in police contacts categorized as Felonies for the 1955 Cohort, this was not unexpected. There were, of course, very few persons in each of the other continuity types with high seriousness scores so that the finding of concentration of seriousness at 18 and older among those with high continuity before 18 remained the same.

SUMMARY

Although the prevalence and incidence of police contacts by juveniles peaked at the ages of 16 to 18 and declined thereafter, males who had at least one police contact during the juvenile period were more likely to have one or more at each subsequent stage than were those who had no contacts. Continuity between age periods had been increasing from cohort to cohort among females, but showed less continuity from period to period than that for males. When each cohort was divided into those who had been socialized in the inner city and interstitial areas vs. those socialized in the remainder of the community, progression was greatest for those in the inner city and interstitial areas.

The proportion of males with continuity for Non-traffic contacts in the periods 6 through 17 and 18 through 20 increased cohort by cohort. The corresponding figure for females was approximately half of that, but it too increased from cohort to cohort. Inclusion of those males who had contacts in the period 6 through 17 and 21 and older raised the proportion with continuity by no more than 10% in any cohort. Although White, Black and Chicano males and females (where comparison was possible) in the inner city and interstitial areas were more similar in continuity than were all Whites, Blacks, and Chicanos, the continuity of Blacks and Chicanos remained higher than that of Whites.

When total male contacts, Traffic contacts, and Non-traffic contacts during the juvenile period were utilized in assessing continuity of careers consisting of only Non-traffic contacts during the 18 through 20 and/or 21 and older period(s), greater continuity was present than for either Traffic or Non-traffic contacts alone.

Socialization in the inner city and interstitial areas increased the probability of continuous contacts before the age of 18 and a continuous career before the age of 18 maximized the probability of a serious career afterward for all cohorts. It was quite apparent that construction of continuity types and controlling for place of socialization enabled one to select out that 10% or 20% from each cohort who were most likely to have serious careers after becoming 18 and whose careers, in addition, included a high proportion of Felonies. But, the fact remains that we have done no more than identify those who were at the greatest risk of having continuity from serious delinquency into serious adult crime. Prediction without unacceptable error is a more difficult endeavor.

NOTE

1. David F. Farrington has recently dealt with several misunderstandings about the alleged invariance of the age-crime curve in "Age and Crime," Michael Tonry and Norval Morris (eds.), *Crime and Justice: An Annual Review of Research* (Chicago: University of Chicago Press, 1985): 189–250.

Chapter 11

CONTINUITY AND DISCONTINUITY AND INCREASING SERIOUSNESS

INTRODUCTION

If a relatively small proportion of the persons in each cohort is responsible for a large proportion of the police contacts by members of their cohort, then most juveniles must cease to have contacts after having only a few. Likewise, since we have found that the more serious reasons for police contacts are even more highly concentrated, attrition must be even greater when only contacts for Felonies are considered.

This chapter focuses upon consecutive police contacts and recurring types of contacts as sequences of events that may have greater or lesser probabilities of continuity leading to adult careers in crime. A sequential model allows the researcher to study the progress of individuals toward greater extremes of delinquency and crime as well as *attrition* from the processes which produce this behavior. We shall concentrate on continuation probabilities.[1]

CONTINUATION PROBABILITIES

Since we commence by comparing our results with Wolfgang, Figlio, and Sellin's 1945 Cohort, most comparable to the 1942 Cohort in Racine, the reader should be reminded that they followed cohort members between the ages of 10 and 18 in their first study and in their restudy followed them to age 30. Contact continuation probabilities for each of the Racine cohorts and the Early and Recent Philadelphia studies are presented in Table 1. In

TABLE 1. COMPARISON OF THE PROBABILITY OF FIRST AND CONTINUING POLICE CONTACTS
FOR MALES AND FEMALES FROM THE RACINE AND PHILADELPHIA COHORTS [1]

| | Philadelphia | | Racine | | | | | |
| | Males | | Males | | | Females [4] | | |
Contact Number	Early [2]	Recent [3]	1942	1949	1955	1942	1949	1955
1	.394	.473	.573	.535	.478	.159	232	243
2	.538	.662	.868	.874	.833	.795	.806	.833
3	.651	.717	.661	.665	.653	.514	.433	.474
4	.716	.798	.726	.726	.800	.500	.733	.576
5	.722	.828	.824	.749	.810	.556	.697	.719
6	.742	.847	.771	.864	.819		.652	.634
7	.791	.836	.833	.824	.838		.533	.885
8	.766	.892	.711	.921	.876		.625	.783
9	.798	.879	.813	.902	.894			.889
10	.827	.900	.846	.905	.871			.688
11	.790	.889	.818	.851	.886			1.000
12	.803	.781	1.000	.912	.885			.727
13	.729	.900	.722	.808	.913			.750
14	.884	.955	.923	.905	.952			.833
15	.697	.814	1.000	.895	.950			

[1] Traffic, Status Offenses, and Contacts for Suspicion, Investigation or
Information omitted to make data comparable to Wolfgang, et al.

[2] Marvin E. Wolfgang, Robert M. Figlio, and Thorsten Sellin, Delinquency in a
Birth Cohort (Chicago: The University of Chicago Press, 1972): 162.

[3] Marvin E. Wolfgang and James J. Collins, Jr., Offender Careers and
Restraint: Probabilities and Policy Implications. Unpublished Final
Report LEAA Project 76NI-99-0089 (Philadelphia: Center for Studies in
Crime, Criminology and Criminal Law, 1978): 19.

[4] Female continuity figures stop when less than 5 had continuing contacts.

order to make the Racine data more comparable to the Philadelphia data
we controlled for sex and removed contacts for Traffic offenses, Juvenile
Condition (status offenses), and Suspicion, Investigation, or Information
from the Racine cohorts.

The first figure in each column is the probability that an initial police
contact would occur, i.e., the proportion of the cohort who had at least
one contact with the police. The probability of having an initial contact in
the Racine cohorts was similar to that in the Philadelphia study with around
half of each cohort having at least one recorded contact. Continuity probabilities for females were considerably lower for the 1942 and 1949 Cohorts
than for the 1955 Cohort, as would be expected from data already presented.

After reaching their fourth contact the 1942 Racine Cohort males and
the Philadelphia males (Early) with similar years of exposure had similar
continuation probabilities. Although the Philadelphia males (Recent) had
the same years of exposure as the 1955 Racine Cohort, the Racine continuation probabilities were slightly higher. While there were small differences

in continuation probabilities from cohort to cohort in the Racine study, this was expected because there were some cohort differences in behavior, and because there were also differences in police tolerance of juvenile misbehavior over time. This was less likely to be revealed, however, when contacts for Juvenile Conditions and Suspicion, Investigation, or Information were removed as they were for comparison of the Racine data with the Philadelphia data. We were more inclusive of reasons for police contact because of our concern about the labeling effect which develops from any type of police contact involving law violation or status offenses.

The probability of a first and subsequent contact for the male and females of each cohort is shown in Tables 2 and 3. Each sequence of probabilities is shown for the entire recorded career of each cohort. Each table is divided into three sets of columns. The Total column contains probabilities of continuation for all contact types, i.e., given that contact of any type has occurred, what is the probability that another contact of any type will follow? Non-traffic columns are a separate category and contain the probability that a contact for a Non-traffic offense will be followed at some time

TABLE 2.   PROBABILITY OF FIRST AND CONTINUING CONTACT BY TOTAL CONTACTS AND BY
           CONTACT CATEGORY: MALES

Contact	Total			Non-Traffic			Felony		
Number	1942	1949	1955	1942	1949	1955	1942	1949	1955
1	.846*	.818	.717	.699	.676	.591	.132	.151	.219
2	.874	.817	.727	.695	.722	.679	.404	.482	.533
3	.802	.802	.749	.775	.773	.761	.474	.556	.654
4	.844	.833	.807	.784	.806	.803	.444	.733	.624
5	.848	.794	.846	.829	.813	.857	.500	.636	.679
6	.861	.889	.828	.908	.831	.893	1.000	.643	.722
7	.854	.845	.890	.861	.842	.895	1.000	.556	.577
8	.874	.878	.877	.882	.883	.872	1.000	.400	.467
9	.907	.838	.885	.917	.885	.871	.500	1.000	.714
10	.920	.869	.906	.818	.920	.915	1.000	1.000	.400
11	.802	.921	.903	.867	.935	.900	.000	.500	.500
12	.892	.888	.914	.846	.930	.915		.000	.000
13	.897	.922	.866	.818	.900	.935			
14	.962	.905	.918	.889	.903	.960			
15	.900	.895	.970	.792	.938	.979			
16	.956	.909	.959	.947	.951	.947			
17	.907	.971	.947	.778	.966	.876			
18	.897	.926	.966	1.000	.875	.859			
19	.914	.968	.930	.929	.939	.910			
20	.875	.902	.913	1.000	.891	.836			
21 or +	.929	.873	.945	.769	.951	.745			

* The number of males with a first contact (301) was divided by the number of
males in the cohort (356) to obtain the probability that a first contact would
occur (.846); the number of persons with a second contact (263) was divided by
the number of persons with a first contact (301) to obtain the probability that
those with a first contact would have a second contact (.874), and so on.   In
each column after the column for Total, the first contact referred to was the
first contact of that category, the second contact of that category, and so on.

TABLE 3.   PROBABILITY OF FIRST AND CONTINUING CONTACT BY TOTAL CONTACTS AND BY
           CONTACT CATEGORY: FEMALES

Contact Number	Total			Non-Traffic			Felony		
	1942	1949	1955	1942	1949	1955	1942	1949	1955
1	.480*	.524	.455	.235	.332	.331	.022	.038	.060
2	.504	.521	.507	.462	.524	.525	.167	.190	.258
3	.478	.618	.594	.633	.639	.617	.000	.250	.625
4	.750	.670	.662	.684	.742	.739		.000	.300
5	.625	.683	.745	.615	.652	.707			.000
6	.667	.698	.743	.875	.700	.776			
7	.700	.800	.865	.857	.714	.822			
8	.857	.625	.911	.833	.867	.946			
9	1.000	.867	.902	.400	.846	.886			
10	.833	1.000	.865	1.000	.818	.839			
11	.800	.923	.750	.500	1.000	.769			
12	.500	.917	.708	1.000	.778	.800			
13	1.000	.818	.882	1.000	.857	.875			
14	1.000	.667	.882	1.000	.833	.875			
15	1.000	1.000	.933	1.000	1.000	.875			
16	1.000	1.000	.714	1.000	.800	.714			
17	.500	.667	.714	1.000	1.000	.714			
18	1.000	1.000	.900	1.000	1.000	.900			
19	1.000	1.000	.900	1.000	1.000	.900			
20	1.000	1.000	.900	1.000	1.000	.889			
21 or +	1.000	.750	.900	1.000	.750	.875			

* The number of females with a first contact (133) was divided by the number of
females in the cohort (277) to obtain the probability that a first contact
would occur (.480); the number of persons with a second contact (67) was
divided by the number of persons with a first contact (133) to obtain the
probability that those with a first contact would have a second contact (.504),
and so on.   In each column after the column for Total, the first contact
referred to was the first contact of that category, the second contact of that
category, and so on.

by another Non-traffic contact. The Felony columns are also separate categories and represent the probability that a contact for a Felony will eventually be followed by another Felony contact.

While the probability of continuing to have any kind of contact was
roughly similar for all cohorts after the first few contacts, there were also
some differences. The same was true if only Non-traffic contacts were considered. Since fewer of each cohort had an initial Felony, there was more
irregularity in the continuation probabilities for Felonies from cohort to
cohort. Although these probabilities were based on different years of exposure, it was obvious that the same general process was at work in each
cohort. The relatively smaller numbers and proportion of females with a
first and succeeding contact made their continuation probabilities even more
subject to fluctuation as the continuation sequence developed.

In order to present a strict comparison of cohorts, exposure time was
held constant in Table 4 for males (females not shown) by including only
those contacts which occurred through the age of 21. Although there were

cohort and sex differences, it was apparent that continuation probabilities were not grossly different from cohort to cohort. Two exceptions were found among males, the lower continuation probabilities for the 1955 Cohort for Traffic contacts and the lower continuation probabilities for Non-felony contacts after the 15th contact. The first may be a reflection of a change in handling procedures for Traffic contacts during the later years of exposure for that cohort and the second related to the increased proportion of Felony vs. Non-felony contacts among persons in the 1955 Cohort.

DISCONTINUATION PROBABILITIES

While we have shown that continuation to a subsequent police contact was highly probable after any given contact, it is important to note the attrition or discontinuity aspect of the police contact sequence. Tables have also been constructed (not shown) which permitted comparison of the cumulative probabilities of *discontinuing* contacts after the Kth contact for males and females by cohort and type of contact. The cumulative probabilities represented the accumulated proportions of persons with a first contact who had terminated at each step in the sequence. For example, in the case of all contacts for the 1942 males, 12.6% (.126) of those with a first contact ceased with that contact. After the second contact, 29.9% (.299) of all with a first contact had no more contacts, and after the 20th contact, 91.4% (.914) of those with a first contact had no further contacts.

A comparison of total contacts of males and females indicated that females were likely to discontinue having contacts after fewer contacts than males. Over 65% of the females in all cohorts had ceased to have contacts after the second contact. Alternatively, only 29.9% of the 1942, 34.5% of the 1949, and 45.6% of the 1955 Cohort males had no more contacts after the second contact. It was not until after the seventh contact for the 1942 males, the sixth for the 1949 males, and the fifth for the 1955 males that two-thirds had terminated. It must be remembered that each cohort had had successively fewer years of exposure and that members of the 1955 Cohort in particular were likely to have additional contacts for Traffic offenses.

The level at which Non-traffic contacts ceased was, of course, much lower; two-thirds of the males from each cohort had stopped after the fifth contact. The females had terminated even more rapidly, at least two-thirds after their second Non-traffic contact.

When only Felony contacts were considered, even more rapid termination was found, with at least two-thirds of the males having no more contacts after their second and more than two-thirds of the females after their first contact.

It was also clear that termination proceeded more slowly after a given

TABLE 4.   PROBABILITY OF FIRST AND CONTINUING CONTACT BY TOTAL CONTACTS AND BY CONTACT CATEGORY FOR COHORT MALES THROUGH AGE 21

Probability of Contact and Continuing Contacts*

Contact Number	Total			Traffic			Non-traffic			Felony			Non-felony		
	1942	1949	1955	1942	1949	1955	1942	1949	1955	1942	1949	1955	1942	1949	1955
1	.688*	.768	.717	.629	.614	.478	.607	.653	.591	.132	.150	.219	.612	.646	.599
2	.934	.850	.727	.790	.643	.404	.764	.739	.679	.404	.486	.533	.798	.709	.661
3	.878	.812	.749	.740	.613	.377	.806	.784	.761	.474	.556	.654	.764	.737	.710
4	.861	.839	.807	.725	.575	.383	.789	.811	.803	.444	.767	.624	.887	.788	.780
5	.867	.796	.846	.695	.650	.484	.838	.819	.857	.500	.609	.679	.771	.827	.820
6	.867	.893	.828	.864	.687	.333	.898	.828	.893	.500	.643	.722	.813	.822	.835
7	.854	.850	.890	.772	.565	.200	.861	.838	.895	1.000	.556	.577	.932	.806	.862
8	.865	.879	.877	.705	.692	1.000	.862	.884	.872	.000	.400	.467	.783	.889	.910
9	.917	.840	.855	.742	.611	.000	.933	.886	.871		1.000	.714	.833	.885	.824
10	.920	.864	.906	.783	.636		.821	.921	.915		1.000	.400	.867	.871	.898
11	.815	.921	.903	.667	.571		.848	.935	.900		.500	.500	.897	.851	.887
12	.894	.897	.914	.833	1.000		.846	.931	.915		.000	.000	.886	.873	.884
13	.881	.914	.866	.800	.750		.818	.901	.935				.903	.927	.842
14	.962	.917	.918	.875	1.000		.889	.918	.960				.788	.902	.891
15	.900	.898	.970	.857	.667		.792	.940	.979				.773	.935	.737
16	.956	.911	.959	.667	1.000		.947	.952	.947				.941	.884	.762
17	.907	.972	.947	.250	.500		.778	.967	.896				.875	.921	.594
18	.897	.914	.966	1.000	1.000		.929	.862	.859				.857	.914	.632
19	.914	.969	.930	.000	1.000		.769	.940	.910				.917	.906	.333
20	.875	.903	.931		1.000		.800	.894	.836				.818	.931	.500
21 or +	1.000	1.000	.945		1.000		.750	.929	.745				.889	.926	.000
# with 1st Contact	245	568	799	224	454	532	216	483	658	47	111	244	218	478	667

* Calculations made as in tables without controls for years of exposure.

145

number of contacts had been reached. The number was higher for males than for females and it was higher for total contacts than for Non-traffic or Felony contacts. It appeared, then, that the high probability of continuation after any given contact was a consequence of the rapid development of a "hard core" of continuers. Most people ceased to have difficulty with the police after a few contacts. Only a relatively small group of individuals continued to have long contact records.

In order to deal with the problem of varying career lengths, discontinuation tables were also constructed with controls for years of exposure. With this control the cohorts were remarkably similar. Each cohort's females again discontinued their contacts sooner than did the males.

The findings may be summarized as follows: 1) the probability of beginning and continuing contact careers of any category was greater for males than females; 2) Traffic and Felony contact careers were shorter than Non-traffic and Non-felony careers, regardless of sex; and 3) similar patterns occurred among males across cohorts and among females across cohorts which implies that a similar systematic process was operating to produce these similarities, e.g., differential selection and/or similarities in behavior and criminal association.

INCREASING SERIOUSNESS WITH SUCCESSIVE CONTACTS

While a number of monographs based on a few case histories have served as an historical basis for the development of a model of delinquency as ever-increasing in seriousness from contact to contact or with increasing age, there have been few longitudinal studies with data adequate to test the model. Wolfgang, Figlio, and Sellin did, however, find little or no increase in severity of offenses from the first through the ninth offense.[2] The Racine data suggest that the conclusions which one reaches about the pattern of increasing severity vary, depending on the unit of analysis selected and the statistical procedure employed.

We approached the analysis in several ways, commencing with the rather simple strategy of drawing curves representing mean seriousness of contacts by contact order from the first to the Kth contact for each race/ethnic|sex group for each cohort. Since there was a certain amount of fluctuation in seriousness scores as contacts proceeded from the first to, say, the 96th for White males in the 1949 Cohort, five-contact moving averages were calculated for all cohorts. Even with these moving averages there was considerable fluctuation for each male race/ethnic segment of each cohort. Although there was some progression in seriousness for each male segment of each cohort from the youngest ages to early peaks at from 15 to 30 contacts and later peaks from 35 to 45 contacts, varying from cohort to cohort and by race/ethnic group, it would be risky to say that average seriousness scores systematically increased for males in any cohort.

Curves were also drawn representing the proportion of all contacts that were serious or the proportion of persons in the cohort who had serious contacts (Misdemeanors and Felonies) by age at contact. The peak proportion of males with serious contacts and the peak proportion of contacts that were serious were at age 15 for the 1942 and 1949 Cohorts. After 15 these proportions declined, became stable at the age of 21, and remained fairly stable thereafter. Similarly, when the proportion of *persons* in the cohort who had accumulated at least one serious contact and the proportion of the *contacts* that were serious were cumulated for males of these cohorts, these proportions stabilized at the age of 15. The 1955 Cohort stabilized at the age of 16 and the proportion of serious contacts remained at that level through the age of 20.

It was more difficult to pick a single peak year of seriousness for the females of all cohorts but the proportion of their contacts that were serious peaked during the early teens, declined to a lower level, and remained stable thereafter for the 1942 and 1949 Cohorts. That level was higher for the 1955 Cohort than it was for the other cohorts.

The next step was an analysis of all cohorts based on categorization of offenses as Part I vs. Part II. These data did not, of course, generate smooth curves at the very early ages because there were relatively few contacts at this period. However, by the early teens a more stable curve developed and this too declined as time passed with a larger percentage of all contacts for Traffic offenses, a Non-index offense.

Since the Racine data included contacts for Suspicion, Investigation, or Information as well as Traffic (these categories making up a large proportion of the total), additional tests were made in which they were eliminated, the data thus more comparable to the Philadelphia data. With these contact types eliminated, the curves represented a better test of increasing seriousness with contact order or age. But here again the curves were so flat for males and females, for males even through the 40th contact (with the exception of the 1955 Cohort males where each race/ethnic group had a different pattern of rise and decline after 20-some contacts but were still without a trend) and for females through the 20th contact (with the exception of the 1955 Cohort's Chicanas where a decline in seriousness was evident after the fifth contact), that it still must be concluded that seriousness of contacts did not systematically increase with contact order.

When age at contact was substituted for contact number there was, however, a gradual rise in seriousness through the late teens for the 1942 and 1949 Cohort males but a flattening effect thereafter and a gradual rise for 1955 Cohort males of each race/ethnic group from age 8 through 20. Females from all cohorts also exhibited a gradual rise through this age period but so few continued past the age of 20 that the flattening effect was less apparent.

At this point we were still dissatisfied with the adequacy of these approaches in determining whether or not the seriousness of acts leading to police contacts or the average seriousness of accumulated careers progressively increased over time. The data in Table 5 enabled us to develop more definitive answers than have yet been presented.

The first series of averages in Table 5 was based on the average of the average seriousness of the contacts that each person in the cohort had at each year of age; i.e., the average seriousness of reasons for police contacts of the person who had contacts at each age. It was apparent that the average seriousness of reasons for police contacts for persons in the 1942 and 1949 Cohorts with contacts fluctuated considerably in the early years when there were fewer contacts on which to base the mean, but that after the age of 12 average seriousness fluctuated within a range that was declining. By contrast, seriousness fluctuated upward for the 1955 Cohort.

When the average seriousness of the averages was based on the number of persons in the cohort (thus reducing average seriousness in the early and later years when fewer persons were having police contacts), it was apparent that seriousness (as well as number of contacts) had peaked by the age of 16 for the 1942 Cohort and by 17 for the 1949 and 1955 Cohorts.

TABLE 5.   AVERAGE OF AVERAGE SERIOUSNESS OF POLICE CONTACTS BY PERSONS AND AVERAGE SERIOUSNESS SCORES BY PERSONS AT AGE

| | Average for Persons with Contacts[1] | | | | | | Average for Cohort[2] | | | | | |
| | Average Seriousness of Contacts at Age | | | Average Seriousness of Careers at age | | | Average Seriousness of Contacts at Age | | | Average Seriousness of Careers at Age | | |
Age	1942	1949	1955	1942	1949	1955	1942	1949	1955	1942	1949	1955
6	3.000	2.078	2.146	3.000	3.636	2.667	.005	.018	.024	.005	.031	.030
7	3.250	3.000	2.533	3.250	3.000	2.630	.021	.025	.054	.021	.025	.056
8	2.600	2.765	2.346	2.600	2.765	3.196	.021	.036	.056	.021	.036	.076
9	2.333	2.540	2.266	2.333	3.775	3.524	.022	.078	.112	.022	.116	.172
10	3.071	2.643	2.549	3.571	3.872	4.277	.034	.096	.133	.039	.140	.223
11	2.800	2.550	2.464	2.800	2.345	4.275	.044	.114	.150	.044	.128	.261
12	2.857	2.630	2.830	3.000	3.753	5.426	.095	.189	.195	.100	.269	.374
13	2.590	2.445	2.755	2.917	3.969	6.588	.098	.247	.255	.111	.401	.610
14	2.677	2.578	2.821	4.125	5.032	8.158	.271	.314	.357	.417	.613	1.033
15	2.897	2.646	2.726	5.988	5.659	7.028	.380	.424	.402	.785	.907	1.037
16	2.291	2.386	2.587	3.476	4.095	6.113	.525	.522	.545	.796	1.074	1.289
17	2.220	2.314	2.719	4.381	4.893	5.895	.487	.582	.568	.962	1.230	1.232
18	2.402	2.136	2.661	4.962	4.545	5.625	.497	.510	.551	1.027	1.086	1.165
19	2.205	2.222	2.716	4.138	4.763	6.116	.380	.478	.489	.712	1.025	1.101
20	2.217	2.095	2.820	3.981	4.574	5.969	.375	.405	.503	.673	.885	1.064
21	2.254	2.242	2.712	4.585	4.975	4.950	.335	.408	.458	.681	.913	.836
22	2.106	2.306		4.124	4.913		.296	.429		.580	.886	
23	2.121	2.381		4.485	5.330		.345	.417		.730	.933	
24	2.171	2.181		3.330	4.621		.322	.328		.509	.695	
25	1.883			3.029			.208			.335		
26	1.995			3.057			.279			.420		
27	2.154			4.838			.337			.757		
28	2.210			4.228			.321			.615		
29	2.397			3.711			.288			.460		
30	2.196			3.987			.260			.479		
31	2.028			3.138			.186			.288		

[1] The first set of averages is based on the average of the average seriousness of the contacts that a person had at a given age and the second set is based on the average seriousness of all contacts that a person had by a given age; both sets of averages were divided by the number of persons with contacts.

[2] These averages were obtained by dividing the averages described above by the number of persons in the cohort.

DIAGRAM 1

AVERAGE SERIOUSNESS OF POLICE CONTACT CAREERS
BY PERSONS AT AGE

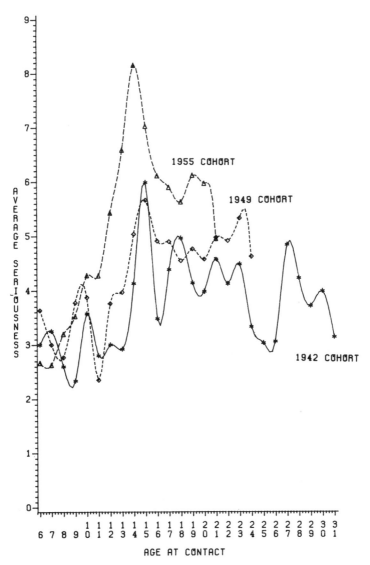

DIAGRAM 2

AVERAGE SERIOUSNESS OF POLICE CONTACT CAREERS
FOR COHORT AT AGE

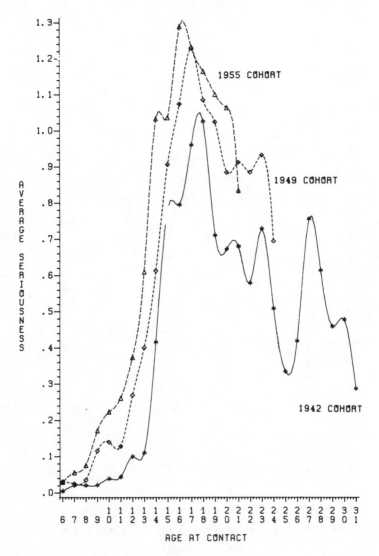

This peak was a function of the high prevalence of offenses at age 16 more than the seriousness of reasons for police contact. What we noted was that seriousness for those with contacts showed very little trend but that seriousness for the cohort reached a peak in the mid-teens and declined slowly thereafter. This does not mean that seriousness of the kinds of contacts that members of the cohort had with the police either rose or declined in a manner comparable to the relationship that prevalence has to age.

Another approach was to observe the average seriousness of all contacts that a person had had by a given age. While this produced a higher mean because accumulated *career* scores at a given age were the basis for the averages rather than the average seriousness at a specified age, this average did not continue to increase because persons without prior careers were added at each age, which tended to counteract the increasing average. How the counter-tendencies worked is shown in Diagram 1. Here the 1942 and 1949 Cohorts reached their peak at the age of 15, the 1955 Cohort at the age of 14, after which the accumulated seriousness of careers for persons in all cohorts then followed a pattern of irregular declines and rises. When the average seriousness of careers based on the entire cohort was considered (Diagram 2), we found that the 1955 Cohort had reached its peak at the age of 16, the 1942 and 1949 Cohorts at the ages of 17 and 18, all declining markedly thereafter, influenced by the fact that fewer members of each cohort remained with an active and accumulating career.

SUMMARY

While it has been the fashion to accept the ideas of repetitiveness, continuity between juvenile and adult careers in delinquency and crime, and ever-expanding careers into more serious delinquency and crime with the passage of time, most juveniles had ceased their delinquent behavior after relatively few police contacts of any kind. Discontinuation rather than continuation was the usual pattern. No matter how seriousness of reasons for police contact was handled statistically, seriousness peaked for most people in their teens and most people in each cohort failed to become involved in increasingly serious misbehavior as time passed. The implications of this for crime control are important. Should we be concerned about early intervention when most youth are unlikely to continue their involvement with the police after their first few contacts?

NOTES

1. Howard S. Becker, *Outsiders* (New York: The Free Press, 1963): 22–39.
2. Marvin Wolfgang, Robert Figlio, and Thorsten Sellin, *Delinquency in a Birth Cohort* (Chicago: University of Chicago Press, 1972): 248–249, 312.

Chapter 12

POLICE CONTACT REFERRALS AND THEIR USE IN PREDICTING CONTINUITY IN CAREERS

INTRODUCTION

During the late 1970s over 30% of the juvenile populations and 40% of the adult populations of institutions in Wisconsin were Nonwhite, this in a state in which less than 5% of the population was Nonwhite. Even if we considered the proportion of Nonwhites in Wisconsin's major metropolitan areas (where percent Nonwhite was double that of the entire state), we would find that minorities were over-represented in the state's institutionalized population.

Although this over-representation has often been attributed to step-by-step discrimination against minorities and/or persons of lower SES in the chain of events between commission of an act and institutionalization, most cross-sectional studies have produced contradictory and/or inconclusive evidence of significant race/ethnic or SES discrimination at any given point in the process. The Racine data suggested that as an individual proceeded through the system, the decision to take the next formal step was more likely to be made if the miscreant was Nonwhite or of lower SES than if he/she was White or of higher SES. Each step, it is hypothesized, adds an increment, perhaps not a statistically significant one, of Nonwhites and/or persons of lower SES to those formally processed and thus brought closer to institutionalization.[1] In the end, a significantly larger proportion of the institutionalized population was Nonwhite and/or from lower SES groups.

Referral rates are dependent upon the action of police and persons in the juvenile justice systems whose attitudes may be long-standing or more recently influenced by sensationalized events or concerns expressed by citizens' groups. At the point of referral, action may be initiated which eventuates in highly disproportionate numbers of institutionalized minority group members, reflecting and reinforcing racial explanations of delinquency and crime.

While it may be that differentials in delinquency and crime rates play a part in determining the disproportionate minority group composition of institutions, the question is to what extent is it race/ethnicity and SES (race/ethnicity is a status and an explanatory sociological category only to the extent that it is indicative of past experiences) combined and to what extent is it race/ethnic definitions (definitions of groups are sociological categories) of what should be done in response to behavior observed by the police? May it not be that the initial screening process, the decision to refer or not to refer, is the first step in a chain of events, each sending a few percent more of the minority or low SES persons on to the next stage of the process?[2]

REFERRAL ALTERNATIVES

Each police contact was disposed of at the time of contact or as a consequence of questioning in one of the following ways: 1) contact, released; counseled and released; 2) referred to County Probation Department; 3) referred to County Welfare; 4) referred to State Department of Public Welfare; 5) referred to Juvenile Traffic Court; 6) referred, other juvenile; 7) referred to District Attorney (Adult); and 8) referred, other adult.

Approximately two-thirds of the male and 80% of the female police contacts in the 1942 and 1949 Cohorts were counseled and released by the police, while about 10% fewer of those from the 1955 Cohort received this disposition. The proportion of police contacts referred to the County Probation Department doubled for the 1955 Cohort from approximately 10% or less to about 20% for both sexes, probably as a function of the fewer years of exposure to the possibility of an adult referral for members of the 1955 Cohort as well as increasing community concern for more formal handling of the problem of delinquent behavior.

Eighty percent of the contacts in the 1942 Cohort were disposed of the same day (usually as a result of counseling and release), as were 73% of the 1949 Cohort and 64% of the 1955 Cohort contacts. Within 15 days 93% of the 1942 and 1949 Cohort contacts and 90% of the 1955 Cohort contacts had been disposed of. No more than 2% of the contacts in any cohort had disposition dates beyond six months from the time of initial police contact.

DIFFERENTIALS IN REFERRAL BY RACE/ETHNICITY, SEX, AND PLACE OF RESIDENCE

Since the cohort data enabled us to examine the progression of careers, we were able to ascertain if referral rates (proportion of contacts referred) increased for some sex, race/ethnic, and residential groups more rapidly than for others. When curves were drawn comparing the proportion of Whites and Blacks who had had at least one contact, at least one referral, and those with contacts who had also been referred by a given age, the most telling curve in terms of its suggestion of differential handling of Blacks was that applying to the percent with contacts who had also been referred. At the peak in the late teens, more than twice as large a proportion of Blacks and Chicanos as Whites were referred. The proportion of Blacks with one referral was greater than that of the Whites; in the 1949 and 1955 Cohorts Blacks and Chicanos were referred disproportionately for their police contacts even before the age of 12 and continued their unenviable status throughout the years covered by the study. The shapes of the curves were similar from cohort to cohort for the ages that they shared but it was apparent that the referral curves for Blacks and Chicanos rose more rapidly and reached their peaks earlier than did the curves for Whites.[3]

Curves based on the accumulated proportion of those with referrals showed that the proportion of the Whites referred reached its peak earlier and at a lower point than that of the Blacks. In other words, all of the Black youth who became involved with the police did so at an earlier age than did the Whites but the proportion who had sufficiently serious contacts to be referred continued above the peak for Whites and continued to rise for several years.

In Table 1, percent of contacts referred by place of residence at time of police contact are shown. Referral has been narrowed to either the Racine County Probation Department or to the District Attorney, the types of referrals most indicative of police concern regarding the seriousness of the behavior resulting in contact. For the males we found some, but not consistent, decline in the proportion of contacts referred as one moved from the poorest to the best residential areas. This decline was not found, however, for females from all cohorts. The inconsistent decline in percentage of contacts referred for the Whites suggested that place of residence at time of contact had relatively little to do with the referral decision. Remember that most Blacks and Chicanos resided in the inner city or interstitial areas at time of referral.

This table does, however, permit one to observe that, in contrast to the overall indication of a higher proportion of contacts referred among Blacks than Whites and the generally higher referral of contacts among Chicanos than Blacks, when area of residence at time of referral was controlled the Blacks and Chicanos did not always have a higher proportion of their contacts referred than did the Whites. Black and Chicano males

TABLE 1. PERCENT OF CONTACTS REFERRED INTO JUDICIAL SYSTEM BY NATURAL AREA OF RESIDENCE AT TIME OF REFERRAL*

Natural Area	MALES White %	N	Black %	N	Chicano %	N	Total %	N	FEMALES White %	N	Black %	N	Chicano %	N	Total %	N
1949: A	19.6	491	25.3	546	27.2	151	23.1	1188	6.0	116	19.1	136	33.3	3	13.3	255
B	21.3	1063	14.1	78	14.9	87	20.4	1228	11.1	162	7.9	38	14.3	7	10.6	207
C	16.9	815	.0	4	35.7	14	17.2	833	10.5	162	40.0	5	.0	6	11.0	173
D	19.5	667	18.2	33	46.5	43	21.0	743	8.9	124	.0	1	100.0	1	9.5	126
E	17.7	300	.0	3	12.5	8	17.4	311	15.2	66	---	---	---	---	15.2	96
	19.3	3336	23.3	664	26.4	303	20.4	4303	10.0	630	17.2	180	17.6	17	11.7	827
1955: A	30.4	411	33.9	998	32.5	151	32.8	1560	18.4	196	19.7	173	17.2	29	18.8	398
B	25.0	1015	33.1	438	44.8	194	29.5	1647	22.9	249	24.7	85	39.6	53	25.6	387
C	19.6	796	14.3	21	35.1	37	20.1	854	22.8	232	16.7	6	.0	3	22.4	241
D	23.5	762	29.4	17	29.2	24	23.8	803	30.1	186	75.0	4	28.6	7	31.0	197
E	15.0	333	22.2	9	.0	7	14.9	349	15.0	133	.0	4	---	---	14.6	137
	23.0	3317	33.2	1483	37.8	413	27.1	5213	22.3	996	21.7	272	30.4	92	22.7	1360

* Includes only contacts for persons who lived within one of the five natural areas at the time of contact(s).

155

from the 1949 and 1955 Cohorts who resided in the inner city (and from the interstitial areas in the 1955 Cohort) did, however, have a disproportionately higher proportion of their contacts referred than did White males who resided in these areas.[4]

RACE/ETHNIC DIFFERENCES IN REFERRAL BY TYPE OF POLICE CONTACT

The percent of the contacts by members of each cohort which were referred to the County Probation Department or the District Attorney (as in Table 1), by reason for contact, race/ethnicity, and sex, is shown in Table 2 for the 1949 and 1955 Cohorts. While the percent of the contacts of Black and Chicano males referred by reason for contact was higher than that of the White males for some types of offenses for the 1949 Cohort, they were very similar for the 1955 Cohort, particularly for the more serious categories. For serious offenses, even though the percent of Black and Chicano males referred was similar to that of White males, it was the disproportionate number of Blacks referred for offenses most likely to result in institutionalization (Felonies Against the Person, for example) that constituted the final step toward the eventual very high proportion of institutionalized minority group members. The proportion of the contacts of females which were referred showed little systematic variation by reason for contact and race/ethnicity, but even were there a pattern, the number of females referred from most race/ethnic groups was small enough that differences would not have been statistically significant.

While Black males produced less than 14.6% of the contacts and 16.3% of those referred from the 1942 Cohort, they were disproportionately represented in the total number referred for the most serious offenses (Felonies Against Property and the Person and Major Misdemeanors). In the 1955 Cohort they again made up a disproportionate share of those referred for the most serious offenses.

Black females and Chicanos were also referred disproportionately to their numbers in the 1949 Cohort, both in the Major Misdemeanor and Juvenile Condition categories as well as overall. The contribution of Black females from the 1955 Cohort to the total number referred was less than their contribution to the total number of contacts by females in the cohort. Although the disproportional referral of Blacks and Chicanas was not found for both of the felony categories for the 1955 Cohort, it was present for Major Misdemeanor and Juvenile Condition contacts. One interesting male/female difference was the disproportionate number of Black females compared to Black males in the 1949 Cohort among those referred for a Juvenile Condition, suggesting that Black females may have been perceived by the police as needing more attention for status offenses than did Black males at that time.

TABLE 2. PERCENT OF CONTACTS REFERRED INTO JUDICIAL SYSTEM BY RACE/ETHNICITY, SEX, AND SERIOUSNESS CATEGORY

	MALES						FEMALES					
	White		Black		Chicano		White		Black		Chicano	
	%	N*	%	N	%	N	%	N	%	N	%	N
1949 Cohort:												
Felony Against Person	56.1	41	71.4	14	50.0	6	21.1	19	.0	1	---	--
Felony Against Property	72.3	137	67.4	46	66.7	9	50.0	4	100.0	2	---	--
Major Misdemeanor	38.7	274	25.8	93	42.3	26	28.0	25	33.3	18	50.0	2
Minor Misdemeanor	28.7	1552	30.3	271	35.8	148	15.7	267	15.2	79	14.3	7
Juvenile Condition	16.5	231	11.1	36	33.3	21	29.2	48	52.4	21	100.0	1
Suspicion or Information	1.1	1385	1.4	208	.0	93	.6	315	.0	61	.0	7
TOTAL	20.1	3620	23.5	668	26.4	303	10.5	678	17.0	182	17.6	17
1955 Cohort:												
Felony Against Person	71.1	142	71.4	112	76.2	21	46.5	43	46.7	15	50.0	2
Felony Against Property	76.3	329	75.0	196	75.6	41	60.6	33	50.0	8	50.0	4
Major Misdemeanor	41.5	410	43.2	308	57.1	77	51.1	94	34.5	55	70.6	17
Minor Misdemeanor	12.4	1279	14.5	422	19.4	129	11.2	374	6.2	97	13.8	29
Juvenile Condition	29.4	633	36.4	209	55.4	74	53.1	209	43.4	53	34.6	26
Suspicion or Information	.1	889	1.5	262	.0	83	.0	319	.0	49	.0	16
TOTAL	23.6	3682	33.2	1509	36.9	425	22.5	1072	21.3	277	29.8	94

* N = Number of contacts.

As we have said, race/ethnicity is a status or characteristic that places persons in areas where police contacts have a somewhat higher referral rate (1949 and 1955 Cohorts) and where the patterns of delinquency and crime that persons are most likely to acquire (Felonies Against Property and the Person and Major Misdemeanors) are those which have higher rates of referral into the justice system than do other offenses. As a consequence, Black males became the most disproportionately referred group in each cohort.

THE ACCUMULATION OF REFERRALS BY PERSONS WITH MULTIPLE CONTACTS

The effect of successive contacts on the probability of being referred became quite apparent upon examination of the percents of those referred with controls for the number of contacts persons had had (1, 2 to 4, or 5 or more). Reasons for contact were dichotomized into Traffic vs. Non-traffic and Non-felony vs. Felony contacts. The proportion of persons referred from each cohort increased in the Non-traffic and the Traffic categories with the frequency of contacts in every instance where there are sufficient cases for comparison. What we saw was a massing of contributions to the official records (referrals) by a relatively small number of chronic offenders. The high proportion of Black and White males with 5 or more contacts who had had at least one referral was particularly noteworthy.

Of those in the 1942 Cohort with Non-traffic contacts, 70.3% of the White males and 83.3% of the Black males had at least one referral, for the 1949 Cohort it was 73.8% and 92.0%, and for the 1955 Cohort it was 86.0% and 86.2%. This suggested, as we have so frequently stated before, that persons who had become recognized, well-known offenders were more frequently dealt with officially. To the extent that minority group members resided in areas which generated recidivists and chronic offenders more than did Whites, they progressively became a larger and larger proportion of those who were dealt with officially, even if they were treated even-handedly by the police at the time of contact.

That the Black male was more likely to become a recognized, well-known offender, either as a consequence of his own behavior or of that of the police and others with a labeling function, was further evidenced by the fact that the 1942 Cohort Black males had a median career between first and last contact of 168 months as compared to 135 months for Whites and 60 months for Chicanos. The median length of careers for males in the 1949 Cohort was 108 months for Blacks, 80 months for Whites, and 92 months for Chicanos. White females in the 1942 Cohort had a median career length of 66 months and Blacks 151 months, while in the 1949 Cohort, White females had a career length of 49 months and Black females 95 months.

The Consequences of Referral

While it is assumed that the juvenile who is referred is being helped by professional persons whose skills will change him or her into a more conforming individual (at least by middle-class standards), the data indicated that this might not have been the case. In order to examine continuities in contacts and referrals, we constructed tree diagrams in which the cohorts were divided into three categories for each period commencing with 6 through 17: 1) those who had at least one contact and referral, 2) those who had at least one contact but no referral, and 3) those who had no contacts. Each of these groups was then further divided for the age period 18 through 20 in the same manner. This produced a total of nine categories or combinations of contact and referral considering both age periods. These nine categories were in turn categorized in the same way for the age period 21 and older, thus creating a total of 27 categories.

Only 2.5% of the 1942 Cohort had a contact and referral in each age period and 31.4% had neither in any age period. Those who acquired at least one contact and one referral had successively higher seriousness scores in the next age period and seriousness scores increased from a median of 7.4 to 10.7 to 34.0. The 1949 Cohort presented a similar picture, with 2.2% having a contact and referral in each age period and 30.9% having neither in any age period. Those who had at least one contact and referral in each age period had successively higher seriousness scores, increasing from 9.0 to 13.1 to 27.0.

By contrast, those who had contacts but no referrals in each age period had very stable median seriousness scores, 2.6, 2.6, and 3.5 for the 1942 Cohort and 3.1, 2.1, and 2.9 for the 1949 Cohort. We have previously shown that referral rates were higher for the more serious reasons for police contact. With few exceptions, the groups who were referred at any stage went on to have higher seriousness scores at the next stage than those who were not referred. At each subsequent stage, however, there was the problem of determining the effects of prior misbehavior and referrals on subsequent behavior and it may be that referrals resulted in more serious delinquent and criminal behavior than in deterrence.

Predicting Continuity from Referrals

Recapitulating the Prediction Problem

Since referral rates were higher for persons who had greater continuity in their careers, prediction of future referrals and frequency of contacts and seriousness scores from referrals could permit improvement over the predictions of future delinquent and criminal behavior based on frequency of police contacts and seriousness scores.[5]

The coefficients of correlation between juvenile and adult measures of frequency and offense seriousness ranged from .500 to .600 but even at the point when prior contacts or seriousness could best be utilized as predictors of future contacts or seriousness, the reduction in error over the modal category of the marginals in predicting future contacts from past contacts was never above 20% for the 1942 Cohort, 17% for the 1949 Cohort, or 14% for the 1955 Cohort. In attempting to predict seriousness in the future from seriousness in the past, the proportional reduction in error never exceeded (at a point when prediction could be useful) more than 27% at age 16 for the 1942 Cohort, 25% for the 1949 Cohort at age 17, and 20% for the 1955 Cohort at age 15. It was not possible to improve on marginal predictions more than 25% even when the data were collapsed following cutting point strategies that minimized errors of prediction.[6]

While it was true that during the late teens and the early 20s those who had not yet had a contact were unlikely to have one in the future and the percent of those with four or five contacts by that age who would have at least one more was very large, the proportion of the cohort with continuity was so small that relatively little improvement could be made over prediction from the marginals. Similarly, a prediction of who would have more than five contacts or a high seriousness score beyond any given age was not greatly improved over the marginal prediction by using prior record as a predictor. At the same time, these percentage differences were great enough to appear quite impressive to persons concerned about the importance of considering errors of omission as well as errors of commission.

Predicting Referrals from Referrals

In developing prediction tables the question arose as to which types of referrals should be included in the analysis. In the first part of this chapter we utilized only the two most serious categories of referral because we were concerned about the extent to which referrals took place at a higher rate for Blacks and Chicanos than for Whites, thus bringing the persons referred one step closer to formal court handling and the possibility of sanctions.

The next analysis included all types of referrals because we were concerned about the possibility that any kind of referral, whether to the Racine County Probation Officer or to the District Attorney, would have some effect on the probability of future referrals and police contacts. Even then there would be, of course, a much smaller percentage of each cohort who had a referral prior to and at any given age than had police contacts, but our assumption was that those who were referred either engaged in more serious behavior which really warranted referral or that their characteristics were those which defined them as persons who needed more formal consideration. In either case, we hypothesized that these were the persons most likely to have had continuity in their careers.

Let us first look at a table showing the percentage of each cohort referred after any given age by the number of referrals they had accrued through that age (Table 3). These correlations peaked about the same time as those obtained between contacts through a given age and contact after that age. The highest correlations were at the ages of 19 through 25 for the 1942 Cohort, at 16 through 22 for the 1949 Cohort, and appeared even earlier, at age 13, for the 1955 Cohort, not because there were cohort differences as much as because of the limited time after the late teens for the 1949 and 1955 Cohorts. What we must emphasize is that at no time was lambda higher than .125 for any age for any of the cohorts, indicating that the predictor (number of referrals through a given age) provided little reduction in errors of prediction over prediction from the marginals. Of course, when we turn to an age such as 18 or 19, those who thus far had no referrals had less than one chance in five of having a referral after that age but those who had had five referrals through that age had at least 9 out of 10 chances of having another referral. This latter group is small, however, and the errors of omission at any age for those who had had no referrals or only one referral through that age were so large that there was relatively little increase in predictive efficiency for any cohort at any age.

Another table was constructed showing the percent with three or more referrals after any age by the number of referrals prior to and at that age. At 16 in the 1942 Cohort, for example, less than 8% of those who had no referrals had three or more after that age, while 100% of those who had five or more referrals had three or more after that age. Similar differences were found for the 1949 and 1955 Cohorts, with proportional differences very high as early as age 13. The problem is illustrated by the fact that at age 13 there were only 29 out of 1,297 persons in the 1949 Cohort who had at least one referral and, although only five of these failed to have another referral, 477 who had not had a referral were referred at some time in the future. And, of these, 146 had three or more referrals in the future. All would have been missed by using past referrals as a predictor. As another example, the knowledge that 12 out of 16 persons who had had five or more referrals through the age of 16 had three or more referrals in the future is a far cry from the ability to predict who out of the entire group would eventually have three or more referrals.

Predicting Number of Contacts and Seriousness Scores from Referrals

In still another table, we examined the percent of each cohort with a given number of referrals through an age who went on to have one or

TABLE 3. PERCENT WITH ANY POLICE REFERRAL AFTER AGE BY NUMBER OF REFERREALS PRIOR TO AND AT AGE: COHORT MEMBERS WITH CONTINUOUS RESIDENCE

PERCENT OF 1942 COHORT WITH REFERRALS AFTER AGE

Number of Referrals Through Age	8	9	10	11	12	13	14	15	16	17	18	19	20	21	22	23	24	25	26	27	28	29	30
0	37	37	37	37	37	37	35	32	26	20	17	15	12	11	10	8	6	6	5	4	3	2	1
1	100	100	100	100	100	75	73	76	56	45	37	34	30	30	26	23	15	13	11	7	4	1	0
2	---	---	---	0	0	0	50	78	68	62	55	41	43	37	37	33	26	23	21	15	19	7	2
3	---	---	---	---	---	---	100	100	100	93	74	61	56	53	50	42	36	38	36	24	17	11	7
4	---	---	---	---	---	---	100	100	100	75	82	57	68	59	50	47	33	33	25	7	6	0	0
5 or +	---	---	---	---	---	---	---	---	100	75	91	94	94	88	83	72	69	67	62	59	41	22	7
Lambda	.004	.004	.008	.004	.004	.000	.004	.009	.030	.028	.018	.034	.044	.083	.081	.047	.056	.048	.066	.079	.087	.080	.125
Somers' D	.697	.697	.707	.506	.623	.420	.463	.548	.432	.401	.386	.343	.356	.343	.327	.296	.251	.241	.220	.184	.139	.064	.024
Pearson's R	.119	.119	.300	.215	.238	.204	.176	.328	.362	.415	.469	.484	.502	.498	.508	.513	.492	.491	.454	.435	.525	.464	.377

PERCENT OF 1949 COHORT WITH REFERRALS AFTER AGE

Number of Referrals Through Age	8	9	10	11	12	13	14	15	16	17	18	19	20	21	22	23
0	37	37	36	36	36	35	34	31	25	17	13	10	8	6	3	2
1	50	80	75	80	86	80	82	73	60	40	32	26	22	16	9	4
2	---	---	---	---	100	100	100	88	71	55	48	44	37	23	16	7
3	---	---	---	---	---	100	100	70	87	63	57	46	34	26	21	9
4	---	---	---	---	100	100	100	100	86	65	65	52	48	41	33	20
5 or +	---	---	---	---	---	100	100	100	88	87	87	74	66	51	41	17
Lambda	.000	.004	.008	.004	.006	.006	.011	.016	.012	.019	.039	.038	.053	.073	.082	.057
Somers' D	.307	.599	.561	.612	.667	.621	.621	.590	.499	.370	.347	.303	.266	.224	.161	.075
Pearson's R	.083	.146	.150	.157	.194	.290	.379	.467	.529	.538	.592	.553	.513	.547	.492	.289

PERCENT OF 1955 COHORT WITH REFERRALS AFTER AGE

Number of Referrals Through Age	8	9	10	11	12	13	14	15	16	17	18	19	20
0	34	33	33	33	32	30	27	24	19	13	10	5	3
1	0	67	86	78	74	76	66	55	37	26	18	12	7
2	---	100	100	100	100	89	87	73	62	46	36	27	15
3	---	---	---	100	100	100	82	88	73	63	45	35	21
4	---	100	---	---	100	100	80	82	67	61	45	39	16
5 or +	---	---	100	75	88	96	95	88	83	69	69	53	35
Lambda	.000	.003	.004	.007	.011	.014	.019	.027	.029	.033	.024	.036	.046
Somers' D	-.336	.689	.794	.704	.680	.687	.608	.526	.412	.320	.257	.224	.136
Pearson's R	-.008	.182	.200	.311	.449	.524	.519	.542	.549	.537	.498	.485	.335

more police contacts. Although very high percentages of those who had referrals through their teens continued to have contacts, particularly those who had frequent referrals, there was practically no increase in predictive efficiency over the marginals for any cohort. When the criterion became five or more contacts after a particular age, a very small percentage of those with no referrals through a given age had five or more contacts after that age but a very large percentage of those who had frequent referrals had five or more contacts after that age, still little improvement over the marginal predictability.

The last table in the series, based on the relationship between referrals through any given age and seriousness scores after that age, showed that persons who had two or more referrals by the age of 15 and those who had four or more by the age of 16 were almost certain to have had high seriousness scores after that age. Overall prediction, however, was improved less than 10% beyond marginal predictability.

That previous records were related to future records has been established in a number of ways but we must emphasize the danger of assuming that significant increases in predictive efficiency over the modal category of the marginals can be made with skewed distributions and relatively modest correlations.

Persons on the firing line know that those who have received frequent referrals through the age of 18 are likely to continue their misbehavior and, from the viewpoint of those who are concerned about the labeling process, it is a considerable concern that far larger proportions of those who have had frequent referrals have five or more contacts after a given age than do those who have had only infrequent contacts. For example, while only 51% of those in the 1949 Cohort who had five or more contacts through the age of 18 had five or more contacts afterward, almost 75% of those with five or more referrals through the age of 18 had five or more contacts after that age. While it can be argued that those who had five or more referrals must have committed more serious types of misbehavior than those who had five or more contacts, the difference in the proportion who continued to have police contacts was so great that the possibility of a labeling effect cannot be disregarded. This led to construction of a table based on the relationship of referrals through a given age to seriousness scores after that age.

When we attempted to predict who from the 1942 Cohort would have a seriousness score of six or more after their 18th year, we found that simply having vs. not having a referral through the age of 18 increased predictive efficiency over the modal category of the marginals by 42%. Almost all of the errors consisted of those who had no referrals through age 18 who acquired a seriousness score of six or more after that age. Almost everyone in the 1942 Cohort who had a referral through the age of 18 had a score of six or more after becoming 19.

In the 1949 Cohort predictive efficiency was increased 21% by predicting that those who had two or more referrals through the age of 18 would have a seriousness score of six or more after that age, but for the 1955 Cohort predictive efficiency increased only 12%, with the most efficient prediction being that those with four or more referrals would have a seriousness score of six or more after that age. As was expected, those persons with a given number of referrals before the age of 18 were more likely to have five or more contacts and seriousness scores of six or more after that age than were those who had the same number of contacts or an equivalent seriousness score.

SUMMARY AND CONCLUSION

When contacts and referrals were plotted against age at time of contact on a series of curves, it was found that the contact and referral curves were similar from cohort to cohort but that Blacks and Chicanos differed from Whites in several respects. Curves for Blacks and Chicanos peaked more rapidly than did those for Whites, particularly the curve representing the proportion of those with contacts who were also referred. Cumulatively, the curves for Blacks and Chicanos not only reached higher levels than did the curves for Whites but continued to rise for several years after passing the peak for Whites.

When the percentage of each race/ethnic|sex group referred by natural area of residence at time of referral was calculated, there was little consistent decline from the poorest to best residential areas in the percent of Whites referred and no regularity for either Blacks or Chicanos or for females of any group.

Higher percentages of Black and Chicano than White males were referred from all cohorts although, when controls for seriousness were introduced, race/ethnic differentials became less consistent. Black males, while disproportionately referred beyond their contribution to the most serious category of contacts in the 1949 Cohort, had similar proportions of their contacts referred in the 1955 Cohort. Whether referrals were for Non-felonies or Felonies, the proportion of persons referred also increased with frequency of contact category and was particularly high among White and Black males with 5 or more contacts. In other words, a larger proportion of the chronic offenders had at least one of their contacts referred, a massing of contributions to the official records, most of all for those who have had five or more contacts for Felonies.

We concluded that although a record of past referrals was correlated with future referrals, number of contacts, and seriousness scores, there was relatively little increase in predictive efficiency over predictions made from the modal category of the marginals.

In summary, minorities made up a disproportionate number of those referred because, however irregular and inconsistent the pattern between cohorts, they had more contacts, more contacts for more serious categories of behavior, and were to some extent disproportionately referred beyond what would be expected considering the categories of behavior into which their reasons for police contact fell.

NOTES

1. After examining the effects of extra-legal factors in determining the length of prison sentences, Bernstein et al., concluded that research strategy should pay more attention to the role of accumulated disadvantage: Ilene Nagel Bernstein, William R. Kelley, and Patricia A. Doyle, "Societal Reaction to Deviants; The Case of Criminal Defenders," *American Sociological Review* 42 (1977): 743–755.

2. How this initial screening process works so as to increase the probability of arrests for Blacks (they are more likely to show disrespect for the police) has been described by Donald Black in "The Social Organization of Arrest," *Stanford Law Review* 23 (1971): 1087–1111.

3. Similar tables may be found in Lyle W. Shannon, "A Longitudinal Study of Delinquency and Crime," Chapter 7, Charles Wellford (ed.) *Quantitative Studies in Criminology* (Beverly Hills: Sage, 1978): 121–146.

4. As Edward Green, "Race, Social Status and Criminal Arrest," *American Sociological Review* 35 (1970): 476–490, concludes, ". . . .the high official rate of crime for Negroes compared with whites results predominantly from the wider distribution among Negroes of lower class characteristics associated with crime."

5. There is an excellent critical literature on the prediction problem, selected items of which follow: Paul Meehl, *Clinical vs. Statistical Prediction: A Theoretical Analysis and Review of the Findings* (Minneapolis: University of Minnesota Press, 1954); Don M. Gottfredson, "Assessment and Prediction Methods in Crime and Delinquency," in James E. Teele (ed.), *Juvenile Delinquency* (Itasca, Illinois: F.E. Peacock, 1970): 401–424; David A. Pritchard, "Stable Predictors of Recidivism: A Summary," *Criminology* 17 (1979): 15–21; John Monahan, "Childhood Predictors of Adult Criminal Experience," Chapter 3 in Fernand W. Dutile, Cleon H. Foust, and D. Robert Webster (eds.) *Early Childhood Intervention and Juvenile Delinquency* (Lexington: Lexington Books, 1982); Leslie T. Wilkins, "Problems with Existing Prediction Studies and Future Research Needs," *The Journal of Criminal Law & Criminology* 71 (1980): 98–101; Steven D. Gottfredson and Don M. Gottfredson, "Accuracy of Prediction Models," in Alfred Blumstein, Jacqueline Cohen, Jeffrey A. Roth, and Christy A. Visher (eds.), *Criminal Careers and "Career Criminals" Volume II* (Washington, D.C.: National Academy Press, 1986): 212–290.

6. The trade-off in costs and consequences of the two types of errors, false negatives and false positives, is discussed at some length by Leslie Wilkins in "Putting

'Treatment' on Trial," *The Hastings Center Report* (Hastings-on-the-Hudson: In-
stitute of Society, Ethics and the Life Sciences, 1975), reprinted in Norman
Johnson and Leonard D. Savitz, *Justice and Corrections* (New York: John Wiley
& Sons, 1978): 670–687. We have also dealt with the prediction problem in Lyle
W. Shannon, "Risk Assessment vs. Real Prediction: The Prediction Problem
and Public Trust," *Journal of Quantitative Criminology* 1 (1985): 159–189.

Chapter 13

SERIOUSNESS OF JUVENILE CAREERS, INTERVENTION, AND ADULT SERIOUSNESS

In this chapter we shall examine the consequences of intervention and sanctions during the juvenile period. A complete description of the adjudication process including alternatives available at each step in handling juveniles who have been referred to juvenile court intake covers 14 pages of schematic diagrams. It was, therefore, not feasible to examine the process in its complexity to determine the consequences of each alternative step for each category of juveniles referred to court. Although some of the effects are lost through simplification, analysis of police contacts, referrals, and sanctions presents some idea of what happened to that proportion of each cohort which came to the attention of the police and courts.

Police and court experiences are encapsulated in a Dispositions Scale to determine if various levels of intervention deterred, had no effect, or seemed to propel cohort members into even more serious misbehavior.[1] Inasmuch as we wished to determine the relationship of severity of sanctions through any given age to later reasons for police contacts, referrals, and sanctions, dismissals were eliminated in a final Severity of Sanctions Scale. Each score on this scale received a rank order based on the level of severity which it represented, with similar levels combined so that scores ranged from 0 to 60. Thus, severity of sanctions during any age period could be correlated with the number and seriousness of offenses during any age period. For example, through age 18, past and present severity of sanctions for the 1942 Cohort had a Pearsonian correlation of .323 with number of police contacts in the future. For the 1949 Cohort, the correlation was .385, and for the 1955 Cohort it was .412.

The Effects of Sanctions on Continuity and Seriousness of Careers

When the number of contacts and seriousness scores through the ages 15, 17, and 20 were controlled and measures of association calculated between severity of sanctions through and number of contacts and seriousness scores after these ages for 45 different groups with and without sex controls, there was not a single correlation that would indicate that those who received more severe sanctions through a given age had fewer police contacts or lower seriousness scores than was the case for persons who received less severe sanctions through that age. Every correlation was positive, indicating that severity of sanctions was related to more contacts or more serious reasons for contacts in subsequent years.

This is such an important point that several examples are presented. In the 1955 Cohort 57% of those males with 1–4 contacts through 17 who had not been sanctioned had already had additional contacts and 75% of those who had been sanctioned had had additional contacts. In the group with five or more contacts through 17, 73% of those who had not been sanctioned had further contacts but 88% of those who had been sanctioned did so. Thus, sanctions had little reformative effect on either group of males.

Given that sanctions had been meted out to juveniles with caution (juvenile court judges were characterized as far too lenient during the period of this study), the consequences of sanctions through age 20 might suggest a greater deterrent effect on future misbehavior.[2] The relationship between severity of sanctions through age 20 and number of contacts afterward for the 1942 and 1949 Cohort males was similar to that obtained when 17 was the cutting point. In the 1949 Cohort segment with 1–4 contacts through 20, 44% of those not sanctioned had additional contacts as did 71% of those sanctioned. Eighty percent and 83% respectively of those who had 5 or more contacts through 20 continued to have contacts. Among those in the 1955 Cohort with from 1–4 contacts through 20, 17% of those not sanctioned continued to have contacts while 32% of those sanctioned continued to have contacts. The percentages were 24% and 53% respectively of those with 5 or more contacts. Sanctioning had relatively less effect in the undesired direction on females with 1–4 contacts than it had on females with 5 or more contacts.

Whatever has been said about continuity in contacts following sanctions is found to a somewhat greater degree for seriousness scores. For example, among those males from the 1949 Cohort with scores of 6 or more who were not sanctioned, only 13% had a score above 31 after the age of 18 but 42% of those who were sanctioned had a score of 31 after the age of 18.

RACE/ETHNIC, SEX, AND PLACE OF SOCIALIZATION DIFFERENCES IN RATES OF INCARCERATION

Although minority groups made up only a relatively small proportion of Wisconsin's population, they constituted a highly disproportionate percentage of those who were dealt with by either the juvenile or adult justice system, ultimately sanctioned, and institutionalized. "Removal from the community" or institutionalization (quite aside from its punishing aspects) is believed by many to be an effective deterrent to further delinquency and crime and one to which the courts should turn with greater frequency.

Very few from the 1942 or 1949 Cohorts had been institutionalized but the proportion of the Blacks (5.0% from the 1942 Cohort and 15.7% from the 1949 Cohort) and Chicanos (12.5% from the 1942 Cohort and 24.1% from the 1949 Cohort) institutionalized from each of these cohorts was much higher than the proportion of Whites (2.8% from the 1942 Cohort and 2.6% from the 1949 Cohort) institutionalized. However, the proportion of Blacks and Chicanos in the 1955 Cohort was sufficient that the high proportion of Blacks (14.6%) who had been institutionalized in comparison to the percent of Chicanos (5.1%) and Whites (3.0%) could not be attributed to chance alone.[4]

The percent institutionalized from the inner city and interstitial areas (3.3%) was essentially the same as the percent of all who had been institutionalized (3.0%) from the 1942 Cohort, but the probability of being institutionalized was greater if one had been socialized there. Compared to the 36.8% of the 1942 Cohort socialized in this area, 42.1% of those who had ever been institutionalized had been socialized in the inner city and interstitial areas. Further, we found that 90.1% of those who were socialized in the inner city and interstitial areas were White but only 75.0% of those institutionalized from the area were White.

Only 33.5% of the 1949 Cohort had been socialized in the inner city and interstitial areas, while 64.7% of those who were institutionalized were from that area. We also noted that 7.3% of those from the inner city and interstitial areas had been institutionalized in comparison to 3.9% of the total cohort. There was an even greater difference in the race/ethnic composition of those socialized in the inner city and interstitial areas of the city with 77.7% of those socialized in the area being White but only 45.5% of those institutionalized being White. The Blacks made up over twice as large a proportion of those from the inner city who had been institutionalized (39.4%) as their proportion socialized there (17.2%). The Chicano differences were even greater proportionately (15.1% vs. 5.1%).

While 26.7% of the 1955 Cohort's members were socialized in the inner city, 56.8% of those who were institutionalized had been socialized there, an even greater difference than found for the 1949 Cohort. Of those socialized in the inner city, 62.0% were White but only 40.0% of those institutionalized from the inner city were White. Again, proportionately twice as many Blacks from the inner city were institutionalized as their proportion socialized there (54.0% vs. 27.9%), but in this case the Chicanos as well as the Whites were institutionalized disproportionately less than would be expected. While only 4.1% of the total cohort had been institutionalized, 8.2% of those socialized in the inner city had had this experience.

It is apparent that socialization in the inner city and interstitial areas generated behavior resulting in disproportional numbers of its residents having contacts, referrals, court sanctions, and ultimate institutionalization, and that the disproportional race/ethnic composition of the inner city played a part in Blacks making up a highly disproportional percentage of those who had ever been institutionalized. We prefer to describe the process in this order although we realize that there are persons who have turned the data around and taken the position that Blacks were more likely to become a part of the records at every stage and ultimately to be institutionalized, their disproportionate numbers in the inner city and interstitial areas generating the disproportional institutionalization of persons socialized in these areas.

THE EFFECTS OF INSTITUTIONALIZATION ON LATER SERIOUSNESS OF CAREERS

We have dealt with the effects of sanctions on the seriousness of police contact records after the juvenile period but have not considered each cohort in terms of differences based on no sanctions, sanctions less serious than institutionalization, and institutionalization. Age 21 was selected as the cutting point for the 1942 Cohort to maximize the number of persons who would have been sanctioned before the age for which before and after mean seriousness were calculated. Ages 18 and 21 were utilized for the 1949 Cohort (to compare results for two cutting points) and age 18 for the 1955 Cohort, the latter to maximize time after age 18 for developing seriousness scores.

The 1942 Cohort segment of the table indicated that there was a reduction in mean after-age seriousness for those institutionalized before 21, mean scores of 21.2 after and 31.9 before. Those with high seriousness scores before 21 who had been institutionalized had about the same after-21 seriousness (21.2) as those sanctioned but not institutionalized (20.9). Both, however, had after-21 seriousness scores almost double that of those who had *not* been sanctioned (12.9). Males with high seriousness scores prior to 21 who had been institutionalized had higher seriousness scores (25.8) than those who had been sanctioned but not institutionalized (20.8), and both had considerably higher seriousness scores than those not sanctioned (13.4).

When the same age cutting point was utilized for the 1949 Cohort, the overall after-age seriousness scores were again lower for those who had not been sanctioned (1.9) and highest for those who had been institutionalized (27.0). With controls for seriousness of prior career, those who had been institutionalized had markedly higher after-age seriousness scores (27.0) than those who had been sanctioned but not institutionalized (8.7), males and females combined, males alone, and Blacks and Whites alone. Those Chicanos who had not been sanctioned had the highest after-21 seriousness scores. Although the mean after-age seriousness scores were not the same for the 1955 Cohort, the pattern of differences was similar to that for the 1949 Cohort with age 21 as the cutting point.

One must conclude that these data provided little support for the idea that institutionalization of juveniles deterred them from continuing to accumulate fairly high seriousness scores as adults. On the other hand, a more precise response to the question of effects of institutionalization must be conducted with even more stringent controls. The number of persons institutionalized made this difficult except with the 1955 Cohort.[5]

MULTI-STAGE MODELS OF THE RELATIONSHIP OF SANCTIONS TO SERIOUSNESS SCORES

We now go beyond percentages and simple first-order correlations, controlling for a variety of variables that may have had underlying or intervening effects on seriousness of adult careers or later juvenile careers. Two-, three-, and four-stage models were constructed for the effect of the independent variable, severity of sanctions, on the dependent variable and seriousness scores at various ages. The first order correlations and Betas for all models, based on uncollapsed data, are shown in Table 1.[6]

Although there were positive relationships between severity of sanctions and seriousness scores during specified succeeding ages in the two-stage model, these effects were reduced when controls for area of socialization, race/ethnicity, sex, age at first contact, and severity of past sanctions were held constant.[7]

The first-order correlations were positive in the three-stage model in all cases but when controls were introduced, as in the two-stage model, severity of sanctions during the ages 18 through 20 had a small inverse relationship with seriousness for persons 21 years of age in the 1955 Cohort. Since this involved a period of only one year, we would maintain that severity of sanctions was not related to a decline in seriousness of careers in age periods following the period of sanctions. Further, it was clear that (with the exception of the 1955 Cohort) the unplanned effects of sanctions were strongest in the period immediately following them.

The four-stage model produced even more interesting results. At every stage the first-order correlations of severity of sanctions and following age

TABLE 1. MULTI-STAGE MODELS OF THE RELATIONSHIP OF SANCTIONS TO SERIOUSNESS SCORES DURING LATE JUVENILE OR ADULT PERIODS

Independent Variable:
Sanctions During Agea[1]   Dependent Variable: Seriousness During Ages

TWO-STAGE MODELS

		Total Cohort	Males
1942 Cohort		18-30	18-30
6-17	r	.245	.229
	Beta	.084*	.097
1949 Cohort		18-23	18-23
6-17	r	.376	.385
	Beta	.100*	.096*
1955 Cohort		18-21	18-21
6-17	r	.420	.403
	Beta	.014	.011

THREE-STAGE MODELS

		Total Cohort		Males	
1942 Cohort		18-20	21-30	18-20	21-30
6-17	r	.274	.201	.260	.184
	Beta	.082*	.014	.095	.017
18-20	r	----	.480	----	.449
	Beta	----	.171*	----	.168*
1949 Cohort		18-20	21-23	18-20	21-23
6-17	r	.350	.320	.345	.327
	Beta	.112*	.017	.105*	.021
18-20	r	----	.454	----	.460
	Beta	----	.007	----	.111*
1955 Cohort		18-20	21	18-20	21
6-17	r	.412	.246	.395	.227
	Beta	.003	.045	.003	.034
18-20	r	----	.281	----	.265
	Beta	----	-.088*	----	-.089

FOUR-STAGE MODELS

		Total Cohort			Males		
1942 Cohort		16-17	18-20	21-30	16-17	18-20	21-30
6-15	r	.157	.249	.115	.138	.262	.114
	Beta	-.026	.134*	-.060	-.036	.177*	-.056
16-17	r	----	.219	.187	----	.197	.167
	Beta	----	.019	.041	----	-.015	.043
18-20	r	----	----	.480	----	----	.449
	Beta	----	----	.176*	----	----	.171*
1949 Cohort		16-17	18-20	21-23	16-17	18-20	21-23
6-15	r	.238	.219	.162	.254	.236	.179
	Beta	-.113*	.034	-.070*	-.097*	.038	-.083*
16-17	r	----	.358	.308	----	.350	.305
	Beta	----	.128*	.017	----	.123*	.021
18-20	r	----	----	.454	----	----	.460
	Beta	----	----	.008	----	----	.113*
1955 Cohort		16-17	18-20	21	16-17	18-20	21
6-15	r	.356	.286	.189	.368	.279	.161
	Beta	-.052	-.095*	.021	-.030	-.127*	-.011
16-17	r	----	.373	.197	----	.354	.182
	Beta	----	.016	.011	----	.013	.002
18-20	r	----	----	.281	----	----	.630
	Beta	----	----	-.087*	----	----	-.088

[1]Beta is the effect of sanctions when natural area, race, sex (for the total cohort), age at first contact, past seriousness, and past sanctions were held constant.

* p < .05.

period seriousness scores were positive, more than half of the relationships between severity of sanctions during the ages of 6 through 15 and later age periods reversed when controls were inserted. Most, however, were very small even if statistically significant. These results did not change the conclusions that sanctions had little or no effect in deterring juveniles from continuing contacts with the police as older juveniles or as adults. Moreover, severity of sanctions during ages 16 and 17, when they were most frequently applied, had significant positive effects on seriousness scores in the immediately following age period 18 through 20, the strongest effects to be found in the 1949 Cohort.

Juvenile Career Patterns and the Seriousness of Adult Careers

Two questions are answered in this section of the chapter: 1) to what extent did adult seriousness differ by juvenile career patterns and 2) to what extent did the seriousness of juvenile police contacts, the number of juvenile police referrals, and the severity of juvenile sanctions affect adult seriousness over and above the influence of career patterns alone?

Cohort members were classified into four juvenile career types according to the presence or absence of juvenile police contacts, juvenile police referrals, and juvenile sanctions. The first type included those who had no police contacts, referrals, or sanctions as juveniles. The second type included those who had at least one police contact as juveniles but no referrals or sanctions. The third type included those who had at least one police contact, at least one referral, and no sanctions. The fourth type included those who had at least one police contact, at least one referral, and at least one sanction. Thus, the four categories reflect increasing involvement in the juvenile justice system but do not necessarily reflect the seriousness of juvenile contacts, the numbers of referrals, or the severity of sanctions.

To answer the questions which have been posed we examined the mean adult seriousness scores for each of the four categories with and without statistically controlling for juvenile seriousness, the number of juvenile police referrals, and the severity of juvenile sanctions. This strategy permitted us to examine predicted adult seriousness scores for each of the four categories as if they were equivalent in terms of the control variables. Obviously, they were not equivalent but the analysis of covariance method allowed us to gain some insight into the effects of juvenile seriousness and official intervention on adult seriousness for persons who had experienced different juvenile career patterns.

We should emphasize that career patterns and control variables are not independent. For example, those cohort members who had no juvenile police contacts necessarily had no juvenile seriousness scores. This means that the career patterns and control variables were artifactually correlated to some extent but dummy variable multiple regression was applied so that these intercorrelations were taken into account. This procedure allowed us to partially address the important substantive issue of how the adult seriousness of the four juvenile career types varied according to the seriousness of juvenile police contact careers, the number of juvenile police referrals, and the severity of juvenile sanctions.

Table 2 presents the unadjusted and adjusted mean adult seriousness scores for the 1949 Cohort. The association of adult seriousness with greater juvenile involvement in the juvenile justice system was considerably diminished for the males when either juvenile seriousness or referrals was held constant, another indication that these variables contributed to increased adult seriousness.

We again found a large difference in juvenile and adult police contacts by sex. As opposed to 36.9% of the males, 71.8% of the females had no juvenile contacts, referrals, or sanctions. Similarly, the mean adult seriousness for the females was 2.377 in contrast to 9.597 for the males.

As with other groups, the mean adult seriousness for the 1949 Cohort females increased with greater juvenile involvement in the juvenile justice system. When juvenile seriousness was held constant, however, these differences between career patterns were markedly reduced.

When juvenile referrals were held constant we found a partial reduction in the differences in adult seriousness by career pattern. This suggested a weak positive relationship between referrals and adult seriousness. In other words, if the 1942 Cohort females had received no referrals they would have had more serious adult careers whereas the 1949 Cohort females would have had less serious adult careers.

In summary, juvenile seriousness and referrals were associated with increased adult seriousness among the 1949 Cohort females. This pattern is similar to that found for the 1942 and 1949 Cohort males but differed from that for the 1942 Cohort females.

The same analysis was conducted for the 1955 Cohort. Let it suffice to say that even with the highest levels of juvenile seriousness, greater numbers of police referrals, and more severe juvenile sanctions associated with increased adult seriousness for the 1955 Cohort males, this pattern was similar to that found for the 1942 and 1949 Cohort males despite the different historical periods involved.

Like the 1955 Cohort males, the seriousness of juvenile careers, number of juvenile referrals, and severity of juvenile sanctions all worked to increase adult seriousness for the females. In addition, we found the interesting effect that, for the 1955 Cohort females, severity of juvenile sanctions produced an increase in adult seriousness that more than accounted for the differences between the juvenile career patterns.

In Table 3 the adult period was defined as ages 18 through 21 to permit direct within-sex comparison across cohorts for males. In effect, we held

TABLE 2.   UNADJUSTED AND ADJUSTED MEAN ADULT SERIOUSNESS (EXPRESSED AS DEVIATIONS FROM THE GRAND MEAN), BY JUVENILE CAREER PATTERN AND SEX: 1949 COHORT

| Juvenile Career Pattern | | | N | % | Unadjusted | Adjusted for: | | | |
Contacts 6-17	Referrals 6-17	Sanctions 6-17				Seriousness 6-17	Referrals 6-17	Sanctions 6-17	Referrals and Sanctions, 6-17
MALES									
No	No	No	273	36.9	-7.180	-2.668	.213	-6.624	3.459
Yes	No	No	208	28.1	-3.713	-1.970	3.680	-3.157	.008
Yes	Yes	No	213	28.8	6.013	2.555	5.403	6.569	1.445
Yes	Yes	Yes	46	6.2	31.555	12.908	16.542	23.272	13.800
			740	100.0					
Grand Mean = 9.597									
FEMALES									
No	No	No	400	71.8	-1.162	.331	-.837	----*	----*
Yes	No	No	110	19.7	.178	-2.306	.503	----	----
Yes	Yes	No	42	7.5	7.742	.636	4.605	----	----
Yes	Yes	Yes	5	.9	24.023	4.409	17.215	----	----
			557	99.9					
Grand Mean = 2.377									

* Too few cases to adjust for sanctions.

175

TABLE 3. UNADJUSTED AND ADJUSTED MEAN SERIOUSNESS DURING AGES 18-21 (EXPRESSED AS DEVIATIONS FROM THE GRAND MEAN), BY JUVENILE CAREER PATTERN: MALES

Juvenile Career Pattern			Unadjusted			Adjusted for Seriousness, 6-17			Adjusted for Sanctions, 6-17			Adjusted for Referrals, 6-17			Adjusted for Referrals and Sanctions, 6-17		
Contacts 6-17	Referrals 6-17	Sanctions 6-17	1942	1949	1955	1942	1949	1955	1942	1949	1955	1942	1949	1942	1942	1949	1955
No	No	No	-3.522	-4.425	-4.613	-1.198	-2.137	-2.108	-2.986	-4.155	-3.112	-1.688	-2.564	-2.405	-1.442	-2.548	-2.521
Yes	No	No	-.847	-2.337	-2.016	-.409	-1.454	-.459	-.311	-2.067	-.515	.987	-.476	.192	1.232	-.460	.075
Yes	Yes	No	4.366	3.826	3.125	1.699	2.072	2.792	4.903	4.096	4.626	1.247	1.657	2.595	2.006	1.494	2.301
Yes	Yes	Yes	8.961	19.114	8.953	2.366	9.659	3.216	-1.113	15.044	4.433	2.859	9.693	3.214	-4.688	10.288	3.624

Grand Means: 1942 = 4.983, 1949 = 5.799, 1955 = 6.364

constant the adult age range so that the length of exposure to the possibility of police contacts was the same for all three cohorts.

When no variables were held constant the career patterns which reflected greater involvement with the juvenile justice system were associated with more serious adult careers, as before. The 1942 and 1955 Cohorts exhibited similar differences in mean adult seriousness by juvenile career pattern; however, the unadjusted deviation from the grand mean for the 1949 Cohort males who had contacts, referrals, and sanctions was more than twice as great as that for either the 1942 or 1955 Cohort males. This difference was all the more striking in that years of exposure were the same for all three cohorts. This is consistent with our previous finding that the percentage of males with no involvement in the juvenile justice system was lower for the 1949 Cohort males than for males in either of the other cohorts.

Differences in adult seriousness by juvenile career pattern were largely reduced when juvenile seriousness was held constant, although the same group in the 1949 Cohort again showed a relatively high level of adult seriousness. Overall, however, this indicated that juvenile seriousness was a major factor in producing adult seriousness over and above the career pattern. As before, an alternate way of stating this is that the adult seriousness scores associated with the various juvenile career patterns would be very similar (with the exception of the 1949 Cohort group) if their levels of juvenile seriousness were equivalent.

A similar pattern emerged when referrals were held constant which suggested that referrals acted in much the same manner as seriousness in terms of their effects on adult seriousness. Again, the one exception was members of the 1949 group who had contacts, referrals, and sanctions. When sanctions were held constant, differences in adult seriousness were again reduced in a manner which was similar across cohorts with the exception of the 1949 Cohort males.

During the ages 18 through 21 the 1949 Cohort was the one exception in seriousness among the males of the three birth cohorts for those who had contacts, referrals, and sanctions during the juvenile period. This group consistently exhibited a high level of adult seriousness relative to the other groups with and without controls. However, the similarity across cohorts was the predominant finding of this analysis despite an upward trend in adult seriousness over time (see the cohort grand means in Table 3).

The inter-cohort comparisons for the females will be dealt with more briefly, and the table is omitted. As with the males, there was evidence of an upward trend in adult seriousness over time. One reason for the overall increase in mean seriousness across cohorts for the females was that a greater proportion of females in the 1955 Cohort were either referred or sanctioned and it was they who also had the highest mean adult seriousness.

A number of different processes may underlie this phenomenon, as has been said before. Perhaps females in the 1955 Cohort were treated more legalistically and therefore were more likely to have serious adult careers. Because females were permitted to play roles with more equality than previously there was also a greater likelihood of exposure to official intervention. Another possibility is that juvenile seriousness had come to have a greater impact on adult seriousness over time. Thus, the greater proportion of females being referred or sanctioned may reflect an increasing articulation between offense and official responses. Increasing adult seriousness may in part be an extension of increasing juvenile seriousness.

Although these data provided some interesting insights into the factors affecting adult seriousness, they did not tell us much about the magnitude of these effects or the strength of their influences when all other variables in the analysis were held constant. To examine these relationships in a more parsimonious and rigorous manner path analysis was applied to the causal model of adult seriousness. To anticipate these findings, we may note two major findings from this analysis which will hold up under more rigorous analysis. First, juvenile seriousness had an important causal relationship to adult seriousness. Second, this relationship persisted despite the intervening effects of juvenile referrals and sanctions; intervention by agencies of social control did not have the effect on later criminality for which the programs were designed. We have suggested that intervention and sanctions had a role in increasing seriousness; with few exceptions, this was the case or their influence on later behavior was negligible.

PATH ANALYSIS RESULTS WITHIN COHORT BY SEX

Path analysis results for the 1942 and 1949 Cohort males showed that juvenile seriousness had a statistically significant effect on adult seriousness holding constant juvenile referrals and sanctions, such that the greater the juvenile seriousness, the greater the adult seriousness. Juvenile sanctions and referrals played essentially no role as intervening variables in the model. We also found that receiving more severe sanctions was associated with a greater number of juvenile referrals but that there was no direct effect of juvenile seriousness on sanctions.

The findings of no effect of referrals and sanctions on adult seriousness are important for both criminal justice policy and criminological theory. From a policy point of view they again imply that intervention by agencies of social control had little to do with later police contact careers. From a theoretical point of view they support neither the view that such intervention deterred deviant behavior nor the view that intervention promoted deviant behavior as proposed by labeling theory.

The most important effect on adult seriousness for the 1949 Cohort males was the moderate positive effect of juvenile seriousness. The severity of juvenile sanctions was influenced directly by juvenile referrals and indirectly by juvenile seriousness. The latter variable showed no direct effect on sanctions. Unlike the model for the 1942 Cohort males, however, we found a weak but statistically significant positive relationship between juvenile referrals and adult seriousness; that is, the greater the number of juvenile referrals, the greater the adult seriousness. Overall, this model indicated that there was a moderate degree of continuity in seriousness from the juvenile to the adult period. While seriousness of contacts was only related to severity of sanctions through referrals, seriousness had an important influence on the number of referrals during the juvenile period. Suffice it to say that the analysis for the 1942 and 1949 Cohort females turned up nothing at variance with previous findings for the females.

Path analysis results for the 1955 Cohort males and females showed again that juvenile seriousness had a significant positive influence on adult seriousness. However, this model differed from previous ones for males in that juvenile seriousness had both a direct effect ($p = .377$) on juvenile sanctions and an indirect effect through referrals ($.381 = .952 \times .400$). This suggested that the seriousness of juvenile careers had become a more important factor in determining the severity of juvenile court sanctions. In addition, the direct effects of seriousness and referrals on sanctions were about the same. As with the previous models for both males and females, seriousness was an important determinant of referrals, explaining over 80% of the variance. Differences between the 1942 and 1949 Cohorts and the 1955 Cohort may partly be an artifact of a change in juvenile court procedures.

The path analysis results for the 1955 Cohort females differed from those of the males in several ways which have implications for intervention. First, juvenile seriousness had a rather substantial impact on adult seriousness ($p = .891$) and juvenile referrals were also related to adult seriousness ($p = -.446$). This latter relationship means that a greater number of referrals during the juvenile period was associated with less adult seriousness holding constant juvenile sanctions and seriousness. However, juvenile sanctions were not related to adult seriousness. Second, there was no direct effect of juvenile seriousness on sanctions but, like most of the male models, there was an indirect effect through referrals. This is the only model examined thus far in which intervention by social control agencies had any effect of substance on adult seriousness.

To summarize the path analysis results, we found that the strongest influence on adult seriousness was juvenile seriousness. At the same time, we must remember that most of the variance remained unexplained, as indicated by the high residuals for seriousness after age 17, results which were consistent with the analyses presented in earlier chapters in which a relationship between delinquency and crime was shown to exist but to be insufficient to permit prediction.

SUMMARY AND CONCLUSION

The first set of analyses described in this chapter indicated that severe sanctions, all other things being roughly equal, have not been followed by a decline in the accumulation of police contacts and high seriousness scores. The extent to which continued police contacts were a response to sanctions and not simply an extension of a pattern of behavior (in spite of the efforts of persons in positions of authority who know the records of juveniles and who exercise their best judgment) was not determined. To the extent that some decline was found following the application of sanctions, the decline may be a part of the general attrition in contacts also found among persons who had not been sanctioned.

We have also found that, step by step, the process of continuation worked to place a disproportional number of inner city Blacks in institutions before the age of 18 and to continue to place them in institutions after that age. As the data indicated, this was a function of the interaction of place of socialization, race/ethnicity, response to intervention, and, even more specifically, to severity of sanctions including institutionalization.

The multi-stage analyses which were conducted supported preliminary conclusions even further, revealing that the unplanned effects of sanctions were strongest in the period immediately following them but that even during the ages 16 and 17, when most frequently applied, had little or no effect or the opposite of that desired in terms of deterring juveniles from continuing contacts with the police as older juveniles or adults.

In the final section of this chapter, multivariate techniques were utilized to determine more precisely how the continuity between the seriousness of juvenile and adult police contact careers was influenced by the intervening variables (number of police referrals and the severity of sanctions during the juvenile period). These multivariate techniques enabled us to reaffirm some of the conclusions which were reached earlier but which were held more tentatively because the analytic technique did not permit us to say, "all other things being equal." At this point we may say that earlier indications about the ineffectiveness of referrals and sanctions as procedures for changing behavior for the better prevailed. Overall, however, neither referrals nor sanctions had an impact on later seriousness comparable to that of juvenile seriousness.

NOTES

1. The initial sanctions coding included all possible categories (sentence suspended, commuted, etc., 20 categories of fines, 11 categories for time in institutions, etc.) which were then combined within each type of category on a basis of degrees of penalties imposed. This process resulted in 21 code categories with

variation in severity of sanctions within major categories. With the data collapsed and the penalty groups rank-ordered, the data were converted to a Dispositions Type Geometric Score by assigning a code of 1 to a single dismissal, 2 to 2–3 dismissals, 4 to 4–5 dismissals, through 1,048,576 for 1 or more years of institutionalization.

Having established this scale, we next constructed an abbreviated version by collapsing categories into basic types of dispositions with no indication of degree within categories and assigning a Geometric score as follows:

1 Dismissals
2 Juvenile controls (supervision and custody transfer)
4 Probation (including suspended sentence)
8 Fines (including forfeit of bail)
16 Driver license suspension/revocation
32 Incarceration (jail, reformatory, prison).

These Geometric scores could range from 1 to 63 for any period of time. Each person's new Dispositions Type Geometric Score was then recoded, age-by-age, according to this scoring system.

While Geometric scores may be utilized in generating tables for analysis by nominal statistical techniques, they should not be used in correlational analyses without the employment of some transformation technique.

2. Some believe that the court deals too harshly with youth, others are concerned because the "punishment" does not fit the "crime" and still others are aggrieved because the circumstances are not given sufficient consideration. David F. Greenberg refers to the Lipton, Martinson, and Wilks survey by saying that, "The blanket assertion that 'nothing works' is an exaggeration, but not by very much." David F. Greenberg (ed.), *Corrections and Punishment*, Beverly Hills: Sage Publications, 1978, Chapter 5, p. 141.

3. A discussion of this may be found in Lyle W. Shannon, "Assessing the Relationship of Adult Criminal Careers to Juvenile Careers," in Clark C. Abt (ed.), *Problems in American Social Policy Research* (Cambridge: Abt Books, 1980): 232–244.

4. The figure that may be used for comparison with other juvenile courts from counties of 50,000 population or over is the percent of those referred who had also been incarcerated, i.e., the overall commitment rate. This average rate for 253 juvenile courts in the United States in a 1974 survey was 5%. This rate for Racine was 8.6% for the 1942 Cohort, 6.5% for the 1949 Cohort, and 7.2% for the 1955 Cohort (that cohort whose historical position was most comparable). See Michael Sosin, *Juvenile Court Commitment Rates: The National Picture*. A Discussion Paper of the Institute for Research on Poverty, University of Wisconsin, Madison, DP#550-79, 1979.

5. Greenberg, et al., contend that studies of crime rates which have appeared over the last decade and which have been interpreted as supportive of the deterrence

position are really not. See David F. Greenberg, Ronald C. Kessler, and Charles H. Logan, "A Panel Model of Crime Rates and Arrest Rates," *American Sociological Review*, Vol. 44, 1979, pp. 843–850.

6. This analysis has been abridged from a lengthy report, "A Multivariate Analysis of the Relationships of Seriousness of Juvenile Careers and Intervention to Adult Seriousness," by James P. Curry, Ph.D., an Assistant Research Scientist in the Iowa Urban Community Research Center at the time of writing.

7. Very few studies have been designed in such a fashion to give a definitive answer to the consequences of incarceration (institutionalization for juveniles), although those who have attempted to introduce appropriate controls conclude that incarceration does not work. For one of the more definitive studies, see Andrew Hopkins, "Imprisonment and Recidivism: A Quasi-Experimental Study," *Journal of Research in Crime and Delinquency*, Vol. 13, 1976, pp. 13–32. Hopkins concludes that incarceration may actually be worse than noninstitutional treatment.

Chapter 14

INTERVIEWING PERSONS IN THE 1942 AND 1949 COHORTS

THE SEARCH AND INTERVIEWING PROCESS

So far only brief mention of the search and interviewing phases of this research has been made. Although we had obtained the most recent addresses of 3,451 persons (or their parents) in the 1942 and 1949 Cohorts from Racine City Directories and Racine area telephone books, we were aware that not everyone would still be at that address when interviewing commenced on June 1, 1976. We were also aware that time in the community from age 6 to the present should be verified for those whom we had been unable to follow through 1975.

Community contact workers, all lifetime residents in the community, were employed to telephone the parents of those Whites whom we had not been able to locate. Since we would attempt to interview all Blacks and Chicanos, the minority group interviewers utilized numerous sources of information (clubs, associations, churches, neighbors, and relatives) to determine the whereabouts of those who were not at the addresses we had in our records. The search for missing Whites commenced while the interviewer training course was in progress but the search for missing minorities did not commence until interviewing had begun.[1]

Prior to the week-long course in interviewer training, other members of the Iowa City staff and those added to the Racine staff had searched a cross-index of married and maiden names in the Racine City Health Department for the married names of females whom we had been unable to locate.[2] This, of course, generated an additional records check in the Police Department in order to complete the police contact records of females.

Interviewers were assigned respondents of their same race/ethnicity and sex. The White interviewers usually found respondents where our records indicated but, if not there, addresses were usually obtained by our community contact workers. Two Black interviewers spent a major portion of their time locating those Blacks who had frequent moves or name changes. They found that, contrary to our experience with older Blacks in previous research, the rate of out-migration of younger Blacks to other states had been very high. Most difficult of all were the Chicanos; they had left the community or moved more than had either of the other groups.

As each interview was returned to the office in Racine, pertinent items were checked against the data in our files on the respondents. This validity check turned up some cases of the wrong person being interviewed (the correct person was located and interviewed) and some cases of inadequate probing by the interviewers. Each interview was read for quality and if interviewers had not obtained responses to the questions but instead had obtained irrelevant comments, they were asked to return (or someone else returned) in an effort to obtain relevant responses.

There were some refusals and some cases where the respondent had left the community. The rule for Whites was to substitute the next person of the same sex on the list. The cohort lists were not in complete alphabetical order, but were in segmented alphabetical order. Statisticians in the department concluded that no systematic bias would be introduced by substitution. It should be noted that a first refusal was not accepted as final. Another interviewer was sent. Interviewers sometimes suggested that an opposite sex interviewer would have better success in establishing rapport with the respondent and, while the intent was to always utilize same sex | race/ethnic interviewers, in some cases, different sex | race/ethnic interviewers were more effective.

The first 180 interviews were read by Center staff to ascertain the range of responses to open-ended questions. Preliminary code categories were developed from these responses. Five members of the staff coded each of the same 20 schedules to determine if responses could be coded with reliability. As expected, it was necessary to clarify and/or collapse some codes before final coding. As schedules were returned from Racine they were coded and check-coded in Iowa City.

The original goal was to interview all of the minority members and 25% of the White members of each cohort. Table 1 tells the story of the interviewing experience from sample selection to the final count interviewed. The percentage of Blacks and Chicanos interviewed from among those available exceeded 50%. This is not what had been originally hoped for but more than believed possible when interviewing such highly mobile young people commenced.

TABLE 1. INTERVIEW STATUS OF 1942 AND 1949 COHORTS

	1942 Cohort							1949 Cohort						
	White		Black		Chicano		Total	White		Black		Chicano		Total
	M	F	M	F	M	F		M	F	M	F	M	F	
Originally Selected or as Substituted														
Interviewed	145	158	10	10	2	8	333	230	229	32	28	17	20	556
Out of Area	97	109	8	4	2	4	224	106	191	17	15	9	5	343
Never Located	61	82	4	3	2	3	155	91	156	10	3	5	2	267
Never Home	17	16	4	1	0	0	38	26	21	4	5	0	0	56
Handicapped, Retarded	1	0	0	0	0	0	1	3	1	2	2	0	0	8
Deceased	7	1	2	0	1	0	11	7	2	1	0	1	0	11
Refused	42	26	3	2	2	0	75	26	46	6	5	1	1	85
Invalid Interview	0	0	0	0	0	0	0	0	0	2	1	0	0	3
Not Selected														
Available	151	127	0	0	0	0	278	333	170	0	0	0	0	503
Out of Area	66	63	0	0	0	0	129	84	57	0	0	0	0	141
Never Located	68	54	0	0	0	0	102	62	58	0	0	0	0	120
Deceased	4	2	0	0	0	0	6	6	0	0	0	0	0	6
Total in Cohort	639	638	31	20	9	15	1352	974	931	74	59	33	28	2099

185

REPRESENTATIVENESS OF PERSONS INTERVIEWED

Since we did not achieve the goal of interviewing all Blacks and Chicanos in the two cohorts or 25% of the Whites without substitution, there was a question of how representative those interviewed were of their segments of the two cohorts. The distributions of the total cohorts and those interviewed were compared in a variety of ways in order to determine if significant differences existed on major characteristics of the interview sample and the cohort.

There was not a single significant difference (.05 level), between those interviewed and those with continuous residence in either cohort among the males or females in number of police contacts for the 6 through 13 age period, the 14 through 17 period, the combined 6 through 17 period, the 18 through 20 period, the 21 and over period, or for total careers. There were also no significant differences in reasons for police contact between those interviewed and persons in the cohort with continuous residence.

We further checked the possibility of significant differences between those interviewed and those who had always lived in Racine on type-seriousness of first contact in each age period, who the complainant was, the number of persons involved in the incident, and whether or not the contact had been referred. There were no statistically significant differences for either sex in either cohort. In another test, those who had been interviewed (males and females from both cohorts) were distributed according to their natural area of residence in Racine, in immediately outlying areas, or in communities adjacent to Racine, including Milwaukee and Kenosha, and were compared to persons in the cohort who were located in 1976 by their place of residence. There were no significant differences at the .05 level.

There was also concern about whether those who were interviewed did or did not have police contact records similar to those who were not interviewed. Perusal of the mean seriousness scores for persons interviewed and not interviewed, for those with contacts, and for the entire cohort revealed little difference in mean seriousness scores for Whites in either cohort, age period by age period. The differences did, however, build up for total careers for the White males from both cohorts so that, for the total, those who were *not* interviewed did have somewhat more serious scores than did those who were interviewed.

Differences between interviewed and not interviewed 1949 Chicano males were quite marked, suggesting that even with the relatively small numbers involved we cannot consider the 1949 Chicano males interviewed to be representative of Chicano males in the cohort (this is not a real problem as far as the overall objectives of the study are concerned, however, since they made up a small proportion of those who were interviewed). Similarly, Black males from the 1942 Cohort who were *not* interviewed had higher seriousness scores than those who were interviewed. Most differences between the 1949 Blacks were in the opposite direction, with those who were interviewed having higher mean seriousness scores than those who were not. Therefore, the Black males interviewed from the 1942 Cohort, the Chicano males from the 1949 Cohort, and the Black females from the 1949 Cohort were less than representative of their race/ethnic|sex group. The total of those interviewed from both cohorts, however, had essentially the same seriousness scores as those who were not interviewed.

We shall next present some of the more basic data obtained from interviews and, at the same time, examine the relationships of those variables to the measures of delinquency obtained from police records. While not all of these variables are antecedent to police contacts that might have taken place in early or late teens, some are and would (if not already known to officers in the juvenile bureau of a police department) have been readily ascertainable in the course of an officer's discussion with the juvenile at the time of contact or during an interview if the juvenile had been taken into custody. Many of the variables could have been utilized by well trained police officers in making a decision to intervene or not to intervene, or to observe the development of the juvenile's career with the possibility of intervening if behavior continued in a given direction. Furthermore, these data establish what might be called the "normalcy" of the cohort of residents of an urban-industrial city with a mix of race/ethnic groups that did not include minority group persons in such disproportionate numbers as do our largest metropolitan areas.

EDUCATION AND POLICE CONTACTS

Much has been written about delinquency and dropouts and the relationship between them has turned out to be less direct than expected. Voss and Elliott determined that juveniles may actually have less police involvement after leaving school than before, depending on their reasons for leaving.[3] This, too, seemed to be the case in Racine for some subgroups with controls for sex and attitude toward school, but the findings were by no means consistent within or between cohorts.

Persons who did not graduate because they were expelled had stronger negative attitudes toward school and disproportionate numbers of those who had negative attitudes failed to graduate. The combination of negative attitudes toward school and being expelled combined to generate higher 18 and after seriousness scores for the males in the 1949 Cohort than for any other group.

Interpreting these complex data was not easy, but they definitely suggested that the seriousness scores of persons in the 1942 Cohort who had a negative attitude toward school did not increase after they left school, while they did for those who professed a more positive attitude. The findings for the 1949 Cohort revealed fewer differences in police records that suggested departure from school as departure from a troublesome situation. On balance, a positive attitude toward school and receiving a diploma, i.e., high school graduation, were associated with lower seriousness scores during and after high school ages, particularly if it can be assumed that respondents from the 1949 Cohort had better memories of events than those from the 1942 Cohort.[4]

OCCUPATION AND REGULARITY OF EMPLOYMENT OF PARENTS AND POLICE CONTACTS OF RESPONDENTS

Rates of juvenile delinquency and crime, as we have previously stated, showed considerable variation in Racine by place of socialization and by place of residence as indicators of the SES of the milieu in which these behaviors were generated.

The findings were not as clear at the individual level. There was practically no linear relationship between occupational level of the head of the household in a respondent's family and the number of contacts the respondent had had with the police. However, when occupational levels were dichotomized (highest three occupational levels vs. others or highest four occupational levels vs. others) and the average number of police contacts calculated, those with parents in either of the lower occupational level groups had higher mean numbers of contacts. White males during ages 6 through 17 in the 1942 Cohort had a mean of 2.0 contacts if their families were in the top four levels and 2.5 if they were in the bottom four levels; for the 1949 Cohort it is 2.0 vs. 3.0. With the exception of the Black males in both cohorts where the means were .7 vs. 4.0 (1942) and 3.4 vs. 5.6 (1949), other race/ethnic|sex differences were less or nonexistent. For ages 18 through 20 there was practically no difference between the Whites but there was for the Blacks.

We next turned to regularity of employment of the head of the household and its relationship to the child's police contacts. Regularity of employment was coded: "Yes, all the time," "Employed during age 6 through 13," "Employed during age 14 through 17," and "Never regularly employed." Although there were no significant relationships between number of police contacts or seriousness scores and regularity of employment, no matter how the data were manipulated for any race/ethnic|sex or age period group of either cohort, those who came from families where the head was not regularly employed did have delinquency score distributions that were either skewed toward the high end of the scale or were less skewed toward the lower end than scores of those where the head was always regularly employed.

EARLY EMPLOYMENT OF RESPONDENTS AND THEIR POLICE CONTACT RECORDS

Although the value of work for youth has been widely accepted and much has been said about how work builds citizenship, the relationship of work to delinquency is not straightforward. Responses to a series of questions on work while in high school were divided into four categories: (1) no work, (2) work during the summer only, (3) work during the school year, and (4) work all year round. Multiple regression analyses were conducted including relevant variables such as SES of area of socialization, race/ethnicity, head of household's employment, and at least a dozen other variables, but significant direct effects of high school employment in reducing either official or self-report seriousness were found for only the 1942 males' official seriousness scores during the ages 6 through 17. Although half of the effects suggested that employment during junior high and high school produced higher seriousness scores, we concluded there were no significant differences in seriousness directly related to employment during high school.

One other way to approach the supposedly deterrent effect of gainful employment at an early age was to determine the relationship of age at first full-time job to number of recorded police contacts at each age period. Those males who began working full-time prior to age 18 had significantly more contacts during that period than did those who began working at or after their 18th year. Does this mean that early entry into full-time work led to early delinquency because the nature of some work made one more likely to have police contacts or was it a function of the fact that those who commenced working full time at an early age were from the lower SES groups? Is it perhaps because employment provided the funds for liquor, drugs, automobiles, and other kinds of activities that led to police contacts?

When police contacts and age at the first full-time job for the age period 18 through 20 were considered, the pattern was similar to that for the previous period but the relationship was not quite as strong. This suggested that the economic factor (as it influenced the decision to enter the work force at an early age) was probably not as much a determinant of the number of police contacts young males had who had entered the labor force during the 18 through 20 age period as it was for young males who entered even earlier. Further decline in this relationship was noted when contacts at 21 and older were arrayed by age of first full-time work. There was a tendency for females whose first full-time jobs came at the ages of 18 through 20 to have more contacts than those who entered the labor force prior to 18, followed, of course, by those who commenced working full time at 21 and older. This raised the question of how commencing to work full-time at the ages of 18 through 20 for females might lead to more police contacts as adults than other entry ages.

We next examined the data age by age, controlled for years of exposure

before and after the first full-time job, and compared number and seriousness of contacts before and after age at first full-time job. Although this
reduced the number of years for which valid comparisons could be made
for the 1942 Cohort, the results were more definitive. There were significant
differences between the average number of police contacts and seriousness
scores before and after full-time employment among those who commenced
work at almost any age. The ratio was two to one (two contacts after the
first full-time job for each contact before) for the males from both cohorts.
Although it was two to one for females in the 1942 Cohort, it was close to
four to one for the 1949 Cohort. How these ratios varied by age of first
full-time employment was our concern.

There were only sufficient persons with a first full-time job for analysis
at ages 17 through 29 for the 1942 Cohort and 16 through 22 for the 1949
Cohort. If first full-time employment of males occurred at the age of 17,
their number of contacts and seriousness scores were greater after employment by a ratio of 3.5 to 1 and 5.2 to 1. There was less difference or
the opposite relationship for those who commenced work at a later age,
the ratios being below or only slightly above the mean. For females, early
first full-time jobs did not generate higher police contact rates but the before
and after ratios for females who first worked at age 20 were similar to the
early age at employment ratios for men.

While it is impossible to say how much the difference in police contacts
among those who commenced work early could be attributed to a different
kind of exposure as a result of employment or to the lower SES of those
who entered work early, the fact remains that those males who did commence work early were not prevented from having a disproportionate share
of police contacts and higher seriousness scores in the years to follow. There
was also the possibility that commitment to work detracted from commitment to school, as suggested by reasons given for leaving school before
graduation.

Family Type, Marital Status, and Police Contacts

Each family was coded into one of 20 different family types depending
on whether or not both parents were present in the household during the
period 6 through 17 or if the family consisted of some combination of the
parents, step-parents, grandparents, etc. Less than 10% of those who were
interviewed from either cohort were in the categories describing some family
type other than both parents present for the age period 6 through 17, although about half of the Blacks in the 1942 Cohort and one-third of the
Blacks in the 1949 Cohort were in categories in which both parents were
not present throughout the entire period.[5]

When the distributions of police contacts were dichotomized (no contacts vs. one or more), those from homes with both parents present for the age period 6 through 17 did have a greater (but not statistically significant) percentage without contacts (from 8% for the 1949 Cohort's females to 21% for the 1942 Cohort's males) than did those who came from families where both parents were not present the entire time. There were also correlations between number of contacts and seriousness scores and family status for males and females of each cohort but all were small (.124 was the highest).

We concluded that there was some relationship between family type, seriousness, and patterns of delinquency for young males but that it was not as strong as the literature suggested, probably because most of the studies had been based on cases referred to the juvenile court, and there is a tendency to refer when both parents are not present in the home.

Although no family type has been found which was an efficient predictor of police contacts or seriousness of careers at any age period, there remained a possibility that respondent's marital status might be related to one or the other of these measures. The same analytic approach was applied that was utilized with age of first full-time employment (determining the number of contacts and seriousness scores for respondents before and after marriage by age of marriage). Whether the marriage was very early or later in life presumably had some influence on the nature of the impact this change in status had on number of contacts afterwards. The impact of age of marriage was, of course, related to a number of other variables, such as employment status.

With the exception of the age of 19 for the 1942 Cohort males, there was no age of marriage that was followed by a marked increase in the average number or seriousness of contacts with the police. By contrast, marriage at either 18 or 21 was followed by a disproportionate increase in number and seriousness of police contacts for females from the 1942 Cohort, while the ages of 17 and 21 produced the most disproportionate increase for those from the 1949 Cohort. We have no theoretical explanation for those sex differences but it was apparent that differences existed in before and after number of contacts and seriousness and that they were patterned by age of marriage.

One remaining and closely related variable must be given consideration, and that is age at which the respondent reported moving away from home. There are conflicting propositions which would suggest differences in police contact records before and after the event, one hypothesizing an increase in police contacts without parental restraints and the other suggesting a decline as a consequence of removal from a conflict situation and the assumption of adult roles. Still another viewpoint would hypothesize that the nature of the conflict situation determines whether moving away from home increases or decreases involvement with the police. The immediate problems faced by the juvenile may be in themselves generative of certain types of police contacts.

Surprisingly enough, the average number of police contacts actually decreased after respondents reported moving away from home but seriousness scores increased for males in the 1942 Cohort. Both increased for males from the 1949 Cohort. Leaving home at the age of 18 seems to have resulted in a marked increase in police contacts and seriousness for those males from the 1942 Cohort and a somewhat lesser increase, but still an increase, for those who left at 17 and 19. The 1949 Cohort males did not produce such a straightforward pattern but leaving home at age 20 seemed to produce the greatest future difference in number and seriousness of police contacts.

There was some indication of a decline in the ratio of before and after number of contacts and seriousness with age at which they left home but it was not consistent for the females of either cohort. Again, while the overall ratio of before and after contacts and seriousness differed from that of the males in the 1942 Cohort, these ratios were similar for the 1949 Cohort. For whatever reason, however, moving away from home at an early age was followed by higher average yearly rates for the females than for the males from both cohorts.

SUMMARY

It was apparent that reason for not obtaining a high school diploma and attitudes toward school were related in a complicated fashion to number and seriousness of police contacts that respondents acquired at the age of 18 and older. For males, a negative attitude toward school and some reasons for leaving school may have combined to produce lower seriousness scores after leaving school.

Those who came from families where the head was not regularly employed did have delinquency score distributions that were either skewed toward the high end of the scale or less skewed toward the lower end than were those where the head was always regularly employed. Although those who worked during both the summer and school year during the years in which most persons would have been in junior high and high school, particularly males, had more police contacts and higher seriousness scores than did others, significant effects were not consistent in the multiple regression analyses. When police contacts before and after age of males' first full-time job were compared, very significant differences were found between the number of police contacts and seriousness scores before and after full-time employment among those who commenced work at an early age, particularly if first full-time employment was at the age of 16 or 17. While contact rates and seriousness scores were higher after first full-time employment than before for females in both cohorts, neither showed an effect of early employment such as that found for males, regardless of age at which they took their first full-time job.

Male respondents who had married at the age of 19 had, on the average, more contacts and contacts of greater seriousness in the years after marriage than did respondents who were married at the ages of 20 to 24. Early marriage seemed to be associated with more frequent and more serious contacts for females but the picture was not clear because a high ratio of average contacts after marriage to the average for years previous to marriage was found for both cohorts at the ages of 18 and 21.

Moving away from home at an early age had a definite impact on the police contact records of males from the 1942 Cohort and a less clear impact on the 1949 Cohort. In both cohorts, moving away from home at a relatively early age seemed to have more impact on police contacts and seriousness scores for the females than for the males.

Notes

1. The Gateway Technical Institute supplied us with an excellent suite of offices without charge. The cooperation of Keith W. Stoehr, District Director of the Institute, Milton C. Millery, Assistant Director, Ralph Troeller, Coordinator of Instructional Services, Tom Bishop, and many others at Gateway facilitated the task of finding interviewers and housing the project. The staff of the Racine Environment Committee was also helpful in securing interviewers. James McKeown (deceased) of the Department of Sociology at the University of Wisconsin-Parkside was particularly helpful to us in finding interviewers.

2. A very large debt is owed to Gabriel P. Ferrazzano, Commissioner of Health, Racine City Health Department, for without his files it would have been impossible to follow such a large proportion of the females under their married names.

3. Delbert S. Elliott and Harwin L. Voss, *Delinquency and Dropout* (Lexington: D.C. Heath and Co., Lexington Books, 1974) and an earlier report by Elliott, "Delinquency, School Attendance and Dropout," *Social Problems* 13 (1966): 307–314, are not alone in their concern about the role of the school in delinquency. We have also previously referred to Kenneth Polk and Walter E. Schafer (eds.), *Schools and Delinquency* (Englewood Cliffs: Prentice-Hall, 1972). There has also been extensive literature on the relationship of school performance to delinquency; see Chapter 9, LaMar T. Empey, *American Delinquency: Its Meaning and Construction* (Homewood: The Dorsey Press, 1978) for an excellent discussion. As he states, the relationship between school performance and delinquency has been established but the question is how it is to be interpreted.

4. The literature on school attendance and attachment to teachers and school suggests that academic success and a positive attitude toward teachers and school are associated with low delinquency rates while in school. See, for example, Gary F. Jensen, "Race, Achievement and Delinquency: A Further Look at Delinquency in a Birth Cohort," *American Journal of Sociology* 82 (1976): 379–387. Also see Chapter 7, "Contexts for Adolescent Socialization: Family, School, and

Adolescent Society," Gary F. Jensen and Dean G. Rojek, *Delinquency: A Sociological View* (Lexington: D.C. Heath, 1980). Jensen and Rojek, in summarizing the literature, conclude that variables related to high in-school delinquency are not predictive of continued delinquency after leaving school. It is very possible that Tittle, Villemez, and Smith have made a major point in noting that social class may have been more important in earlier years than at present. Just as we have shown that differences between males and females were declining, so may socioeconomic status differences in rates. See Charles R. Tittle, Wayne J. Villemez, and Douglas A. Smith, "The Myth of Social Class and Criminality," *American Sociological Review* 43 (1978): 643–656. But there is again a question of whether behavior has changed or is a matter of converging rates because the police are more even-handed in record keeping and referrals.

5.   Although there has been a lengthy literature on the relationship of family type and family interaction to juvenile delinquency with inconsistent findings, one obtains the impression that those with a positive finding (broken or disrupted homes associated with delinquency) are more frequently cited. Roland J. Chilton and Gerald E. Markle, "Family Disruption, Delinquent Conduct and the Effect of Subclassification," *American Sociological Review* 37 (1972): 93–99, find differences in referral rates based on family status. For an example of negative findings, see Robert E. Dentler and Lawrence J. Monroe, "Social Correlates of Early Adolescent Theft," *American Sociological Review* 26 (1961): 733–743. Jensen and Rojek, op. cit., refer as well to the self-fulfilling prophesy nature of the system.

Chapter 15

A RETROSPECTIVE DESCRIPTION OF HOW JUVENILES PERCEIVED THEIR JUVENILE (MIS)BEHAVIOR

WHAT ADULTS REPORTED ABOUT THEMSELVES AS JUVENILES

We have shown that very few juveniles continued to have police contacts after they became 18 and that attrition was very rapid after that age, with only a small percentage of each cohort continuing to have contacts throughout the period covered by this study. How a sample of cohort members perceived their juvenile misbehavior which resulted in police contacts and how they perceived their juvenile misbehavior that did not result in police contacts (even with allowance for selective reporting) revealed why we should not have expected a large proportion of them to continue their misbehavior beyond the late teens.

Before Age-18 Misbehavior That Resulted in Police Contacts

Over half of each cohort (53.2% of the 1942 Cohort and 59.6% of the 1949 Cohort) stated that they had been stopped by the police before the age of 18 for doing something wrong or something the police suspected was wrong, but only 37.5% and 48.0% had ever had their contacts recorded by the police. About 45% of those who reported being stopped by the police of each cohort had had only one incident of this nature and almost 70% had reported being stopped only once or twice before the age of 18. Nearly 60% of each cohort indicated that their contact(s) with the police had taken place around the age of 16 or 17. So, just as our official data have shown, relatively few began to have contacts with the police at an early age and most police contacts took place around the age of 16 or 17.

TABLE 1.   REASON FOR WHICH RESPONDENTS WERE STOPPED BY POLICE BEFORE AGE 18,
            ACCORDING TO RESPONDENTS AND ACCORDING TO WHAT RESPONDENTS REPORTED
            THE POLICE SAID

| | Percent of Total Incidents Described by Respondents* | | | |
| | 1942 | | 1949 | |
	Police Statements	Respondent Statements	Police Statements	Respondent Statements
Traffic Offense	43.0	31.1	37.5	25.5
Disorderly Conduct	16.3	13.3	16.9	13.3
Liquor Violation	5.9	8.9	6.4	8.9
Theft	5.6	6.3	7.7	6.0
Incorrigible, Runaway	5.6	6.3	11.8	9.9
Sex Offense	1.1	5.2	1.1	6.0
Vagrancy	7.8	4.4	7.1	5.3
Truancy	.7	1.5	.6	.4
Auto Theft	1.1	1.1	.9	1.7
Burglary	1.5	.7	2.4	1.3
Robbery	.4	.4	.0	.2
Violent Prop. Destruction	.7	.4	.2	.0
Assault	.0	.0	.2	.4
Drugs	.0	.0	.2	.0
Forgery, Fraud	.0	.0	1.0	.6
Weapons	.0	.0	.6	.4
Unintentional or Mischievous Behavior		20.4		18.6
Suspicion, Investigation	10.4		5.4	
	100.1	100.0	100.0	100.0

                         N = 270   N = 533

* "How many times before you were 18 did the police stop you for doing something
wrong or something that they suspected was wrong? (1942 N = 333; 1949 N = 556)

"Tell me about the ones you remember best." "According to the police, what were
you doing that attracted their attention?" "What were you (respondent) really
doing?"

What the police said the juveniles were doing, according to respondents, differed somewhat from what the respondents said they were actually doing, but in both cases more of the contacts centered around an alleged Traffic offense than any other reason (see Table 1). Between 16% and 17% of the contacts were reportedly perceived by the police as involving Disorderly Conduct on the part of the juveniles, with the juveniles agreeing with this to a somewhat lesser extent. In approximately 20% of the cases the juveniles saw their misbehavior as unintentional or as simply mischievous and did not consider what the police said to be correct. Even as the police saw it, only a small percentage of the contacts involved what would be considered a felony if the respondents had been adult, 4.9% of the 1949's contacts and 6.2% of the 1942's contacts.

Misbehavior Before Age-18 Which Did Not Result in Police Contact

Another line of questioning dealt with misbehavior before the age of 18 which did not result in being caught by the police. Over 66.4% and

69.6% of the two cohorts stated that they had done things before they were 18 for which they could have been caught by the police. When asked what things they had done, Liquor violations headed the list (31.5% for the 1942 Cohort and 38.9% for the 1949 Cohort), followed by Theft (24.8% and 20.1%) and Disorderly Conduct (12.2% and 11.8%). In contrast, Liquor violations constituted only 5.9% and 6.4% of the offenses for which they admitted being stopped. Theft constituted only 5.6% and 7.7% of the offenses for which they said they had been stopped. Relatively few admitted Traffic offenses for which they were not caught (10.0% and 5.4%) but 43.0% and 37.5% said that they had been stopped for Traffic offenses. The contrastingly higher proportion of police contacts for Traffic or alleged Traffic violations suggested that Traffic offenses were either more visible or that (as recorded police policy suggested) more effort was directed toward moving vehicles than toward other categories of potential delinquency, while Liquor violations were either relatively less visible or there was comparatively less concern about enforcement of liquor laws.

Only between 10% and 15% of the offenses described by cohort members would have been considered serious misdemeanors or felonies if committed by an adult. We must remember that these offenses were committed by that two-thirds who said that they had done things for which they could have been caught but were not. If their responses are accepted as complete, only a relatively small proportion of each cohort had engaged in serious misbehavior for which they were not apprehended.

Cohort members admitted offenses involving Drugs, Forgery, Fraud, and Weapons for which they were not caught (5.1% and 9.6%) disproportionately to their mention of offenses for which they had been caught (.0 and 1.8%). The wide range of juvenile misbehavior, detected and undetected, which was reported (in a range comparable to the range found for the cohort in official police records) inclined us to accept their responses to both questions as representative of the misbehavior of persons in the 1942 and 1949 Cohorts.

The Fullness of Participation

When those persons from each cohort who were stopped by the police or who had engaged in undetected misbehavior (by their own accounts) were combined, they added up to well over 90% participation in youthful misbehavior of one type or another for the males and 65% to 70% for the females. As Table 2 reveals, female participation increased in the 1949 Cohort over that of the 1942 Cohort by more than 15%.

Remember that whether official or self-report data were utilized, Traffic contacts constituted a greater proportion of all juvenile police contacts than any other type of contact.[1] It was not without evidence that we stated that police contacts for moving vehicle and other automobile violations were part and parcel of the larger picture of delinquency and crime. A high pro-

TABLE 2.   PERCENT OF THE 1942 AND 1949 COHORTS INTERVIEWED WHO ADMITTED MISBEHAVIOR
           BEFORE THE AGE OF 18 (DETECTED AND UNDETECTED), BY SEX AND COHORT

	1942			1949		
	M	F	T	M	F	T
Stopped by police and did things	62.3	21.6	40.4	65.3	28.2	46.8
Stopped by police but didn't do things	13.9	11.9	12.8	12.3	13.4	12.8
Not stopped by police but did things	19.2	31.3	25.7	16.2	29.6	22.9
Not stopped and didn't do things	4.6	35.2	21.1	6.1	28.9	17.5
	100.0	100.0	100.0	99.9	100.1	100.0
Either stopped or did things	95.4	64.8	78.9	93.9	71.1	82.5
N =	151	176	327	277	277	554

portion of affirmative responses to the question, "Did you and your friends spend much time driving around in a car just for something to do?" revealed that understanding a large proportion of the trouble that juveniles had with the police might come from recognizing how juveniles acquired contacts of a related nature, contacts that could reasonably stem from leisure-time use of an automobile. Having asked the question in reference to the high school period, it was not difficult to see how leisure-time use of the automobile could have led to police contacts for a variety of reasons at the ages of 16 and 17. In the 1942 Cohort, 50.2% responded "yes" to the driving around question and 16.5% were in the "Some, but not a lot" category, 44.4% and 17.3% in the 1949 Cohort responded accordingly. More Blacks and Chicanos in both cohorts reported that they never had access to an automobile (over 50%) than reported all of the other categories (unlimited, frequent, and casual), while only 29.9% and 24.3% of the Whites reported never having access. Surely race/ethnic differences in types and patterns of delinquency must stem in part from differential access to and use of an automobile.

Responses to the question about time spent driving around produced low positive correlations with the number of police contacts during the juvenile period (none were higher than the 1949 Cohort's males, .176) and the 18 through 20 age period (none were higher than the 1942 Cohort's males, .235); however, the group nature of driving around would tend to lower the correlation because the driver would be most likely to acquire the police contact.

Further investigation turned to age when respondents became licensed drivers. The question was not just whether more police contacts were generated after a license was obtained but whether or not the seriousness of contacts changed and, of course, how all were related to the age at which the license was obtained. For example, those males and females who obtained their licenses at the age of 16 or younger had police contacts and seriousness scores that were significantly greater after than before obtaining the license. There were no significant differences in before and after police contacts among those who received their driver's license between the ages of 17 and 21.

This did not answer the question quite precisely enough so the age-by-age data were pursued even further, with the mean before and after license seriousness scores adjusted for years of risk before obtaining a driver's license and years of risk afterwards, the latter including the year that a driver's license was obtained. This analysis shed little light on the matter other than to reveal that the ratio of average yearly after-license seriousness to prior-to-license seriousness was not greater for younger ages for males in either cohort.

Having detoured a bit, we now return to further examination of what respondents had to say about their police contacts before becoming 18 and what they said about their undetected behavior which could have led to a police encounter but didn't.

How They Happened to Do It

When respondents were asked "Why were you doing this?" over 50% of the incidents described were seen as just for fun, use of unstructured time, unintentional behavior, or they just happened to be there. Responses permitted classifying only about 35% of the behavior as deliberate violations of the law. Even then we must remember that most of these were not very serious violations. Around 40% of the incidents described by respondents were the respondent's own idea but 37.5% of the 1942 Cohort and 31.6% of the 1949 Cohort stated that the incidents were a collective or group idea. Only 16.5% and 25.5% blamed these incidents on somebody else. In fewer than 20% of the incidents the respondent was the only one involved; in about 28% of the incidents two persons were involved; in 13.6% and 16.5% of the incidents three persons were involved. In over 85% of the incidents with others involved, they were people the respondent usually ran around with.

Although respondents indicated that they commenced doing things for which they were not caught somewhat earlier than the things for which they had been caught, about 60% stated that they had started to do these things at the age of 15 or older. Here again when asked, "Why did you do it?" (referring to things for which they had not been caught), 48% of the 1942 Cohort and 40% of the 1949 Cohort stated that they had done it just for fun or to use their unstructured time, even higher percentages than given for the behavior that resulted in police contacts. Peer influences were given as the reason by 27% of the 1942 Cohort and 31% of the 1949 Cohort. Relatively small percentages of each group gave a reason suggesting that there was anything close to what might be considered willful or malicious intent. Over 70% said that they acted with others.

One additional question was asked about why respondents had done things for which they were stopped or could have been stopped. We found that as they looked back and thought about these things, fun and leisure time activity was still the top response (36.9% and 34.0%), followed by peer influence (26.2% and 28.2%) and curiosity or experience (12.9% and 16.0%). While retrospective judgments about behavior may be questioned, most gave responses which indicated that their behavior could be viewed as part of growing up, as a part of the process of learning how one must behave while eager to become an adult but still a juvenile.

In both categories (behavior which had or had not resulted in a police contact) respondents were involved in group activity in 70% to 80% of the incidents reported, further attesting to the position that most juvenile mis-behavior is group activity and fun. The official reports for all cohorts re-vealed essentially the same finding. Police contacts with juveniles showed that through the age of 15 over 70% of the 1942 Cohort's police contacts had involved more than one person, as had 57.0% of the 1949 Cohort's through the age of 14 and 66.3% of the 1955 Cohort's through that age.

What happened when they were caught and what happened when they were not? How much does this tell us about why so few juveniles continued to have police contact after police contact? In the next section we shall go a step further in putting it all together.

THE AWFUL CONSEQUENCES OF GETTING CAUGHT

How the police disposed of these contacts and how the respondents reacted gave us further indication of why most contacts or incidents did not lead to continuity in misbehavior. In over half of the cases the police released the juvenile after counseling (50.4% and 55.0%) and in almost another 20% they released them but notified their parents. In over 17% of the cases the juveniles were taken to the police station but only a third of these cases were referred to the juvenile court or some agency.

The most frequent consequence consisted of revocation of driver's li-censes following an appearance in traffic court (37.1% and 33.3%) or bicycle court (11.4% and 20.3%) or some similar disposition. Less than 15% were even put on probation or under supervision. Only 20% had been sent to a detention home, training school, or jail. In other words, however brief it might have been, 20% did experience some juvenile institutionalization.

Perhaps even more important in understanding why so few continued to get into trouble with the police was their response to the question, "How did you react to the police and what they did?" While 11% of the 1942 Cohort and 18% of the 1949 Cohort stated that they reacted with hostility and rebellion, most stated that they reacted with courtesy, deference, obe-dience, compliance, fear and anxiety, casually, or had no reaction at all.

Obviously the police dealt with juveniles in such a way as to not instill hostility and rebellion in most of them.

This is not to say that there were no differences among juveniles in attitudes toward the police. When asked, "What kind of attitude did you and your two or three closest friends have toward the police when you were in junior high and high school?" (responses were coded as positive, negative, or indifferent), most responses were positive or indifferent with the exception of the 1949 Cohort males where 33% were positive, 39% indifferent, and 28% negative. Although persons with low mean seriousness scores generally had positive attitudes toward the police and those with higher mean seriousness scores had negative attitudes, the correlation of attitudes toward the police and seriousness scores was rather modest, the highest being a tau of .443 for the age period 6 through 17 for males from the 1949 Cohort.

It was difficult to decide if attitude toward the police was predictive of continuity in careers or if continuity developed negative attitudes toward the police. Furthermore, attitudes toward the police during junior high and high school were significantly correlated with police contacts during the 6 through 17 and the 18 through 20 age periods. One might be inclined to surmise that attitudes toward the police during earlier years carried over and were related to the generation of continuing police contacts during the 18 through 20 period, but this is a bit difficult with retrospective data when the two periods in question could be intertwined in the memory of respondents.

Interpretation became even more difficult when the correlations of seriousness scores between the age period 6 through 17 and 18 and older within attitude toward the police categories were examined. Juvenile and adult seriousness scores had a lower relationship among persons with a positive attitude toward police from the 1942 Cohort (.370) than among those from the 1949 Cohort (.599). Persons from the 1942 Cohort with indifferent attitudes toward the police had only modest (.473 and .250) correlations between seriousness scores in the juvenile and adult periods and those from the 1949 Cohort had even lower correlations. The greatest consistency between cohorts was found among those with negative attitudes toward the police; whether they had relatively high or low seriousness scores during the juvenile period, those with positive or negative attitudes toward the police continued to have similar seriousness scores as adults (.775 and .678).

In 77% of the cases nothing happened to the juveniles outside of what the police had done but in about 10% or more of the cases parents took additional action. When we asked them what their parents thought about their behavior, it was quite obvious that those who knew disapproved (43% and 38%). It was also obvious that a large proportion did not tell their parents about the experience (27% and 37%) and that their parents apparently did not learn about it from another source. In very few cases did the parents have an attitude that could be considered supportive of the juvenile.

When we looked at groups and persons whom the juveniles considered important in influencing their lives, we saw that 67% in the 1942 Cohort stated that their parents had a positive influence on them, as did 71% of those in the 1949 Cohort. It was quite evident that relatively few of the parents had attitudes which were contributory to the misbehavior of their children.[2] It was also apparent that relatively few juveniles received any kind of disapproval from their peers, with a sympathetic attitude expressed by them in about 40% of the cases described.

Before leaving this discussion, a word must be said about those who said that they had never done anything that could have resulted in a police contact. We asked this group, predominantly females, "How does it happen that you never did anything that could have attracted the attention of the police?" There were 106 persons in the 1942 Cohort in this group, of whom 50.0% gave a response that was categorized as referring to parental control and, of the 145 persons in the 1949 Cohort in this category, 53.8% did so. Responses indicative of a good self-concept characterized 24.6% and 22.7% of the 1942 and 1949 Cohorts. Only 6.6% referred to social pressure.

When we looked at respondents' total reactions to the contact experience, "What effect did this experience have on your behavior?" only a very small percentage indicated rebellion towards authority (2.2% and 7.3%), while the others stated that it had either no, or very little, effect on their behavior (52.7% and 59.0%), or had a deterrent effect (42.5% and 33.0%). When they were asked, "Why do you think you reacted that way?" or "What people or parts of the experience made you react that way?" very few mentioned a negative reaction to the police and what the police said or did. Aside from the 30% or more who stated that they really hadn't done anything wrong or that the incident was of too minor a nature to have much effect and that everyone does it, the largest group was those who stated that they learned from the experience and that it had a generally deterrent effect. While some of the responses could be interpreted as not indicating that the experience had had much impact on the juvenile, what most of them had done was really not very serious. When the various reactions were lumped together, it could be said that 35% or 40% thought that the experience was generally beneficial in terms of their future behavior. All of this suggested that police monitoring of juveniles had more positive than negative effects.

Only about 20% of those who misbehaved but did not get caught by the police were caught by anyone else; if caught, it was most often someone in their own family or the victim (circa 65%) and the usual reaction was a verbal or physical reprimand (circa 60%).

Eighty percent of the respondents said that they no longer did these things and most of those who stated that they had stopped doing these things said that they did so because they had changed their self-concept, values, reassessed their behavior (60.5% and 52.9%), and/or recognized the responsibilities associated with new life statuses. The decision to cease these behaviors could be attributed to the normal consequences of socialization into adult groups. In fact, the effect of getting caught or the fear of the consequences of getting caught made up less than 15% of these responses. Bolstering the position that misbehavior declined and/or decreased during the process of socialization is the fact that cessation of the behavior took place by the age of 18 for most respondents. This is an appropriate point at which to examine the seriousness scores of the kinds of friends that members of each cohort reported.

DIFFERENTIAL ASSOCIATION AND SERIOUSNESS OF REASONS FOR POLICE CONTACT

Sutherland's differential association hypothesis, tested and retested, cannot really be tested with these data but the findings are consistent with what would be expected. The question, "Did any of your 2 or 3 closest friends get into trouble with the police during the junior high and high school years?" produced significant correlations between friends with trouble vs. no friends with trouble and the number of police contacts at ages 6 through 17 for males and females in both cohorts, males having higher correlations than females, .362 for the 1942 Cohort males and .295 for the 1949 males, .144 and .173 for the females.

A similar question was asked in reference to their adult friends, "How about your closest friends since you have been an adult? Have any of them been in trouble with the police?" There were relatively few who had adult friends who had been in trouble, with the exception of the 1949 males (about 40% of the Black males as compared to 23% of the White males) and it was only with the 1949 males that any significant relationship was found (tau = .326).

If they, as juveniles, had friends in trouble with the police, their mean juvenile and adult seriousness scores were higher than scores for those who did not have friends in trouble. Those with friends in trouble with the police as both juveniles and adults had the highest mean adult seriousness scores in the 1949 Cohort and the second highest mean juvenile seriousness score. This pattern was not as evident in the 1942 Cohort since those who had no adult friends in trouble with the police, although they had had them as juveniles, had higher mean seriousness scores than did their counterparts with adult friends in trouble.

Turning to those who had no friends in trouble with the police as juveniles, we found that those who did have adult friends in trouble with the police had higher mean adult scores than did those who did not have adult friends in trouble with the police. Those who never had friends in trouble with the police had the lowest seriousness scores, first as juveniles and second as adults.

We shall later see how much friends in trouble with the police contributed to the ability to predict who would continue from juvenile delinquency into adult crime. Unfortunately, we were not able to determine whether juvenile misbehavior preceded delinquent associates or delinquent associates preceded serious delinquent and criminal behavior.

One other related associational issue should be considered at this point, and that is the impact of juveniles' perception of patrolling their neighborhood on their police contacts.

The squirrel-cage effect (areas highly patrolled have more police contacts than other areas with resulting statistics increasing the number of police officers in an area with further increases in police contacts) has been frequently considered a factor in explaining the notably higher police contact rates in some areas than in others. If it has merit and if respondents had an accurate perception of the extent to which their neighborhoods were patrolled, there should be a relationship between responses to "When you were in junior high and high school, was your neighborhood heavily, moderately, or lightly patrolled by the police, or not patrolled at all?" and the frequency of police contacts by juveniles at the two earliest age periods. When responses were dichotomized (high and medium vs. low and not patrolled) it could readily be seen that a higher proportion of those from the low or unpatrolled areas had had either no police contacts or very few.

It has not yet been determined, however, if patrolling in fact was greater in areas in which respondents perceived it to be and did increase the number of police contacts or if these were simply the low SES areas in which juvenile misbehavior was perceived by the police to merit more official recognition.

HOW JUVENILES PERCEIVED THEIR FAMILIES, FRIENDS, SCHOOL, AND ADULT FIGURES IN THE LARGER SOCIETY

In another section of the interview, respondents were asked to respond to several groups of people, one at a time, in terms of whether someone in the group was particularly important in influencing them in one direction or another in terms of their decisions, attitudes, and/or behavior. While coding a question of this nature presented some difficulties, Table 3 indicates the extensiveness of positive and negative influences of each of the groups mentioned. As indicated, over two-thirds of each cohort said that their parents had a positive influence on their lives, followed by siblings, entire family, and in almost 40% of the cases, by teachers at school. About 25%

TABLE 3.   INFLUENCES ON LIVES OF PERSONS INTERVIEWED

"I'm going to name several groups of people, one at a time. If the group or someone in
the group was particularly important in influencing you in one direction or another in
terms of your decisions, attitudes, and/or behavior, we would like to know what
happened and how old you were."

	1942 Cohort Percent*				1949 Cohort Percent			
	Posi-tive	None	Pos. from Neg.	Nega-tive	Posi-tive	None	Pos. from Neg.	Nega-tive
Brothers, sisters	19.5	48.9	4.2	2.4	28.2	42.4	3.2	2.0
Parents	67.0	8.4	1.8	3.6	70.7	4.7	2.0	5.4
Entire family	27.6	38.4	1.5	.9	23.8	46.2	1.3	1.1
Students at school	21.9	42.6	1.2	6.0	20.3	41.4	2.2	10.6
Teachers at school	38.1	25.8	.0	3.3	39.2	28.8	.0	3.8
Police	8.9	37.5	.0	2.1	7.4	39.7	.0	3.4
Judges, probation officers, etc.	4.5	14.1	.0	1.2	2.5	12.4	.0	.9
Landlords	2.7	17.1	.0	1.2	1.4	16.0	.0	3.2
Employers or supervisors	24.6	35.4	.0	4.5	26.6	35.3	.0	6.3

"Is there any person or group we left off this list whose influences you think we
should know about?"

Grandparents	10.2	.0	.3	.3	7.7	.0	.0	.0
Spouse, boy/girl friend	17.1	.0	.0	1.2	8.5	.0	.0	.4
Religious figures	13.5	.0	.0	.3	11.2	.0	.0	.4
Friends	2.4	.0	.6	.6	3.4	.0	.2	.0
Military figures	4.2	.0	.0	.0	5.8	.0	.2	.5

* Percents do not add across to 100% because some groups were inapplicable for some
respondents, e.g., no siblings, some were not mentioned in any way by respondents, and
some stated that influence was both positive and negative.

of each cohort even stated that their employers or supervisors had had a
positive influence on their lives. In terms of a negative influence, only 7%
of the 1942 Cohort and less than 11% of the 1949 Cohort stated that students
at school had had a negative impact on their lives. This was followed in
both cases by the mention of negative impacts from employers. All other
groups had smaller negative influences.

SUMMARY

Responses obtained from the lines of questioning described in this
chapter made it clear that the process of socialization into adult roles works
for most juveniles.[3] While a large percentage of each group had contacts
with the police before age 18 and an even larger percentage admitted being
engaged in behavior for which they could have had police contacts, most
ceased these behaviors by the time they became 18. The impact of being
caught had generally had a positive rather than a negative effect. Very few
had developed broadly antisocial attitudes as a consequence of their juvenile
misbehavior and whatever consequences followed.

NOTES

1. In their research on juvenile delinquency in Denver, Colorado, Conger and Miller operationally defined as delinquent those whose cases had been accepted by the Juvenile Court. This would eliminate those who were involved in trivial incidents. Yet they report that joyriding was the most frequent offense (of 410 offenses, 71 were joyriding) followed by incorrigibility (64 offenses). John Janeway Conger and Wilbur C. Miller, *Personality, Social Class, and Delinquency* (New York: John Wiley & Sons, 1966).

2. The Jessors conceive of a person's perceived environment as consisting of a distal and a proximal structure. The influence of the more remote distal structure is diminished or enhanced by perception of whether agreement or disagreement exists between parents and friends. The Jessors found that persons with problem behavior had less compatibility between parents and friends than those who did not have problem behavior. They also found greater friends' than parents' influence.

    The proximal structure refers to the juvenile in terms of the kinds of role models around him or her, the types of role models in the neighborhood and in the school. The Jessors found that proximal aspects of the environment were more closely related to problem and contentional behaviors than distal aspects, for both sexes. See Richard and Shirley L. Jessor, *Problem Behavior and Psychosocial Development: A Longitudinal Study of Youth* (New York: Academic Press, 1977): 26–42, 113–125, and 127–142.

3. The Jessors concluded in their final chapter that problem behavior was more or less part of the process of socialization. "It would be an important step forward for prevention and control if problem behavior in youth came to be seen as part of the dialectic of growth, a visible strand in the web of time." Jessor and Jessor, op. cit., p. 248.

Chapter 16

COMBINING SELF-REPORT AND OFFICIAL DATA FOR A BETTER UNDERSTANDING OF OFFICIAL STATUSES

PERCEPTION OF BEHAVIOR AND POLICE CONTACTS AS A PRE-PREDICTION CLASSIFIER

Respondents' accounts of their own behavior varied from being almost identical to those obtained from police records to being so different that it was almost impossible to believe that the respondent was attempting to provide an accurate description of his/her behavior and experience with the police. In this chapter people have been placed in categories based on their perceptions of their experiences and behaviors to see if this would permit better prediction of later official criminal careers from juvenile mis-behavior (police contact records).

Table 1 presents data for the 1942 Cohort and Table 2 for the 1949 Cohort. Commencing at the top of each table are data for those who stated that they had not been stopped by the police before age 18 and hadn't done things for which they could have been caught. At the bottom of each table are data for those who stated that they had been stopped before 18 and had done things for which they could have been caught (but were not). Note that the highest associations between before-18 and 18-and-after official police contact records were for those who claimed that they had not been stopped and had done nothing for which they could have been caught before age 18.

It is particularly interesting to note that only 11.6% of those who claimed no police contacts or misbehavior before 18 (top of Table 1) had records of any contact but that 58.3% of those who claimed police contacts and mis-behavior before 18 (bottom of Table 1) had recorded police contacts. It was

TABLE 1. RELATIONSHIP OF SELF-REPORTED POLICE CONTACT AND BEHAVIORAL STATUS BEFORE AGE 18 AND OFFICIAL POLICE CONTACT STATUS AFTER 18 TO POLICE CONTACT STATUS BEFORE 18: PERSONS INTERVIEWED, 1942 COHORT

Before Age 18

Not Stopped by Police Before 18 and Didn't Do Things for Which Not Caught

Police Contacts After 18

Police Contacts Before 18	No	Yes	Total
No	35 (57.4)	26 (42.6)	61 (88.4)
Yes	0 (0.0)	8 (100.0)	8 (11.6)
Total	35 (50.7)	34 (49.3)	69 (100.0)

R .367 Lambda .235

Felonies or Misdemeanors After 18

Police Contacts Before 18	No	Yes	Total
No	50 (82.0)	11 (18.0)	61 (88.4)
Yes	3 (37.5)	5 (62.5)	8 (11.6)
Total	53 (76.8)	16 (23.2)	69 (100.0)

R .337 Lambda .125

Felonies After 18

Police Contacts Before 18	No	Yes	Total
No	61 (100.0)	0 (0.0)	61 (100.0)
Yes	7 (87.5)	1 (12.5)	8 (11.6)
Total	68 (98.6)	1 (1.4)	69 (100.0)

R .335 Lambda .000

Not Stopped by Police Before 18 but Did Things for Which Not Caught

Police Contacts After 18

Police Contacts Before 18	No	Yes	Total
No	35 (53.0)	31 (47.0)	66 (78.6)
Yes	6 (33.3)	12 (66.7)	18 (21.4)
Total	41 (48.8)	43 (51.2)	84 (100.0)

R .162 Lambda .098

Felonies or Misdemeanors After 18

Police Contacts Before 18	No	Yes	Total
No	53 (80.3)	13 (19.7)	66 (78.6)
Yes	10 (55.6)	8 (44.4)	18 (21.4)
Total	63 (75.0)	21 (25.0)	84 (100.0)

R .235 Lambda .000

Felonies After 18

Police Contacts Before 18	No	Yes	Total
No	64 (97.0)	2 (3.0)	66 (78.6)
Yes	18 (100.0)	0 (0.0)	18 (21.4)
Total	82 (97.6)	2 (2.4)	84 (100.0)

R .082 Lambda .000

Stopped by Police Before 18 but Didn't Do Things for Which Not Caught

Police Contacts After 18

Police Contacts Before 18	No	Yes	Total
No	12 (42.9)	16 (57.1)	28 (66.7)
Yes	5 (35.7)	9 (64.3)	14 (33.3)
Total	17 (40.5)	25 (59.5)	42 (100.0)

R .069 Lambda .000

Felonies or Misdemeanors After 18

Police Contacts Before 18	No	Yes	Total
No	21 (75.0)	7 (25.0)	28 (66.7)
Yes	9 (64.3)	5 (35.7)	14 (33.3)
Total	30 (71.4)	12 (28.6)	42 (100.0)

R .112 Lambda .000

Felonies After 18

Police Contacts Before 18	No	Yes	Total
No	28 (100.0)	0 (0.0)	28 (66.7)
Yes	11 (78.6)	3 (21.4)	14 (33.3)
Total	39 (92.9)	3 (7.1)	42 (100.0)

R .082 Lambda .000

Stopped by Police Before 18 and Did Things for Which Not Caught

Police Contacts After 18

Police Contacts Before 18	No	Yes	Total
No	24 (43.6)	31 (56.4)	55 (41.7)
Yes	20 (26.0)	57 (74.0)	77 (58.3)
Total	44 (33.3)	88 (66.7)	132 (100.0)

R .185 Lambda .000

Felonies or Misdemeanors After 18

Police Contacts Before 18	No	Yes	Total
No	39 (70.9)	16 (29.1)	55 (41.7)
Yes	38 (49.4)	39 (50.6)	77 (58.3)
Total	77 (58.3)	55 (41.7)	132 (100.0)

R .216 Lambda .018

Felonies After 18

Police Contacts Before 18	No	Yes	Total
No	53 (96.4)	2 (3.6)	55 (41.7)
Yes	72 (93.5)	5 (6.5)	77 (58.3)
Total	125 (94.7)	7 (5.3)	132 (100.0)

R .063 Lambda .000

TABLE 2. RELATIONSHIP OF SELF-REPORTED POLICE CONTACT AND BEHAVIORAL STATUS BEFORE AGE 18 AND OFFICIAL POLICE CONTACT STATUS BEFORE 18 TO POLICE CONTACT STATUS AFTER 18: PERSONS INTERVIEWED, 1949 COHORT

Before Age 18

Not Stopped by Police Before 18 and Didn't Do Things for Which Not Caught

Police Contacts After 18

Police Contacts Before 18	No	Yes	Total
No	49 (62.0)	30 (38.0)	79 (81.4)
Yes	8 (44.4)	10 (55.6)	18 (18.6)
Total	57 (58.8)	40 (41.2)	97 (100.0)

Lambda .050 R .139

Felonies or Misdemeanors After 18

	No	Yes	Total
No	67 (84.8)	12 (15.2)	79 (81.4)
Yes	13 (72.2)	5 (27.8)	18 (18.6)
Total	80 (82.5)	17 (17.5)	97 (100.0)

Lambda .000 R .129

Felonies After 18

	No	Yes	Total
No	78 (98.7)	1 (1.3)	79 (81.4)
Yes	18 (100.0)	0 (0.0)	18 (18.6)
Total	96 (99.0)	1 (1.0)	97 (100.0)

Lambda .000 R -.049

Not Stopped by Police Before 18 but Did Things for Which Not Caught

Police Contacts After 18

Police Contacts Before 18	No	Yes	Total
No	51 (59.3)	35 (40.7)	86 (67.7)
Yes	13 (31.7)	28 (68.3)	41 (32.3)
Total	64 (50.4)	63 (49.6)	127 (100.0)

Lambda .238 R .258

Felonies or Misdemeanors After 18

	No	Yes	Total
No	70 (81.4)	16 (18.6)	86 (67.7)
Yes	21 (51.2)	20 (48.8)	41 (32.3)
Total	91 (71.7)	36 (28.3)	127 (100.0)

Lambda .000 R .313

Felonies After 18

	No	Yes	Total
No	85 (98.8)	1 (1.2)	86 (67.7)
Yes	39 (95.1)	2 (4.9)	41 (32.3)
Total	124 (97.6)	3 (2.4)	127 (100.0)

Lambda .000 R .114

Stopped by Police Before 18 but Didn't Do Things for Which Not Caught

Police Contacts After 18

Police Contacts Before 18	No	Yes	Total
No	27 (69.2)	12 (30.8)	39 (54.9)
Yes	17 (53.1)	15 (46.9)	32 (45.1)
Total	44 (62.0)	27 (38.0)	71 (100.0)

Lambda .000 R .165

Felonies or Misdemeanors After 18

	No	Yes	Total
No	36 (92.3)	3 (7.7)	39 (54.9)
Yes	21 (65.6)	11 (34.4)	32 (45.1)
Total	57 (80.3)	14 (19.7)	71 (100.0)

Lambda .000 R .334

Felonies After 18

	No	Yes	Total
No	39 (100.0)	0 (0.0)	39 (54.9)
Yes	29 (90.6)	3 (9.4)	32 (45.1)
Total	68 (95.8)	5 (4.2)	71 (100.0)

Lambda .000 R .232

Stopped by Police Before 18 and Did Things for Which Not Caught

Police Contacts After 18

Police Contacts Before 18	No	Yes	Total
No	50 (53.2)	44 (46.8)	94 (36.3)
Yes	40 (24.2)	125 (75.0)	165 (63.7)
Total	90 (34.7)	169 (65.3)	259 (100.0)

Lambda .067 R .292

Felonies or Misdemeanors After 18

	No	Yes	Total
No	71 (75.5)	23 (24.5)	94 (36.3)
Yes	70 (42.4)	95 (57.6)	165 (63.7)
Total	141 (54.4)	118 (45.6)	259 (100.0)

Lambda .212 R .320

Felonies After 18

	No	Yes	Total
No	89 (94.7)	5 (5.3)	94 (36.3)
Yes	149 (90.3)	16 (9.7)	165 (63.7)
Total	238 (91.9)	21 (8.1)	259 (100.0)

Lambda .000 R .077

also interesting to note that 49.3% of those who claimed no involvement before 18 (top of Table 1) had police contacts at or after that age and that 66.7% of those who claimed contacts and misbehavior before 18 (bottom Table 1) had recorded contacts after reaching that age. A similar progression was noted for felonies and misdemeanors. But again, and we cannot emphasize this type of finding too frequently, the group with the highest percent who had a felony contact at age 18 or later (only 7.1%) were those who admitted contacts before 18 but who said they didn't do things for which they were not caught.

How consistent are these findings with observations for the 1949 Cohort? All of the measures of association were still modest and only two lambdas indicated a proportional reduction in error greater than 20%, but not for the same groups as in the 1942 Cohort. A larger percent of those 18.6% who claimed no police contact and no misbehavior prior to 18 had higher police contact records prior to 18 than did those in the 1942 Cohort and those who admitted contacts and misbehavior before 18 (63.7%) had the highest percent of any group with official records before that age. Fewer of those admitting no contacts or misbehavior before 18 (41.2%) had contacts after reaching that age, while 65.3% of those who admitted contacts and misbehavior did so.

Progression in the percent who had contacts at various seriousness levels was not quite as consistent among the 1949 Cohort's groups as it was among the 1942 Cohort's groups. However, among those who had felony contacts at 18 and older we found a nice geometric progression from those who had admitted no contacts or misbehavior before 18 to those who admitted both: 1.0%, 2.4%, 4.2%, and 8.1%. Even then, only 8.1% of those whom we might have expected to have serious involvement after becoming 18 did so. One other statistic worth noting was that almost half of the persons who admitted contacts and undetected misbehavior before 18 had contacts at age 18 or later.

Similar findings were made for the males of both cohorts when considered separately (table not included). As one moved from the group who did not admit contacts or misbehavior prior to age 18 to those who admitted both, the percent who had recorded contacts before age 18 increased in both cohorts, from 14.3% to 63.8% in the 1942 Cohort and from 29.4% to 71.8% for the 1949 Cohort. The percent who had contacts at various levels of seriousness at age 18 or later did not increase as systematically as it did for the total cohorts.

Even more than in the total cohort, those males who had police contacts prior to age 18 were likely to have had them at 18 or later. In fact, in the group composed of those who had police contacts and engaged in undetected misbehavior and who, in addition, had police contact records before 18, more than four times as many had police contacts at age 18 and after than before. Also, over half of the males in the "admit everything" category had police contacts at age 18 and after.

The females differed from the males in that the percentage with police contacts before 18 showed more progression from those who were not stopped by the police and did not admit undetected misbehaviors to those who admitted contacts and undetected misbehavior, changing from 11.3% to 44.7% in the 1942 Cohort and from 16.3% to 44.9% in the 1949 Cohort. After becoming 18, progression in the proportion with police contacts at various seriousness levels from those who made no admissions to those who admitted contacts and undetected misbehaviors was not consistent on any seriousness level for which there were sufficient persons with age 18 and after contacts to make a comparison. Probably the most consistent finding for the females was the very small number of persons who had contacts before 18 and contacts at and after that age regardless of what they admitted in terms of police contacts or misbehavior prior to 18.

We must again conclude that no matter how interesting these inter-relationships are and how much general consistency they show in dispro-portional continuity for high-risk groups, it was not possible to predict future behavior of the type which we wish to predict from past behavior and associated prediction groupings.

THE RELATIONSHIP OF SANCTIONS TO OFFICIAL AND SELF-REPORT DATA

When everyone was classified according to their combined official and self-report seriousness, the percent in each of the eight categories who had been sanctioned or severely sanctioned did not progressively increase from those with no police contacts and a low seriousness self-report to those who were *high in both respects*, but the percentage who were severely sanc-tioned was higher for the latter group than for either high official seriousness or for high self-report seriousness alone and was most similar to that for official seriousness.[1] The incremental increase from combining categories was even greater for the 1949 Cohort, but sanctions were more frequently applied to this cohort than to the 1942 Cohort so that such an increase would be expected.

The same percentage of persons with high scores on self-report and low scores on official seriousness or the opposite fell in the highest category for sanctions for the 1942 Cohort at age 21 and older but for the 1949 Cohort these same groups were similar only if both categories of sanctioned persons were combined, and then more so for the 18 through 20 age period than for the 21 and older period. Any high official seriousness category, re-gardless of the seriousness level of self-report, produced more severely sanctioned persons than other combinations, as would be expected.

Summary

Continuity in police contact records between juvenile (6 through 17) and adult (18 and older) periods was related to what juveniles did and were caught for and what they did and were not caught for, but the degree and seriousness level of their continuity was not consistently related to their pre-age 18 reported behavior and experience with the police. Although there was a degree of continuity for each group as categorized by pre-age-18 descriptions of their own behavior, this did not enable us to achieve predictability above that previously determined without this information, however intriguing these data may be.

Persons with high official and self-report seriousness scores were sanctioned more severely than those who had low scores and the relationship was consistently higher for official seriousness, overweighing self-report seriousness regardless of the combination of official and self-report seriousness. The fact that increasing self-report seriousness had only a small incremental impact on severity of sanctions for combinations of self-report and official seriousness should provide a small degree of satisfaction for those who believe that there is little, if any, relationship between "real" seriousness of careers and the severity of sanctions that are meted out in the courts.

Note

1. For an excellent discussion of the literature and a report on the related problem of a sense of injustice, see Marvin Krohn and John Stratton, "A Sense of Injustice: Attitudes Toward the Criminal Justice System," *Criminology* 17 (1980): 495–504. Also see: Goeffrey P. Alpert and Donald A. Hicks, "Prisoners' Attitudes Toward Components of the Legal and Judicial Systems," *Criminology* 14 (1977): 461–481. Is it possible that the "uncaught" cohort members have also been caught enough times that they too have been sanctioned proportionately to those who have been caught?

Chapter 17

SUMMARY OF THE RESEARCH AND
RECOMMENDATIONS

INTRODUCTION

Inherent in any research on the relationship of juvenile delinquency and crime to the changing ecological structure of the city is the premise that delinquency and crime are products of the ongoing social life of the community. Rather than delinquency and crime having some single or underlying antecedent or cause, different types of delinquency and crime are generated in different social milieus and are as normal to their setting as are other behaviors more highly valued in the larger society.

Much of the concern about juvenile delinquency has also been based on the premise that it leads to adult crime. Although a variety of analytical techniques and measures of continuity and seriousness of careers have generated the conclusion that there is some relationship between juvenile delinquency and adult criminality, the relationship is neither sufficient nor of such a nature to permit prediction of who will or will not become adult criminals from their juvenile behavior. Furthermore, to the extent that a relationship exists between juvenile and adult behavior, it may be explained by the operation of the juvenile and adult justice systems as well as by continuities in the *behavior* of juveniles and young adults. It is unrealistic to continue to posit juvenile delinquency as the almost inevitable precursor to adult crime and to intervene as though the facts were different from what they are.

Neither sex nor race/ethnicity was conceptualized as an important explanatory variable in this research; neither would add much to our knowledge about delinquency and crime because we already know that males have higher rates than females and that race/ethnic minority groups have higher rates than does the White majority. Sex and race/ethnicity are statuses which may have some predictive value but, in themselves, do not explain delinquent and criminal behavior. Race/ethnic differences in neighborhood of residence and neighborhood of daily interaction with others may play a dominant role in the acquisition of values and behaviors and are important in understanding how race/ethnic differences in delinquency and crime come about. In other words, race/ethnicity has value only as examined in its social context. The community's perception of these statuses must be taken into consideration if we wish to understand how recorded contacts with the police, contacts for more serious forms of misbehavior, referrals, and dispositions eventuate in the incarceration of disproportionate numbers of people with specific race/ethnic and sex characteristics.

INCREASING INVOLVEMENT, SERIOUSNESS, AND CONTINUITY OF RELATIONSHIPS FROM COHORT TO COHORT

Total rates of contact with the police did not increase from cohort to cohort as much as did rates of contact for the more serious offenses such as Assault, Burglary, Theft, Robbery, and other Part I offenses. The proportion of contacts with the police which involved Part I offenses more than doubled from the 1942 to the 1955 Cohort for the age period 6 through 17 and more than tripled for the age period 18 through 20. Delinquency among females increased from cohort to cohort even more, regardless of the measure of frequency or seriousness employed.

During the 30-year period covered by our research, measures of delinquency and crime neither rose nor fell as Racine's economy fluctuated, nor did they share a pattern of lag behind economic trends. Crimes against property (neither property offenses in general nor Theft alone) did not fluctuate with unemployment rates or with other measures of the economy's vitality so as to support an economic cycle or trend explanation of the crime rate in Racine. What we did find, as have others, was that crime rates were highest in those inner city and interstitial areas whose residents were employed at lower level jobs, whose residents were frequently unemployed, and whose youthful members were less integrated into the world of rewarding work.

Important to our own assessment of change impacting on crime rates was the fact that the city had undergone rapid growth during the 1950s, growth that carried on into the 1960s. This growth had been accompanied by increasing individual mobility, as evidenced by automobile registrations and traffic counts, both of which had increased disproportionately to the city's population growth. As Racine's residential and commercial-industrial areas grew, it became obvious that many of the changes that took place could have led to increased involvement of the police with both juveniles and adults.

The more the growth and development of the city was considered, the easier it was to see how delinquency and crime had become part of a cyclical pattern of change which, while it involved decline and deterioration in the inner city and interstitial areas, was likewise an outgrowth of population movement to and commercial and recreational development in peripheral areas that were readily accessible by auto or bus. Rather than be surprised and mystified by increases in delinquency and crime and changing spatial patterns for these phenomena, the observer sees them as natural and expected developments.

Having recognized the cyclical nature of the phenomena, the next step was to develop an understanding of the complex interrelationship of variables that kept the process going. Not until more is known about this process and the crucial variables can we effectively go about breaking the cycle of decline, deterioration, delinquency, crime, and further population movement.

At another level of conceptualization, although not likely when the problem has been placed in an ecological framework, focus is on the individual and his/her behavior so that programs, rather than aiming at breaking the cycle, aim at breaking the delinquent and criminal. This type of approach, on which we shall later comment more fully, makes the error of assuming that if delinquent and criminal elements are removed from the community the cycle is broken. It disregards the normalcy of most delinquent and criminal behavior, behavior which will continue to be a part of community life because others will take the place of those who are removed.

The Ecology of the City and Its Relationship to Delinquency and Crime

Setting the stage for an approach that would lead to a better understanding of trends and cycles was our central concern in the fourth chapter. We had proposed that a variety of spatial systems or sets of units should be utilized to determine if the same findings were made regardless of unit of measurement. Since the literature has been replete with contradictory findings, would we have the same experience if the results of research with a variety of units were compared: census tracts, police grids, natural areas, and neighborhoods? Would neighborhoods present a more precise picture of changing patterns of delinquency and crime and also be more sensitive to changes in the social organization of the community than were larger spatial units?

The chapter concluded with the inner city and interstitial areas of each system delineated and with other areas grouped to achieve maximum within-group homogeneity on the characteristics hypothesized to either provide a milieu for in-area delinquency and crime or the production of it by residents of the area. That the areas in each spatial system were of different sizes and created similar but not identical inner city and interstitial areas guaranteed that there would be differences in the findings from one system to the other. At the same time, the general process of change should generate similar findings when identical measures of delinquency and crime were utilized.

The stage had been set for the analysis in Chapter 5 of Racine's changing rates and patterns of Part I offenses by place of offense for census tracts (1970 through 1978) and police grids (1968 through 1979) and arrests for Part I and II offenses by place of residence in census tracts (1968 through 1979).

The description of trends in Chapter 6 was non-statistical, with the metric variables trichotomized to produce tables which would readily indicate if offense and arrest rates were related to the ecology of the city. High offense and arrest rates were characteristic of the inner city and interstitial areas and low rates were (with explainable exceptions) associated with the middle and higher socioeconomic status areas on the periphery of the city. Although the pattern was far from perfect, changes in the characteristics of tracts and police grids were related to measures of delinquency and crime.

The pattern of change, however, was not the same for all variables, nor could one discern a neat pattern of cyclical change in variables from time period to time period. Instead, there were a variety of combinations and permutations characterizing the tracts and grids between the inner city and the highest SES areas on the periphery. While offense rates and arrest rates rose throughout most years of the study, they commenced to decline in 1974 or 1975, even in the inner city.

It was also apparent that historical trends in offense and arrest rates overshadowed the trends that were expected in some tracts and police grids. This does not mean that the model of expected spatial variation in rates has been rejected, only that the cyclical phenomenon is best seen in the inner city and interstitial areas and that the rates in other areas may be more of a response to general trends than to other changes within the area.

This brought us to Chapter 7 in which cohort data were used to compare the results obtained by analyzing the same data within each of the spatial systems. The emphasis was on cohort time period change (by place of contact and place of residence) by the units of each spatial system. We were concerned, not with simply whether police contact rates, seriousness rates, referral rates, and severity of sanctions scores were highest in the inner city and lowest in the peripheral areas *and* for those who resided there, but with whether those inner city and interstitial areas *and* their residents could be characterized as having progressively higher rates, time period by time period.

Some of the interstitial and other transitional areas were quite obviously much like the inner city and others were not sharply differentiated from the stable residential areas of the community. There was also variation depending upon the basis for computing rates or the measure of involvement with the police and justice systems. This led us to refer to the hardening of the inner city that appeared to be taking place at the same time when delinquency and crime were increasing in some other areas, particularly if rates for the 1970s were considered. Finally, there was a strong suggestion that when measures of serious involvement were observed the hardening was even more apparent.

Our concern with the trend toward hardening of the inner city led to further examination of the data (Chapter 8), first in terms of the proportion of each cohort who had contacts with the police at each age in the areas within each spatial system and second in terms of the linkage between high seriousness rates in areas, age group by age group, as seriousness built up in each cohort. Both approaches provided further evidence of this hardening. Continuity remained in the inner city areas and it was evident that seriousness of reasons for police contact had uniformly high ecological correlations for the 1949 and 1955 Cohorts from age group to age group, particularly during the ages 15 through 17 and 18 through 20. Areas with high mean seriousness scores by cohort residents continued to have high mean seriousness scores and, to the extent that these correlations were not higher, it was because seriousness of reasons for police contacts had at the same time increased in some interstitial and peripheral transitional areas.

When mean seriousness of all earlier age groups was regressed on seriousness 18 through 20, the impact of ages 15 through 17 on later ages was significant for three out of four spatial systems. In addition, an analysis of mean seriousness scores before and after moves confirmed the generally deleterious effects of movement to lower SES areas, most of which involved moves to inner city or transitional areas which had increasing delinquency and crime rates. This section concluded with an analysis which showed that sanctions failed to have a deterrent effect on the future behavior of persons who resided in areas which received the most severe sanctions.

The Concentration of Delinquency and Crime by Cohorts

Police contacts, particularly for more serious reasons, had their highest incidence in the inner city and interstitial areas. Chapter 9 revealed that approximately 5% of each cohort, the persons with two or three felony contacts, was responsible for about 75% of the felonies (and much of the other crime) in each cohort. While police contacts for delinquent and criminal behavior were highly concentrated among a few individuals in each cohort, they were also widely dispersed, 60% to 70% of the males in each cohort having at least one contact for an offense other than a Traffic violation.

Combining continuity types and controlling for place of socialization permitted selection of a relatively small percentage of offenders who were most likely to have criminal careers after the age of 18, those whose careers included a large number of felonies (Chapter 10). In a high risk group composed of that 11.7% of the 1942 Cohort who had been socialized in the inner city and interstitial areas and who had continuous careers before 18, 53.3% had high seriousness scores after 18. No other area and no other continuity type had even close to 50% with high seriousness scores after 18. Findings were similar for the 1949 and 1955 Cohorts. As promising as this sounds, one must look at the total picture. While 43.8% of the inner city group with continuous contact careers before 18 and high later seriousness scores committed at least one felony after 18, they comprised only 26% of the persons in the 1942 Cohort and 29% and 22% of the persons with felony contacts in the 1949 and 1955 Cohorts. The other felony offenders, some of whom never had a police contact before the age of 18, were spread throughout the community.

In every other manner in which the data were examined there was a high degree of concentration, i.e., there were certain categories of persons who had a high probability of having serious careers that included felonies. There was also a high degree of dispersion in that people scattered throughout the community who either had no juvenile record or only had intermittent contacts for minor offenses ultimately were charged with serious offenses by law enforcement agencies. Without extensive records as juveniles there was no basis for the prediction of later criminal behavior. Knowing that a high percent of those from a high risk group will have serious offenses as adults is not the same as predicting who in a total cohort will commit serious offenses as an adult, but it is the latter with whom we are most concerned.

Tables and diagrams in Chapter 11 showed that the most prevalent pattern of delinquent behavior was one of declining seriousness and discontinuation after the teenage period. The few who continued to have police contacts into their late 20s with an increase in seriousness (and finally a decline) were those who had become well known to the juvenile and adult justice systems and thus created the impression of continuity and increasing seriousness in delinquent and criminal careers. The careers of these persons were atypical of all who had had contacts with the juvenile and adult justice systems. This "hard core" group of continuers suggested that there was a relatively small group on whom attention should have been focused, assuming that they had been accurately identified.

PREDICTING FROM ACCUMULATED EXPERIENCE

Although there were relationships between frequent and more serious contacts in the early years and continuity of careers, these relationships alone did not permit much improvement in predictive efficiency over the prediction that no one would have a continuing career. Chapter 12 revealed that similar problems were encountered when police referrals were used as the predictor. By the age of 18, only 17% of those who had had no referrals had a referral after that age, while 91% of those who had had five or more referrals by 18 had at least one referral afterwards. However, while 10 of the 11 persons in the cohort who had had five or more referrals *before* the age of 18 had future referrals, there were *82 people who had had no referrals at all through the age of 18 who had at least one later referral*. In short, while it was predictable that a large proportion of those who had frequent contacts and a large proportion of those who had frequent referrals would continue to be referred, there were numerous others who had contacts and referrals after their teens who had not had them to that time.

It was apparent that many of those who had frequent contacts and numerous referrals as juveniles continued to have them, but was this a characteristic of the persons or a matter of responses by authorities to prior behavior which resulted in fulfillment of the prophecy regardless of how the individual behaved in the future? Did early identification and intervention effectively deter juveniles from further misbehavior or did it ensure that they would continue to be identified as miscreants?

We have reported little success in predicting continuity and a word should be said about the kinds of discontinuities that made prediction so difficult. The first has to do with what appeared to be discontinuities in behavior which may really have been discontinuities in contacts with the police because of undetected offenses. These discontinuities are interruptions in the sequence in the official records of police contact and make it difficult to predict from any given year or two to the future. Similarly, past contacts cannot be utilized in predicting to any present or several relatively present years. While this problem did not have much effect upon the prediction of past to the future in any middle range of years for the 1942 Cohort and had only slightly less effect for the 1949 Cohort, we have shown that prediction from past to future became rather difficult for later years for the 1955 Cohort.

The second problem refers to discontinuities that came about as police patrols changed, as emphasis on referrals changed, as proneness to send juveniles to court for formal disposition changed, as emphasis on sanctions and their severity changed, and as emphasis on record keeping changed over the years. Thus, while juvenile behavior (at least as measured by police contacts) was undoubtedly changing over the years, police and court behavior were changing as well. The meaning of a referral changed if there was an increased emphasis on street dispositions and the meaning of a court disposition changed if there was a change in the behaviors for which people were likely to be sent to court. If formal sanctions were meted out with greater regularity than at earlier periods of time, involvement would have changed from cohort to cohort; the impact would have come in the later years for the 1942 Cohort, in the intermediate years for the 1949 Cohort, and earlier for the 1955 Cohort. All did have their effects on the proportion of each cohort which experienced increasing involvement in the juvenile justice system, on measures of association between past and future recorded behaviors, and on our ability to increase predictive efficiency.

It is not surprising, therefore, that the various findings which we have described differed for the 1955 Cohort from those of the 1942 and 1949 Cohorts. With the entire juvenile and adult justice systems in the process of change, and producing records indicative of change, it is indeed difficult to speak about the ability to predict into the future from prediction tables developed with the data from earlier cohorts. Even then, the ability to make a prediction about future behavior from past behavior (with a high proportional reduction in error) that was better than the prediction that could be made from the marginals was not demonstrated to be great for any of the cohorts.

With all that has been presented on continuities and prediction, it is difficult to understand how the officer on patrol may be faulted if he/she misjudges who should be referred and who should be handled by counseling and release. Considering the fact that police training has been in the ordinances and laws which must be enforced, on procedures for taking people into custody, and on procedures for dealing with people who appear at time of contact as dangerous to themselves or to society, how can he/she be expected to be an expert in determining who is most likely to continue their misbehavior if some sort of formal intervention is not initiated?

Going a step further, if the police officer who had contact with the juvenile made a referral to the juvenile bureau, officers in the bureau were faced with the same problem of deciding what to do. Even given that they may have been able to readily ascertain the number of contacts that a juvenile had previously had and the seriousness of the behavior that resulted in these contacts, could they be expected to take only that into consideration in making the decision to refer the juvenile on to county probation or juvenile court intake? Surely one cannot expect them to refrain from considering such additional items as the area of the community in which the juvenile lived, the attitude of the juvenile while being questioned, the nature of the juvenile's associates insofar as this may be known from previous encounters, knowledge of the juvenile's family situation, and so on? For that matter, it is understandable when the juvenile bureau utilizes sex and race/ethnicity as predictors since they are indicative of a status which carries with it a greater or lesser likelihood of future police encounters.

If people in the community demand police action and demand increasing formality and intervention, those on the firing line must determine if better indicators are available than those upon which they have traditionally relied. It is a question of whether traditional methods have resulted in intervention in the appropriate cases at the appropriate times to maximize discontinuity in behavior, or whether intervention has simply maximized continuity and created the impression that traditional predictors are somehow associated with continuities in delinquent behavior rather than continuities in police behavior.

Juvenile probation and juvenile court intake have a similar problem. The data upon which the county probation or intake officer must rely are previous records available in that office with some data from the juvenile bureau. One would expect the probation or intake officer to have a wider variety of relevant information upon which to base a decision. The framework within which decisions are made is quite different from that faced by the police in that the professional staff may obtain data on school performance, adjustment in the family, prior attempts at intervention by private agencies, and so on. Here, again, the literature in the field has frequently been based on case studies of dubious value. These case studies have been accepted as supportive of a position not really established by empirical research on either large samples of the population or through longitudinal studies of cohorts. To the extent that the community demands action, the court is forced to respond even though it may doubt that the limited alternatives available are appropriate for most of the cases at hand.

THE EFFECTIVENESS OF SANCTIONS

What was found, in numerous analyses and with considerable consistency, was an increase in frequency and seriousness of misbehavior in the periods following those in which sanctions were administered. This was more the case for males than females. The best that can be said is that sanctions had a benign effect on the females.

A variety of multivariate analyses led to the conclusion that the significant effect of juvenile seriousness on adult seriousness persisted even when the intervening effects of juvenile referrals and sanctions were held constant. With few exceptions, intervention by the agencies of social control did not play even a modest role in decreasing the seriousness of adult contacts.

WHAT THE INTERVIEWS TOLD US

Interviews with persons from the 1942 and 1949 Cohorts were valuable in enabling us to see how persons from these cohorts viewed themselves and how their reports of their own misbehavior related to their official records.

It was as important to understand why so *few* juveniles went on to careers in adult crime as to explain the continuity of a few. Almost 70% of those from each cohort who admitted they had been stopped by the police said that they had been stopped only once or twice before 18, around 60% of them at about the age of 16 or 17. Most had not been stopped for anything serious. Two-thirds of each cohort also admitted doing things for which they were not caught.

When official contact records and self-report measures were combined, well over 90% of each cohort's males appeared to have engaged in youthful misbehavior, as had 65% to 70% of the females. Nevertheless, few continued to get into trouble after 18 and even fewer were involved in serious trouble after 18. Among those who had been both stopped by the police and had done things for which they could have been caught (the group that would be most likely to continue their misbehavior into adulthood), only 10.6% of the 1942 Cohort and 13.9% of the 1949 Cohort had a major misdemeanor or felony police contact after 18. Only 5.3% and 8.1% had a felony-level police contact after that age. From 30% to 50% of the incidents described by members of each cohort were "just for fun," and were shared in with someone else in four out of five cases, usually the persons with whom they ran around. Furthermore, most of those who were caught and most of those who were not caught stated that they had reappraised their behavior and ceased to engage in the acts which either got them or could have gotten them into trouble.

While negative attitudes toward the police were related to high seriousness scores regardless of age, relatively few in each cohort had negative attitudes toward the police. Those few who did were likely to have had higher juvenile and adult seriousness scores than those who did not. Coupled with what appeared to be considerable police understanding of the juveniles was the failure of persons close to them (with the exception of some sympathy from peers) to condone their delinquent behavior. Relatively few had friends in trouble with the police during the juvenile *and* adult periods (2.4% in the 1942 Cohort and 9.8% in the 1949 Cohort).

Over two-thirds of each cohort stated that their parents had a positive influence in their lives. Only 7% of the 1942 Cohort and less than 11% of the 1949 Cohort stated that students at school had a negative impact on their lives. Most misbehavior ceased as a consequence of the process of socialization into adult roles and most had ceased for positive reasons rather than from the fear of getting caught (less than 8% stopped because they feared getting caught).

WHAT DOES IT MEAN?

These are the basic findings. What do they mean to persons on the firing line? The crime problem continues to be more complex and deep-rooted than commonly realized. It is not just a matter of hired killers or sadistic murderers scattered here and there throughout the country. It is not a matter of individual avarice and greed. Nor can it be said that patterns of crime are related to regional variations in skull thickness, nostril width, endocrine imbalance, overconsumption of jelly rolls (this has been seriously proposed at criminology meetings even within the past few years), or the lack of corrective eye glasses and shoes (which has also been proposed and which received more publicity than some scientifically grounded sociological explanations).

Criminal behavior is one of the diverse varieties of human behavior. However reprehensible, most misbehavior can be understood as an outgrowth of interaction with others in the larger social milieu or in a smaller social milieu which is a variant of the larger. Unless one commences with some comprehension of this, what could really be understood seems to be hopelessly incomprehensible, aberrant behavior. When the juvenile ceases to misbehave by the age of 18 or, as in most cases, by the age of 21, his/her explanation of "why" substantiates the normality of most earlier misbehavior.

People in the justice system will do a better job (not as much harm) if they understand how crime comes about in various settings. They will not be so inclined to see themselves as warehousemen or zoo keepers, however much that may seem to be their role in their darkest moments. It is just as important that the guard on the wall and the cell block custodian understand this as it is for the warden and the deputy warden to do so. Breaking the outlaw may appear necessary if the warden is to keep his/her job but has little or nothing to do with effectively responding to the crime problem in America. It is just as important that the executive branch of government, the legislative branch, and the judicial branch understand this if they wish to make a positive impact on the problems of delinquency and crime.

This is the broader view of the problem. While it may seem philosophical, it is not. This position is an outgrowth of research that has been conducted at the lowest level (that is, closest to misbehavior by the self-report method and by victim surveys) and at the highest level which involves the analysis of Uniform Crime Reports for the entire United States for lengthy periods of time. The most sophisticated multivariate statistical analyses and interviews with participants in barroom disturbances culminate in essentially the same conclusion, that understanding how delinquent and criminal behavior comes about is the first step to learning what to do about it.

For some years (perhaps since the time when the pyramids were built) varying proportions of the population have professed the almost certain "knowledge" that increasing youthful and adult misbehavior (however it has been characterized) must be followed by swift and sure action. There are others who would commence with leniency and understanding but, if that does not bring forth repentance and cessation of delinquent and criminal behavior, turn to punishment as the appropriate remedy.

While punishment may not always be in vogue, sanctions whose severity may go as far as institutionalization, incarceration for adults (incapacitation is popular now), is considered the final step. No research exists which supports the effectiveness of such an approach (popularizations of misreadings of other peoples' research does not count, however eminent the authority) but there is abundant evidence that programs directed at the offender (juvenile or adult) neither deter potential offenders because they fear the same thing will happen to them nor serve as corrective measures for those who are thus sanctioned.[1]

With growing concern about the problem, the danger lies in presuming that a policy of increasingly severe sanctions will serve as a deterrent. If sanctions have a deterrent effect the consequences should be seen and responded to in the area where the sanctioned person is known. Ecological and other data suggest that this is not correct.

The findings in the first half of this volume revealed that areas of delinquency and crime were being solidified. The position that there is a cyclical type of process with areas changing in all major respects followed by increasing delinquency and crime probably overstates the case. If a variety of indicators are selected, some will account for more of the variance than others in one spatial system and others will account for more of the variance in another spatial system, and, of course, some will appear to be powerful determinants no matter which spatial system has been selected. Still the variable may simply be one of many indicators of something which is the real antecedent of delinquency and crime.

That target density and residential vacancy were correlated with offense and arrest rates by census tracts and police grids tells us that a large segment of the offenses in an area were probably target-related, directly or indirectly, and that arrest rates by place of residence were also high in these areas. It neither explains delinquency nor tells us that a policeman at the door of every store is a viable solution to the problem in the United States.

In the inner city and transitional areas residential vacancies are indicative of an attitude and a change in population and population composition that make delinquent and criminal behavior more normal or at least more available as alternate forms of behavior. Residential vacancies in an outlying, developing area mean that new homes have not been sold and new apartments have not been rented. It is an oversimplification to take research findings literally and to assume that whatever differences in housing or other variables are found between the inner city and interstitial, high delinquency and crime rate areas and other areas must be eliminated as a solution to the problem of delinquency and crime.

WHERE TO BREAK THE CYCLE: THINGS TO STOP DOING AND THINGS TO DO

Large areas of major cities are wastelands and for a multitude of reasons it would be desirable to see them rebuilt whether or not this impacts on delinquency and crime.[2] It can be argued that the long-run costs of not rebuilding the inner city will be greater than the short-run costs of attacking the problem. If crime and delinquency rates show significant decline, so much the better. What can be done short of revitalization of the inner city and transitional areas as a basic step toward changing people's lives in these high delinquency and crime areas?[3]

One reasonable step would be to slow the trend toward official handling of juvenile delinquency and youthful crime, i.e., encourage street-level handling of minor offenses[4] and other informal dispositional alternatives as opposed to referral to the juvenile bureau or to juvenile court intake.[5] This involves training police officers to understand human behavior in addition to the training that they must have in how to deal with violent offenders.[6]

Official statistics on police contacts and referrals generate a societal response as it is, and the more that juveniles are contacted and referred (and this will happen more in areas that are defined as delinquent and criminal areas), the greater the attention to that area will be. As the composition of the population changes and more youth and minority groups reside in transitional areas or in areas whose land use and other physical characteristics mark them as "new slums," the more likely it is that attention will be focused on their youthful misbehavior.

Although the court will, of necessity, deal with a certain proportion of the juveniles, the second step must be to resist the argument of those who believe that increasing the severity of sanctions and sanctioning a greater proportion of the youth earlier will have a favorable impact on the problem of delinquency and crime.[7] If severe sanctions are followed by increasingly serious delinquency and crime, this too speeds up the cycle, for this serious delinquency and crime is followed by even more severe sanctions. There is no evidence, contrary to recent and popular opinion and suggestions from Washington, that making the punishment fit the crime leads to greater court effectiveness.

A third step would be to determine through social accounting how extensive the savings from such a policy would be (in the billions every year if the trend toward severity of sanctions continues). It is not just the cost of institutionalization with which we are concerned, but the cost of processing from time of referrals (including detention and court dispositions) that must be taken into consideration. While the cost to victims is sometimes incalculable, it is also sometimes very small, stolen wheel covers, etc.

The cost of crime other than what has sometimes been called "the ordinary garden variety," i.e., the sometimes multimillion dollar cost to financial and investment institutions of a single sophisticated offense must also be considered if we are truly interested in the "cost" of crime. This cost in lost confidence in major economic institutions may be just as incalculable as violence against persons. These savings should be made available for a more positive approach to the problems of delinquency and crime.

It is apparent that a proportion of the youth socialized in the inner city and its interstitial areas (and in other areas as well) have not seen the existing organization of society as one into which they can fit and through which they can progress toward life goals that are acceptable in the larger adult society. The school discipline problem is a prime example.[8]

To place youth in the "troublemaker" category for classroom or school misbehavior early in their school careers may only result in treatment which maximizes the fulfillment of the prophesy.[9] Even if we take the position that the acquisition of a history of being difficult at an early age places some students in a high-risk category (labeling),[10] should action be taken which maximizes the probability that, rather than being integrated into the larger group, they will be even more likely to have as their friends and associates persons who are also in trouble? Rather, is it not a matter of determining how to channel students into activities that they will find more rewarding than their disruptive behavior?

It is difficult for adults in and out of the school system (who have already reaped the rewards of secondary and higher education, rewards which do not come as readily to this generation) to realize that the rewards for conformity and diligence in school are not clearly defined and may be perceived by students as unevenly distributed in school and in the world of work. Completion of high school or college does not have the same pay-off for all, no matter that there are relationships between years of education, income, and various other valued goals in the larger society.[11]

The question is, of course, can anything be done to change the school and the student? There has been considerable interest in alternative education programs which may serve to keep young people in school. Whether concern about this approach has its roots in an appreciation of the fact that neither the traditional college preparatory track nor a strictly vocational track provides viable experiences for all students or in the realization that there is an over-abundance of youthful manpower is irrelevant. What will work or what works best is a matter of question (which will take extensive research and some years to answer).[12]

Coupled with this is the necessity of developing opportunities for all persons that are commensurate with their abilities. Formal education must have a pay-off, whether it is in terms of occupational level, income, or increased opportunities for satisfying social participation. The school can provide education but it is up to the community to provide opportunity. This suggests that there should be closer ties between the school and the community. What can be done to redefine the school as a center for juveniles and adults? Development of the school as a place for activities by persons of all ages may well be the first step toward its redefinition by youth.[13] Perhaps the solution to keeping some youth in school is a greater emphasis on alternative education programs tied in with the world of work, programs in which opportunities for the acquisition of adult status are provided along with formal education.[14]

The creation of opportunities that are appealing to the disenchanted who also perceive themselves as the disinherited is not easy.[15] If we can consider spending billions on intervention strategies which we know do not produce a solution but only create a greater problem, is it completely naive to suggest that we couldn't be worse off if more creative approaches are tried? Even if careful evaluation reveals that not all programs for integrating youth into the larger society are successful, the impact of a positive approach would not have the negative consequences that have been shown for traditional but increasingly punitive approaches. We must remember that *the ultimate question is not one of how to most expeditiously remove miscreants from the community but how to integrate them into the larger social structure so that their talents will be employed in socially constructive ways.* This should be our major concern, for, if it is not, the cost will become increasingly higher, postponed only to the future.

NOTES

1. The question, broadly defined, is one of social control. Diverse perspectives on this problem and the difficulty of assessing effectiveness is dealt with by Jack P. Gibbs, "Social Control, Deterrence, and Perspectives on Social Order," *Social Forces*, Vol. 56, December 1977, pp. 408–423. The following articles are also suggested: Harold G. Grasmick and George J. Bryjak, "The Deterrent Effect of Perceived Severity of Punishment," *Social Forces*, Vol. 59, December 1980, pp. 471–491; Robert Nash Parker and M. Dwayne Smith, "Deterrence, Poverty, and Type of Homicide," *American Journal of Sociology*, Vol. 85, November 1979, pp. 614–624; David P. Phillips, "The Deterrent Effect of Capital Punishment: New Evidence on an Old Controversy," *American Journal of Sociology*, Vol. 86, July 1980, pp. 139–148; Charles R. Tittle, "Sanction Fear and the Maintenance of Social Order," *Social Forces*, Vol. 55, March 1977, pp. 579–596. An excellent summary of the research into the 1970s may be found in Charles R. Tittle and Charles H. Logan, "Sanctions and Deviance: Evidence and Remaining Questions," *Law and Society Review*, Spring 1973, pp. 372–392.

   Those who advocate increasing either the severity of sanctions or the certainty of their application must have some consequence other than deterrence, general or specific, as their rationale.

2. This is by no means a plea for additional public housing projects. However desirable they may be as alternatives to rat-infested tenement houses, they have not been the solution to delinquency and crime for their occupants have not been integrated into the larger society by rehousing them. See Leo A. Schuerman and Solomon Kobrin, "High Risk Delinquency Neighborhoods and Public Housing Projects." Presented at the 1981 Annual Meeting of the Society for the Study of Social Problems, Toronto, August 22, 1981.

3. See Congressman Ronald V. Dellums' published hearings, *Problems in Urban Centers*, Oversight Hearings before the Committee on the District of Columbia, House of Representatives, Ninety-Sixth Congress, Second Session on Problems in Urban Centers, Washington, D.C., and the Federal Government Role June 25–27, July 23, 25, and 30, September 30, 1980, Serial No. 96-17. These hearings and the papers and reports included as part of the testimony make it clear that there are no simple answers to the problems of urban centers.

4. See Edwin M. Schur, *Radical Non-Intervention* (Englewood Cliffs: Prentice-Hall, 1973).

5. For a description of various models of diversion and graphic presentation see: Daniel Katkin, Drew Hyman, and John Kramer, *Juvenile Delinquency and the Juvenile Justice System* (North Scituate, Mass.: Duxbury Press, 1976), Chapter 12, pp. 404–455. For a useful reader on this subject, see: Robert M. Carter and Malcolm W. Klein (eds.), *Back on the Street: The Diversion of Juvenile Offenders* (Englewood Cliffs, N.J.: Prentice-Hall, 1976).

6. There are a number of books that could be used as a supplement to regular police training or by police officers with the responsibility of training and developing youth programs: Edward Eldefonso, *Youth Problems and Law Enforcement* (Englewood Cliffs, N.J.: Prentice-Hall, 1972); C.J. Flammang, *Police Juvenile Enforcement* (Springfield, Ill.: Charles C. Thomas, 1972); Robert Portune, *Changing Adolescent Attitudes Toward Police* (Cincinnati: W.H. Anderson, 1971).

7. Edwin Lemert, "The Juvenile Court—Quest and Realities," in the President's Commission on Law Enforcement and Administration of Justice, *Task Force Report: Juvenile Delinquency and Youth Crime* (Washington, D.C.: U.S. Government Printing Office, 1967). For a sociological analysis of how the juvenile court functions, see: Aaron V. Cicourel, *The Social Organization of Juvenile Justice* (New York: John Wiley, 1968); Robert M. Emerson, *Judging Delinquents* (Chicago: Aldine, 1969).

8. See, for example: Herbert L. Foster, *Ribbin', Jivin', and Playin' the Dozens: The Unrecognized Dilemma of Inner-City Schools* (Cambridge: Ballinger, 1974) and Robert J. Rubel, *The Unruly School* (Lexington, Mass.: Lexington Books, 1977). For a short but perceptive chapter on the school, see Chapter 8, "The School and Delinquency," in Peter C. and Lucille Dunn Kratcoski, *Juvenile Delinquency* (Englewood Cliffs, N.J.: Prentice-Hall, Inc., 1979).

9. How teachers influence outcomes, perhaps unwittingly, is described by Delos H. Kelly, "The Role of Teachers' Nominations in the Perpetuation of Deviant Adolescent Careers," *Education* 96 (1976): 209–217. Also see: Jackson Toby, "The Differential Impact of Family Disorganization," *American Sociological Review* 22 (1957): 502–512, for a critical evaluation of early identification and intensive treatment programs.

10. For an excellent discussion of conflicting findings see Gary F. Jensen and Dean G. Rojek, *Delinquency: A Sociological View* (Lexington, Mass.: D.C. Heath, 1980), pp. 274–285.

11. Arthur L. Stinchcombe, *Rebellion in a High School* (Chicago: Quadrangle Books, 1964), deals with the problem of easily discernible links for students between

high school studies and future status in the adult world. In an earlier Racine study it was shown that education had only limited relationships to occupation and income level, Lyle W. Shannon and Patricia Morgan, "The Prediction of Economic Absorption and Cultural Integration Among Mexican-Americans, Negroes and Anglos in a Northern Industrial Community," *Human Organization* 25 (1965): 154–162.

12.   Some pertinent reports from the literature are: Winston M. Ahlstrom and Robert J. Havinghurst, *400 Losers* (San Francisco: Jossey-Bass, 1971); Ernst A. Wenk, *Delinquency Prevention and the Schools: Emerging Perspectives* (Beverly Hills, Calif.: Sage Publications, 1978). Although most of their volume is devoted to a description of the school problem, see Section 4 of Kenneth Polk and Walter E. Schafer (eds.), *Schools and Delinquency* (Englewood Cliffs: Prentice-Hall, 1972).

13.   Chapter 13, "Implications of the Study for Community Action," Lyle W. and Magdaline W. Shannon, *Minority Migrants in the Urban Community: Mexican-American and Negro Adjustment to Industrial Society* (Beverly Hills: Sage, 1973).

14.   For a description of the success that the California Youth Authority had in its Benica Arsenal program where young "felons" worked side-by-side with civilian men and women during World War II, see John R. Ellingstron, *Protecting Our Children from Criminal Careers* (New York: Prentice-Hall, 1948), Chapter 9, pp. 98–118.

15.   As a starting point for those who wish to consider the neighborhood, we do suggest Rolf Goetze, *Understanding Neighborhood Change: The Role of Expectations in Urban Revitalization* (Cambridge: Ballinger Publishing Co., 1979).

SELECTED BIBLIOGRAPHY

Black, Donald J., 1971. "The Social Organization of Arrest," *Stanford Law Review* 23:1087–1111.

Block, Richard, 1979. "Community, Environment, and Violent Crime," *Criminology* 17:46–57.

Bursik, Robert J., Jr., 1980. "The Dynamics of Specialization in Juvenile Offenses," *Social Forces* 58:851–864.

Carter, Robert M. and Malcolm W. Klein, (eds.), 1976. *Back on the Street: The Diversion of Juvenile Offenders*. Englewood Cliffs, N.J.: Prentice-Hall.

Chilton, Roland J., 1964. "Continuity in Delinquency Area Research: A Comparison of Studies for Baltimore, Detroit, and Indianapolis," *American Sociological Review* 29:71–83.

Chiricos, Theodore G., Phillip D. Jackson and Gordon P. Waldo, 1972. "Inequality in the Imposition of a Criminal Label," *Social Problems* 19:553–572.

Cloward, Richard A. and Lloyd E. Ohlin, 1960. *Delinquency and Opportunity: A Theory of Delinquent Gangs*. New York: Free Press.

Cohen, Lawrence E. and Marcus Felson, 1979. "Social Change and Crime Rate Trends: A Routine Activity Approach," *American Sociological Review* 44:588–608.

Elliott, Delbert S. and Harwin L. Voss, 1974. *Delinquency and Dropout*. Lexington: D.C. Heath and Co., Lexington Books.

Farrington, David F., 1985. "Age and Crime," in Michael Tonry and Norval Morris (eds.), *Crime and Justice: An Annual Review of Research*. Chicago: University of Chicago Press.

Ferdinand, Theodore N. and Elmer C. Luchterhand, 1970. "Inner-city Youths, the Police, the Juvenile Court, and Justice," *Social Problems* 17:510–527.

Goetze, Rolf, 1979. *Understanding Neighborhood Change: The Role of Expectations in Urban Revitalization.* Cambridge: Ballinger Publishing Co.

Gottfredson, Steven O. and Don M. Gottfredson, 1986. "Accuracy of Prediction Models," in Alfred Blumstein, Jacqueline Cohen, Jeffrey A. Roth, and Christy A. Visher (eds.), *Criminal Careers and "Career Criminals" Volume II.* Washington, D.C.: National Academy Press.

Grasmick, Harold G. and George J. Bryjak, 1980. "The Deterrent Effect of Perceived Severity of Punishment," *Social Forces* 59:471–491.

Green, Edward, 1970. "Race, Social Status and Criminal Arrest," *American Sociological Review* 35:476–490.

Greenberg, David F. (ed.), 1978. *Corrections and Punishment,* Beverly Hills: Sage Publications.

Greenwood, Peter W., Joan Petersilia, and Franklin E. Zimring, 1980. *Age, Crime, and Sanctions: The Transition from Juvenile to Adult Court.* Santa Monica: Rand.

Hopkins, Andrew, 1976. "Imprisonment and Recidivism: A Quasi-Experimental Study," *Journal of Research in Crime and Delinquency* 13:13–32.

Jensen, Gary F., 1976. "Race, Achievement and Delinquency: A Further Look at Delinquency in a Birth Cohort," *American Journal of Sociology* 82:379–387.

Jessor, Richard and Shirley Jessor, 1977. *Problem Behavior and Psychosocial Development: A Longitudinal Study of Youth.* New York: Academic Press.

Kelly, Delos, H., 1976. "The Role of Teachers' Nominations in the Perpetuation of Deviant Adolescent Careers, *Education* 96:209–217.

Kobrin, Solomon, Joseph Puntil, and Emil Peluso, 1967. "Criteria of Status Among Street Groups," *Journal of Research in Crime and Delinquency* 4:98–118.

Krohn, Marvin and John Stratton, 1980. "A Sense of Injustice: Attitudes Toward the Criminal Justice System," *Criminology* 17:495–504.

Lerman, Paul, 1968. "Individual Values, Peer Values, and Subcultural Delinquency," *American Sociological Review* 33:219–235.

Lizotte, Alan J., 1978. "Extra-legal Factors in Chicago's Criminal Courts: Testing the Conflict Model of Criminal Justice," *Social Problems* 25:564–580.

Mack, John, 1963. "Full-Time Miscreants, Delinquent Neighborhoods and Criminal Networks," *British Journal of Sociology* 15:38–53.

Miller, Walter B., 1958. "Lower Class Culture as a Generating Milieu of Gang Delinquency," *The Journal of Social Issues* 14:5–19.

Monahan, John, 1982. "Childhood Predictors of Adult Criminal Experience," Chapter 3 in Fernand W. Dutile, Cleon H. Foust, and D. Robert Webster (eds.), *Early Childhood Intervention and Juvenile Delinquency.* Lexington: Lexington Books.

Parker, Robert Nash and Allan W. Horwitz, 1986. "Unemployment, Crime, and Imprisonment: A Panel Approach," *Criminology* 24:751–773.

Petersilia, Joan, 1980. "Criminal Career Research: A Review of Recent Evidence," in Norval Morris and Michael Tonry (eds.), *Crime and Justice, Vol. 2.* Chicago: University of Chicago Press.

Pillai, Vijayan Kumara, 1981–82. "Ecology of Intra-Urban Delinquency and Crime," *Journal of Environmental Systems* 11:101–111.

Polk, Kenneth and Walter E. Schafer (eds.), 1972. *Schools and Delinquency*. Englewood Cliffs, N.J.: Prentice-Hall.

Pritchard, David A., 1979. "Stable Predictors of Recidivism: A Summary," *Criminology* 17:15–21.

Pullum, Thomas W., 1977. "Paramatizing Age, Period, and Cohort Effects: An Application to U.S. Delinquency Rates, 1964–1973," in Karl F. Schuessler, *Sociological Methodology 1978*. San Francisco: Jossey-Bass.

Scheuch, Erwin K., 1969. "Social Contact and Individual Behavior," in Mattei Dogan and Stein Rokkan (eds.), *Quantitative Ecological Analysis in the Social Sciences*. Cambridge, Mass.: M.I.T. Press.

Schur, Edwin, 1973. *Radical Non-Intervention*. Englewood Cliffs, N.J.: Prentice-Hall.

Sellin, Thorsten and Marvin Wolfgang, 1964. *The Measurement of Delinquency*. New York: John Wiley and Sons.

Shannon, Lyle W., 1978. "A Longitudinal Study of Delinquency and Crime," in Charles Wellford (ed.), *Quantitative Studies in Criminology*. Beverly Hills: Sage Publications.

Shannon, Lyle W., 1980. "Assessing the Relationship of Adult Criminal Careers to Juvenile Careers," in Clark C. Abt (ed.), *Problems in American Social Policy Research*. Cambridge: Abt Books.

Shannon, Lyle W., 1985. "Risk Assessment vs. Real Prediction: The Prediction Problem and Public Trust," *Journal of Quantitative Criminology* 1:159–189.

Shannon, Lyle W., 1986. "Ecological Evidence of the Hardening of the Inner City," in Robert M. Figlio, Simon Hakim, and George F. Rengert (eds.), *Metropolitan Crime Patterns*. Monsey, New York: Criminal Justice Press.

Short, James F., 1968. *Gang Delinquency and Delinquent Subcultures*. New York: Harper and Row.

Skogan, Wesley G., 1977. "The Changing Distribution of Big-City Crime: A Multi-City Time-Series Analysis," *Urban Affairs Quarterly* 13:33–48.

Thornberry, Terence P., 1973. "Race, Socioeconomic Status and Sentencing in the Juvenile Justice System," *Journal of Criminal Law and Criminology* 64:90–98.

Wellford, Charles F. and Michael F. Wiatrowski, 1975. "On the Measurement of Delinquency," *Journal of Criminal Law and Criminology* 66:175–188.

Wilkins, Leslie T., 1980. "Problems with Existing Prediction Studies and Future Research Needs," *The Journal of Criminal Law & Criminology* 71:98–101.

Wolfgang, Marvin E., Robert M. Figlio, and Thorsten Sellin, 1972. *Delinquency in a Birth Cohort*. Chicago: The University of Chicago Press.

INDEX